AN OUTLINE OF ROMANTICISM IN THE WEST

An Outline of Romanticism in the West

John Claiborne Isbell

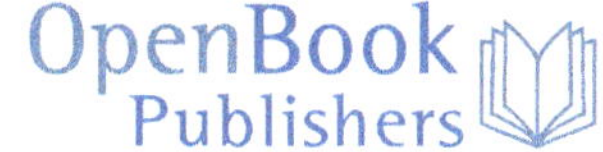

https://www.openbookpublishers.com

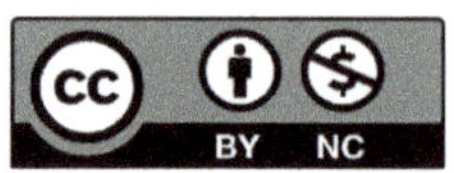

Updated digital material and resources associated with this volume are available at https://doi.org/10.11647/OBP.0302#resources

ISBN Paperback: 9781800647428
ISBN Hardback: 9781800647435
ISBN Digital (PDF): 9781800647442
ISBN Digital ebook (EPUB): 9781800647459
ISBN Digital ebook (AZW3): 9781800647466
ISBN XML: 9781800647473
Digital ebook (HTML): 9781800647480
DOI: 10.11647/OBP.0302

Cover image: Théodore Géricault, *The Raft of the Medusa* (1818–1819), https://commons.wikimedia.org/wiki/File:Th%C3%A9odore_g%C3%A9ricault,_la_zattera_della_medusa,_1819,_07.jpg

Cover design by Katy Saunders

Table of Contents

Acknowledgements

This book was conceived and largely written during the COVID-19 pandemic and without access to any research library beyond my own collection. I am sincerely grateful therefore to the various libraries I was able to access as they reopened: The University of Massachusetts Amherst W.E.B. Du Bois Library, the British Library, the Bodleian Library, the Taylor Institution Library, Hertford College Library, the Cambridge University Library, Trinity College, Cambridge's Wren Library, the Bibliothèque municipale de Bordeaux, the Bibliothèque de l'Arsenal, and the Bibliothèque nationale de France. Trinity College, Cambridge's Trinity Visiting Scholars Fund enabled a return to Cambridge in which much was accomplished. My sponsor there, and the immediate inspiration for this book, was Roger Paulin, who had earlier introduced me to the German Romantics as Dave Kelley had to the French. Others too left their welcome mark on this project: Gerald Gillespie, Kilho Lee, Todd Sjoblom, Gene Stelzig, Eunsil Yim, my friends, colleagues, and students in the University of Texas - Rio Grande Valley who encouraged my interest in Latin America, and the whole team at Open Book Publishers—Cameron Baillie, Laura Rodríguez Pupo, Luca Baffa, Melissa Purkiss, Katy Saunders, and Alessandra Tosi.

Two chapters of this book appeared in earlier versions with John Benjamins B.V. as well as the Association Internationale de Littérature Comparée: J.C. Isbell, "Romantic Disavowals of Romanticism, 1800–1830," pp. 37–55 in *Nonfictional Romantic Prose: Expanding borders*, ed. S.P. Sondrup et al. (2004), and J.C. Isbell, "Romantic novel and verse Romance, 1750–1850: Is there a Romance continuum," pp. 496–516 in *Romantic Prose Fiction*, ed. G. Gillespie, et al. (2008). Published by John Benjamins Publishing Company Amsterdam/Philadelphia and Association Internationale de Littérature Comparée. Their online catalogue is at: https://benjamins.com/catalog/chlel.xviii. A third chapter appeared in an earlier version in the *Rivista di letterature moderne e comparate* (1999), 52/2, 115–136: "*Racine et Shakespeare*'s Sleeping Partners: The Return of the Repressed."

Finally, this book would not exist without the unfailing support of my wife and partner, Margarita. I dedicate this book to her.

Introduction

It seems pretty clear—indeed, it is likely uncontested—that Romanticism was an international movement. It crossed borders. Over the two centuries since its appearance, work on the phenomenon has, perhaps regrettably, tended to silo into uniquely national studies, but there has also been a significant comparatist tradition to which this present outline is indebted. We open, therefore, with an overview of the field.

Let us begin with three precursors. Paul Van Tieghem's *Le Romantisme dans la littérature européenne* (1948) is a 538-page volume in four books: "Le Préromantisme," "La Révolution romantique," "Les Sentiments, les idées, l'art," and "Les Œuvres." In keeping with the study's age, it starts with Preromanticism and ends with Realism, two choices to trouble a modern scholar. But it is quite complete, covering Germany, Britain, the Netherlands, Scandinavia, France, Italy, Spain, Portugal, the Slavic world, and Greece. One has the impression that Van Tieghem read much of this in the original. Sadly, the book does not stretch to the Americas. Seven years later came René Wellek's *A History of Modern Criticism, The Romantic Age* (1955), with twelve chapters: on the Germans, the British, the French, the Italians, the younger Germans, and the German philosophers. In short, four national traditions are covered, specifically as to their criticism, though the book is thorough within those parameters from a mid-century perspective. Marshall Brown's *Preromanticism* (1991) covers early French, German, and British Romanticisms. The book is thorough, and has an overarching thesis, built around a term Brown later questions in the *Cambridge Companion to British Romanticism*, edited by Stuart Curran (2010). It has thirteen chapters, including five on British eighteenth-century texts and two others on specific authors. These three monographs, from Van Tieghem, Wellek, and Brown, separate from the comparatist field in not being anthologies: they are instead each the work of one person, which allows

 https://doi.org/10.11647/OBP.0302.07

them to have a coherent and overriding thesis. All are very good at what they do, though time has marked all three, and only Van Tieghem attempts a comprehensive overview, though without the Americas. The remaining studies here cited are anthologies, building their thesis—to the extent that they do so—in mosaic fashion.

A Comparative History of Literatures in European Languages (1988–2008) devotes five thick volumes of articles to European Romanticism. Let's review them in turn. *Romantic Irony*, edited by Frederick Garber (1988), contains twenty articles by authoritative Romanticists, covering irony in Germany, France, Portugal, Britain, the Netherlands, Scandinavia, Romania, Hungary, Poland, Russia, Eastern Europe, and the United States. It thus lacks Spain, Italy, and Latin America. Romantic Irony is a somewhat narrow topic, but this is a remarkably thorough mosaic treatment, i.e., this is not a monograph, but a collection of shorter studies by authorities with local expertise.

Romantic Poetry, edited by Angela Esterhammer (2002), contains twenty-seven articles in four sections: "The Evolution of Sensibility and Representation," "The Evolution of Genre," "Romantic Poetry and National Projects," and "Interpretations, Re-creations, and Performances of Romantic Poetry." These sections offer different approaches to the Romantic project: in terms of sensibility, in terms of genre or formally, in terms of subject matter and nationhood, and finally in terms of public performance. The third title is close to that of this outline, but contains just one comparatist article: others concern, say, specifically Greek or Romanian or Irish Romantic verse. Spain and Latin America appear along with, say, Hungary, and one comparatist article does mention Leopardi.

Nonfictional Romantic Prose: Expanding Borders, edited by Steven P. Sondrup and Virgil Nemoianu (2004), contains twenty-five articles, including an early version of a chapter published here. It has nine sections, on "Romantic Theoretical and Critical Writing," "Expansions in Time," "Expansions in Space," "Expansions of the Self," "Generic Expansions," "Intersections: Scientific and Artistic Discourses in the Romantic Age," and "Intimations of Transcendence." The trope of "Expansions" provides a certain coherence to the global vision presented; regions covered include Germany, Britain, France, the United States, Scandinavia, Latin America, and Spain. In short, Spain and Latin America feature, but Italy remains absent. Some articles cover multiple nations, while others cover psychology, music, and the visual arts: the volume is thus comparatist and interdisciplinary, with a focus on non-fiction.

Romantic Drama, edited by Gerald Gillespie (2007), contains twenty-six articles in four sections: "Renewal and Innovation," "Themes, Styles, Structures," "Affinity, Dissemination, Reception," and "The Romantic Legacy." Articles cover the reception of Shakespeare and of Calderón, as well as Italy, Spain, Latin America, Poland, Russia, Bohemia, Hungary, Scandinavia, Canada, and the United States. Other articles cover opera and *Faust*, for a quite comprehensive overview.

Romantic Prose Fiction, edited by Gerald Gillespie, Manfred Engel, and Bernard Dieterle (2008), contains thirty-seven articles in three sections: "Characteristic Themes," "Paradigms of Romantic Fiction," and "Contributions of Romanticism to 19th and 20th century writing and thought." The volume is perhaps more comparatist than others, with few articles on a single national tradition and several international or interdisciplinary texts. It appears less generic than topical. An early version of my chapter on novel and verse romance also features.

In sum, these five volumes represent a comprehensive approach to the Romantic phenomenon, undertaken in mosaic form: they are anthologies and lack an overarching thesis. The Western world is represented sometimes incompletely (Italy's or America's absence) and, in keeping with the lack of thesis, there is not much focus on Romanticism as a national art: just one section in the *Romantic Poetry* volume covers that topic.

Two recent comparative studies are sizeable and have special interest. *European Romanticism: A Reader*, edited by Stephen Prickett (2010), offers sixteen short essays (two pages apiece) on a range of national Romanticisms, followed by about nine hundred pages of bilingual extracts from a broad and thorough range of texts. Mácha's important long Czech poem "May," for instance—not an easy text to find—is here in bilingual entirety. This is a splendid sourcebook for European Romanticism (the Americas are missing), but the commentary is generic and very brief. There is no overarching thesis. *The Oxford Handbook of European Romanticism*, edited by Paul Hamilton (2016), covers a variety of European literatures from a mostly literary angle. It contains forty-one sections in two parts: "Languages" and "Discourses."

Nations include France, Germany, Hungary, Italy, Spain, Russia, Poland, Scandinavia, and Greece. Absent nations include Britain, Portugal, the Netherlands, Belgium, the Southern Slavs, and the Baltic nations. Within these parameters, the volume is incisive, like most of these studies, with articles by authorities in the field. The Americas are naturally missing.

To conclude, there may be a new push for comparatism in Romantic studies. The new edition of the *Cambridge Companion to British Romanticism*, for instance, has a chapter on German idealism. It is welcome to see these two heavy new volumes, one of unfindable texts, the other of articles by authorities in the field. Yet, as with the *Comparative History*, both lack an overarching thesis: they are constructed in mosaic style, which also does something to explain the blind spots both volumes present. Croatian, Ukrainian, Estonian, or Flemish Romanticism might welcome a mention. Or in fact Cuban, Brazilian, or Argentinian Romanticism, all of which emerge before 1848. And I believe those blind spots have consequences, contributing to hide from participants what I describe as the national underpinnings to the Romantic enterprise.

One quite recent monograph is that rare thing, both comparatist and single-authored. It is by Paul Hamilton, the editor of *The Oxford Handbook of European Romanticism*. His *Realpoetik: European Romanticism and Literary Politics* (2013) is focused on three countries: France, Italy, and Germany. It has an overarching thesis, anchored in sociopolitical context: namely that, in the new nations of the nineteenth century, there was a necessity to imagine the kind of nation which would be desirable. Hamilton examines this thesis in the writings of Germaine de Staël, Friedrich Schlegel, Giacomo Leopardi, and others.

Three additional texts tangential to comparative Romanticism seem to offer useful models for the present outline. First, Jerome J. McGann's *The Romantic Ideology: A Critical Investigation* (1983) is a slim volume, offering a sociopolitical reading of British Romanticism, which went a long way to overturning the traditional focus on the Romantic individual, at least for Britain and for me. Second, Anne K. Mellor's *Romanticism & Gender* (1993) returns women authors to the discussion of British Romanticism, thereby exposing a missing half to the British Romantic universe and doing so with a thesis as to what distinguishes the two. This work clearly remains to be done for the other female Romanticisms waiting to be discovered, of which there are many. And third, Paul Johnson's *The*

Birth of the Modern: World Society 1815–1830 (1991) covers precisely what it says. It is extensive and universal, and that was an inspiration as the initial work began on this comparatist project some decades ago.

The present outline, then, proposes an argument for the global coherence of Western cultural production between 1776 and 1848. Furthermore, the Romantic enterprise here presented bleeds back into the 1760s in France and the United Kingdom—in Rousseau or Ossian, for instance—and on into the 1850s in the Americas, as in Eastern and Northern Europe. This proposed continuity to Romanticism in the West can be located in the concept of *nationality* and, specifically, *national credit*, marking a watershed in Western thought that continues to shape the modern world. Here is that dialectic: from the nation's rich soil arises a genius speaking the nation's voice. The nation, which sits within a patchwork of nations—rather as the UN or the EU imagine themselves—is subsumed and literally embodied in that unique national individual, an elect and alien figure who represents it and to whom it gives credit. This Romantic concept still elects our national representatives; it determines the incomes of our celebrities; it has led nations from Russia to Argentina to erect monuments to Romantic authors; it is why Percy Bysshe Shelley, who sold poorly, writes that "Poets are the unacknowledged legislators of the world."[1] Focus on the Romantic individual may then have it precisely backwards: 'Romantic' and 'national' are two sides of the same coin, I argue, and to speak about the Romantic individual without speaking about the represented nation is to study a circuit's anode without its cathode.

The present outline aims to restore the Romantic era as it was lived by its creators and citizens, in a global overview that bypasses some common divisions. For instance, the Classic-Romantic-Realist distinction. Neoclassical and Romantic art coexist in the painter David as in the writers Foscolo or Hölderlin, while talk of 'subsequent' Realism, a term passing from the near-forgotten Champfleury to Soviet work on Gogol, or to Lukács on Balzac, deletes major creators—Balzac, Gogol, Dickens—from the Romantic universe. This survey also avoids the term 'Preromantic,' which historically has served to silo national Romantic movements from international chronologies, and subdivisions such

1 Percy Bysshe Shelley, *A Defense of Poetry*, ed. by Albert S. Cook (Boston: Ginn & Co., 1890), p. 46.

as *Trivial, Schauer*, or *Afterromantik*, which tend to narrow 'German Romantic' production to the decade or so from 1798–1808. German lands remained strongly regional, and that may matter more. On the other hand, the book notes Romantic elements in the plastic arts throughout this period—in Géricault, Blake, Goya, and Friedrich for instance—and even in music, where musicologists label Mozart and Beethoven Classical, though the two composers have clear debts to Romantic thought. Romantic elements can be traced across a variety of disciplines—in architecture, in fashion, in landscaping where the term appears early. They can also be traced in the era's politics. Sidestepping a series of received divisions may offer a fresh and holistic view of the period, one that includes Dickens and Rousseau; Lermontov, Andersen, and E.T.A. Hoffmann; Bishop Percy and Leopardi; Poe, Berlioz, and Bernardin de Saint-Pierre. It may help return the West's diverse Romantic-era creators to a lived continuum.

An ancillary point. 'Realism' makes for a constricting uniform into which to try to shoehorn authors of the Romantic era. As Albert Béguin argues in *L'Âme romantique et le rêve*, it is characteristic of Romanticism to open a window onto dream, with its floating affect, its weight of meaning, and its aleatory structures. Dream, the fantastic, and the arabesque routinely determine the Romantic horizon, from Novalis to Poe. Thus, the Romantics value fairy tale and ballad. Thus, Gogol's narrator meets his own nose in Kazan cathedral. Thus, Balzac's shagreen skin shrinks with every wish it grants. Thus, also, Stendhal's Julien Sorel finds a newspaper clipping recounting his own death. Thus, indeed, Dickens's Pip and Magwitch are bound in a bizarre web of coincidence—an arabesque, a pattern shaped not by lived reality but by abstract principles, rather like an algebraic formula. At such moments, 'Realism' simply does not apply, and such moments—such indeterminacy—are not tangential to these texts, they lie at their heart. That is why the present study returns to fantastic elements found in allegedly 'Realist' Romantic-era texts—to heuristic conflict, to night, dream, and the arabesque.

Philosophy is not foregrounded here. Outside of Coleridge or Villers, Kant and the post-Kantians had their contemporary impact mostly in German lands; meanwhile, Rousseau, an overwhelming influence in the West, gets less credit for that influence than he merits. British empiricists had been shaping European thought for a good century, but Romantics had cause to dislike Bentham, and Godwin was an anarchist. In general, the Romantics' philosophical treatises, which exist, are not the primary reason we read Romantic authors. We read the Romantics for plots and speakers, to meet people, like Wordsworth's Idiot Boy or Balzac's Eugène de Rastignac, and watch them interact with the world. There is good philosophical prose in the period—Kant writes better prose than often credited, and Rousseau's prose is splendid—but that story has been told.

This outline instead proposes a unified political and historical framework. Authors can choose whether or not to open a given book, but they cannot choose their system of government. If their nation is occupied by French, Russian, Turkish, or Austrian troops—or liberated by Washington, Bolívar, or Louverture, by Spanish *guerilleros* or Garibaldi—that will have an impact which deserves review. This was a revolutionary age: deemphasizing the revolutions that played out across the region will falsify the texts we read. Here, too, one may witness that watershed in thought which defines our extended Romantic period. There is a reason all continental America bar Canada won independence in the half-century 1776–1826, and that the many nations of Eastern Europe—Poland, Serbia, Croatia, Hungary, Ukraine, Estonia, Finland—now produced foundational Romantic epics. There is a reason Italian Romantics were rounded up in 1821 by the Austrian police, and that so many Romantic authors wrote in exile. This is not the solipsistic glorification of a Romantic individual, but its opposite: a popular or *national* ideology at its birth.

In short, this outline aims to retrace a unified field, replacing some of the divides that still shape the Romantic enterprise. How could that totality have hidden away so long? Various factors suggest themselves. First, the Romantic choice to write in the vernacular—the people's voice—and not, say, in French, conceals key texts in various languages: Frederick the Great of Prussia wrote in French, while a generation later German authors elected to write in German. Second, the world's nation-states pursue national agendas, which impacts specialists living within them: comparative Romanticism remains a minority occupation alongside a sea of national Romantic studies, and even we comparatists draw frontiers inside the map to define what we will treat. Third, a century divide bisects the Romantic period, while many scholars spend entire careers working within one century's borders. Fourth, the political context is complex: there are scholars with libraries devoted to the French Revolution alone. Fifth, credit theory and economics are unusual topics in literary scholarship: discipline boundaries in general conceal the totality here outlined. Sixth, scholars have over the years endorsed various agendas that partition the Romantic continuum—for instance, focusing on Realism and the search for its roots in the European novel, 1750–1850. All these seem understandable choices, and Romanticism had its hand in their launching. This does not, however, mean we must remain their prisoners.

My 1996 Lilly Library exhibition catalogue, *The People's Voice: A Romantic Civilization, 1776–1848,* shows a draft constitution for Bolivia with President Sucre's handwritten corrections: presidential elections will be held "popularmente conforme a la ley de junio" [popularly in accordance with the June law]. This is the Romantic age of the nations of the West, with states discovering nationhood, like France after 1789, or defining nationhood for themselves, like the United Kingdom. In addition, nation-states began emerging, as throughout the Americas, along with nations absent from the map but aspiring to appear on it, as in Italian or German lands, or almost the whole of Eastern Europe. This story, not that of some solipsistic Romantic individual, is the West's cultural matrix during the years 1776–1848, from Moscow to Montevideo. The entire region was a concert of new nations, real and imagined—and thus *international,* to use a word coined at the time. This book presents key texts reaching from Russia to Argentina, showing the history of these nations' art within the timeframe of their struggle for nationhood. If 'Romanticism' is to mean anything, as the Lovejoy-Wellek debate once wondered—that is, if the term is to mark a historical moment—then we may expect Romantic data points across the broad field of cultural production. And we can perhaps identify such data if we look. This is a wide range of information, but it is held together by nationhood and by the ideas of representative government and credit in which it is grounded.

The outline has some interdisciplinary scope. It engages beyond literature with the spectrum of cultural production, touching not only on the humanities—literature, politics, economics, philosophy, music, the fine arts—but also on technology and the sciences. It oversteps century, nation, and language boundaries in an effort to present the Romantic phenomenon as it was once lived by its creators and audience.

Chapter One, "Romanticism and the Nations of the West," echoes Erich Auerbach's *Mimesis* in format, presenting twelve different Romantic artifacts in ten European languages and reviewing each piece and its context in turn. The format is: a painting or short text in verse or prose; an English translation if needed; a brief biography of the creator; and a contextual commentary. The works covered are: Novalis, *Heinrich von Ofterdingen*; Germaine de Staël, *Corinne ou l'Italie*; Francisco Goya, *Tres de mayo 1808*; Mary Shelley, *Frankenstein; or, The Modern Prometheus*; Alexander Pushkin, *Evgenii Onegin*; James Fenimore Cooper, *The Last of the Mohicans*; Adam Mickiewicz, *Pan Tadeusz*; Hans Christian Andersen, *Eventyr*; Giacomo Leopardi, *Canti*; Esteban Echeverría, *El Matadero*; Hendrik Conscience, *De Leeuw Van Vlaanderen*; João de Almeida Garrett, *Viagens na minha terra*. That means this long chapter covers the years 1800–1846 and, globally, German lands, France, Spain, the British Isles, Russia, the United States, Eastern Europe (Poland), Northern Europe (Denmark), the Italian peninsula, Latin America (Argentina), the Low Countries (Belgium), and Portugal. It thereby sketches out a substantial Romantic field.

Chapter Two, "The Frankenstein Conundrum. Romantic Disavowals of Romanticism, 1800–1830," argues that a common thread indeed unites Europe's Romantics, from Saint Petersburg to London: it is precisely their disavowal of what they created. The chapter further proposes that what is at work is not simply dislike of the term, but instead a synthetic vision shared by these artists seeking to reconcile Neoclassical and Romantic art, past and future within a new, Hegelian synthesis—a vision obliterated by less subtle hangers-on, as the term and original agenda were co-opted, if not hijacked.

Chapter Three, "Romantic Novel and Verse Romance. Is There a Romance Continuum?" follows the hypothesis that verse romance and the historical novel—Romantic verse and prose respectively—are complementary, with a genre border between them that is more porous than sometimes thought. It follows the two genres across the century 1750–1850, and through German lands, the British Isles, France, the Italian peninsula, Northern and Eastern Europe, Iberia, the Low

Countries, then finally the Americas, for an extensive tour of Romantic extended narrative, a topic which is sometimes neglected. It further makes the argument that Romantic novel and verse romance represent a lost corpus, indeed a lost continuum in Romantic-era production, long hidden by a focus on short lyrics and 'the Realist novel.' This corpus is marked by epistemological crisis and the arabesque, for which the tools of a Lukács are gravely, if not grotesquely, unsuited.

Chapter Four, "*Racine et Shakespeare*'s Sleeping Partners. The Return of the Repressed," offers an in-depth case study in what the French long called 'Preromanticism' and in the hermeneutic consequences of an exclusively national approach. Stendhal's *Racine et Shakespeare* (1823–1825) seems well suited to a case study both in Romantic internationalism—our proposed method—and in the nationalism or parochialism it supersedes. A detailed review of French, German, English, and Italian sources for Stendhal's famous manifesto reveals the systematic plagiarism—disguised to some extent by misrepresentation—at the root of this famous treatise. Sources uncovered include Staël, A.W. Schlegel, and various British and Italian Romantics. The chapter reviews Stendhal's complex relations with his international sources, some of whom he had met, across two decades, 1803–1825, and the factors involved both in his decision to borrow from them extensively and lie about it, and in the French tradition's willingness to accept his complex and playful text at face value. Foundational national texts are not always what they appear from a national perspective, and that seems worth underlining.

Chapter Five, "Thoughts on the Romantic Hero, 1776–1848," ranges from Rousseau to Heine and from Russia to South America, in order to investigate the nature of the Romantic hero—that Protean being. It argues that the originary act constituting the Romantic hero, across seven decades and a wide geographical and linguistic sweep, is one of compassion, if not empathy. In 1755, Voltaire found Rousseau unintelligible: for the Romantics, almost to a man, existence in human society involves recognizing not just the Other, but the downtrodden, the outsider and the outcast—Quasimodo or Jean Valjean, Ourika or Byron, Heathcliff or Jane Eyre, Faust, Werther or Ortis, Pechorin or Onegin, Hester Prynne—and making of them not just an interlocutor, but the hero of the story: a 'Hero for Our Time,' in Lermontov's words.

This act of faith is taken not, in fact, by the character on the page, but by author and reader together. Romantic heroes exist in a liminal space, and the chapter points out that like Vigny's Moïse, these liminal individuals, outside the common run as they are, find themselves caught in a contract with the nation of solitary readers from which they arise—they represent it. In that Romantic social contract, a better dream of the social order is juxtaposed (as, say, in the interleaved verso-page autobiography of E.T.A. Hoffmann's bourgeois Tomcat Murr) with the social order as constituted. This may suggest a revolution brewing, and the age is not without them, from 1776 through 1848. The chapter ends with a section on Romantic drama, and another, "Romantic Women Authors: The State of the Field," which follows up on the women authors featured notably in Chapter One by searching for women Romantics throughout the period and asking why broadly speaking, they will not be found. It adds various French and German women Romantic authors to the better-known British list, inviting readers to join this search and to ponder what its necessity tells us. Finally, the book ends with an overview of Romanticism outside the Western ambit: in the Ottoman Empire, in Japan, in South Asia.

What, then, remains to be done? A few things, which may come down to a different way of seeing. First, the curious might read fresh texts: foundational Romantic texts from Eastern and Northern Europe, from the Caribbean and Latin America, or by women Romantics outside the British Isles, in France and Germany to begin with. Indeed, any rediscovery of a substantial women's corpus lying outside the British Isles, France, and Germany—where some documentation does already exist—might well complicate a variety of hypotheses put forward here. Second, readers might extend their gaze both forward and back, looking from that explosion for the Western world which was the 1776 Declaration of Independence, on to 1848, the year which saw both the *Communist Manifesto*—a different vision of the folk or people—and Metternich's Restoration Europe in revolt. "We, the people," begins 1787's United States Constitution, and this contested era devoted considerable energy and imagination to enacting that vision of citizenship. Third, readers might focus on overcoming disciplinary divides—between history, economics, and political thought; between gardening, fashion, music, and architecture—in order to sense the Romantic continuum as it was lived then. From this perspective, readers might find some subsequent received ideas losing their explanatory power. A web of *a posteriori* distinctions and divisions might fall away from the field, much as a chrysalis falls away to reveal the adult. It seems time.

1. Romanticism and the Nations of the West

1. German Lands, 1800
Novalis, *Heinrich von Ofterdingen*

Die Eltern lagen schon und schliefen, die Wanduhr schlug ihren einförmigen Takt, vor den klappernden Fenstern sauste der Wind; abwechselnd wurde die Stube hell von dem Schimmer des Mondes. Der Jüngling lag unruhig auf seinem Lager, und gedachte des Fremden und seiner Erzählungen. Nicht die Schätze sind es, die ein so unaussprechliches Verlangen in mir geweckt haben, sagte er zu sich selbst; fern ab liegt mir alle Habsucht: aber die blaue Blume sehn' ich mich zu erblicken. Sie liegt mir unaufhörlich im Sinn, und ich kann nichts anders dichten und denken. So ist mir noch nie zu Muthe gewesen: es ist, als hätt' ich vorhin geträumt, oder ich wäre in eine andere Welt hinübergeschlummert; denn in der Welt, in der ich sonst lebte, wer hätte da sich um Blumen bekümmert, und gar von einer so seltsamen Leidenschaft für eine Blume hab' ich damals nie gehört. Wo eigentlich nur der Fremde herkam? Keiner von uns hat je einen ähnlichen Menschen gesehn; doch weiß ich nicht, warum nur ich von seinen Reden so ergriffen worden bin; die Andern haben ja das Nämliche gehört, und Keinem ist so etwas begegnet. Daß ich auch nicht einmal von meinem wunderlichen Zustande reden kann! Es ist mir oft so entzückend wohl, und nur dann, wenn ich die Blume nicht recht gegenwärtig habe, befällt mich so ein tiefes, inniges Treiben: das kann und wird Keiner verstehn. Ich glaubte, ich wäre wahnsinnig, wenn ich nicht so klar und hell sähe und dächte, mir ist seitdem alles viel bekannter.

The parents had already retired to rest; the old clock ticked monotonously from the wall; the windows rattled with the whistling wind, and the chamber was dimly lighted by the flickering glimmer of the moon. The young man lay restless on his bed, thinking of the stranger and his tales.

 https://doi.org/10.11647/OBP.0302.08

> "It is not the treasures," said he to himself, "that have awakened in me such unutterable longings. Far from me is all avarice; but I long to behold the blue flower. It is constantly in my mind, and I can think and compose of nothing else. I have never been in such a mood. It seems as if I had hitherto been dreaming or slumbering into another world; for in the world, in which hitherto I have lived, who would trouble himself about a flower? — I never have heard of such a strange passion for a flower here. I wonder, too, whence the stranger comes? None of our people have ever seen his like; still I know not why I should be so fascinated by his conversation. Others have listened to it, but none are moved by it as I am. Would that I could explain my feelings in words! I am often full of rapture, and it is only when the blue flower is out of my mind, that this deep, heart-felt longing overwhelms me. But no one can comprehend this but myself. I might think myself mad, were not my perception and reasonings so clear; and this state of mind appears to have brought with it superior knowledge on all subjects.[1]

Novalis, pen name of **Georg Philipp Friedrich Freiherr von Hardenberg** (2 May 1772–25 March 1801). **Works**: poems—*Hymnen an die Nacht*; novels—*Heinrich von Ofterdingen, Die Lehrlinge zu Sais*; treatises—*Die Christenheit oder Europa, Das allgemeine Brouillon*. Hardenberg was born at the family seat founded in 1287. He studied law at Jena, Leipzig, and Wittenberg from 1790 to 1794, meeting Goethe, Herder, and Jean Paul and befriending the philosopher Schelling and the brothers Friedrich and A.W. Schlegel. He attended Schiller's lectures and they became friends. In 1795, he became engaged to the thirteen-year-old Sophie von Kühn, who died in 1797 of tuberculosis. In 1795–1796, Hardenberg entered the Mining Academy of Freiberg. His first fragments appeared in 1798 in the Schlegels' journal *Athenäum*, under the pseudonym "Novalis." In 1799, he met Tieck and other Jena Romantics. In 1800, he contracted tuberculosis, dying in 1801. His unfinished novels and various fragments were published posthumously by his friends Ludwig Tieck and Friedrich Schlegel.

My own interest in comparative Romanticism began with the question of why the French and German Romantics seemed to have different periods, even centuries; different priorities; and a quite different esthetics. Here, we open with an opening: the first few sentences, after

1 Novalis, *Henry of Ofterdingen*, trans. by John Owen (Cambridge, MA: Cambridge Press, 1842), p. 23.

a short dedicatory poem, of Novalis's historical novel *Heinrich von Ofterdingen* (1802), a key text from the German *Frühromantik* circle led by Tieck, the two Schlegel brothers, and Novalis himself. Novalis died young the following year, and he wrote in loss: his teen fiancée died in 1797, bringing him from mine management to writing, at first in the lyric poems of the *Hymnen an die Nacht* (1800), and then in this long unfinished novel, or novel fragment.

How after all does a story begin? In this third-person narrative, we begin in the night and under the sign of dream. The parents are asleep. The first sentence, with its clock, its windows, its flickering Moon, might be the start to one of the Grimm brothers' fairy tales a decade or so later. This inanimate world is pregnant with meaning, a theme that will continue throughout Novalis's text. Scholars have argued that *Frühromantik* separates from its predecessor *Sturm und Drang* in its self-awareness, its sense of lucid mission, and that may be. Certainly, Novalis is working from the outset to create a space in which dream and reality, world and hero, bleed into each other. The text is notable for its weight of thought in art—a characteristic of German *Frühromantik*.[2]

Novalis's Germany in this novel is fundamentally that of fairy tale. As in his essay *Die Christenheit oder Europa*, Novalis turns his back on the changing territories the French were then invading in favor of a timeless, medieval space: that of the thousand-year-old Holy Roman Empire which Francis II was finally to end in 1806.[3] In some ways, the Middle Ages lasted longer in German lands than elsewhere in Western Europe; journeymen still traveled, as in Goethe's two-part novel *Wilhelm Meister* (1795–1821), to which *Ofterdingen* was written in answer, or indeed in Schubert's 1823 song cycle *Die schöne Müllerin*. German lands, as Staël notes in *De l'Allemagne* (1813), lacked a capital city to exert its pull.[4] Heinrich, then, meets a stranger and is inspired to travel for his craft. Ofterdingen has a historical basis in the medieval world where Novalis

2 Romantic philosophy *per se* is not our topic in this book. Samuel Taylor Coleridge in his *Biographia Literaria* (1817) has extensive debts to Friedrich Wilhelm Joseph Schelling, the post-Kantian philosopher.

3 Novalis, *Die Christenheit oder Europa. Ein Fragment* [Christianity or Europe. A Fragment] (1799). Francis II reordered the Empire dramatically with the *Reichsdeputationshauptschluss* (1803); Napoleon created the Confederation of the Rhine in July 1806 and Francis II abdicated weeks later.

4 Germaine de Staël, *De l'Allemagne* [On Germany], 5 vols, ed. by Comtesse de Pange (Paris: Hachette, 1958–1960), I p. 37: "cet empire n'avoit point un centre commun."

places him—there was a *Minnesinger* of that name—but such a figure was also not yet alien to Novalis's German readers, as he would have been to the British or the French. It matters too that, like a fairy tale, Novalis conducts his narrative in the world of dream. The tale opens in dream, as we have seen. It continues via a succession of embedded narratives, and it ends, elegantly enough, in an embedded narrative from which Novalis does not provide an exit. This may be a simple consequence of the story being unfinished; but German *Frühromantik*, beginning with Friedrich Schlegel, was interested in the fragment as art, and it seems equally possible that Novalis came to prefer leaving his readers lost in a dream, like Heinrich himself.[5] Let us add that Mary Shelley's *Frankenstein* (1818) uses exactly the same framing device—leaving us lost in an embedded narrative—to end her story of creature and creator.

Heinrich begins his tale *unruhig* [restless] like Kafka's Gregor Samsa.[6] He is at once immersed in story: a stranger arrives in town with tales to tell, inspiring Heinrich alone with sleepless enthusiasm. Heinrich then notes his own indifference to wealth and his yearning for the blue cornflower that was to become a symbol for the early German Romantics. Storytelling, moreover, is an interesting occupation. First, it is oral; Heinrich may come to writing—his vocation is poetry—but his call comes via the spoken word. It is, in that sense, popular, not courtly; it is typical of the folk that Fichte celebrated in his 1808 *Reden an die deutsche Nation*. This is an epiphanic moment: Heinrich feels as if he has woken from sleep and dream, or as if he had slumbered "into another world," the text reads, as one might in the *Upanishads*. It is mystical. Heinrich rightly contrasts his prosaic surroundings, where none would trouble themselves about a flower, with his new passion and vision. The

5 Novalis's notes of February 11, 1800, indicate that *Ofterdingen* was conceived as a poetic response to Goethe›s "unpoetic" *Wilhelm Meisters Lehrjahre* [Wilhelm Meister›s Apprenticeship]; see *Novalis. Schriften. Die Werke Friedrich von Hardenbergs*, 5 vols, ed. Paul Kluckhohn and Richard Samuel (Stuttgart: Kohlhammer, 1960–1988), III 645–652 (11 February 1800). August Wilhelm and Friedrich Schlegel largely constructed their journal *Athenaeum* (1798–1800) in fragments and devoted some thought to that form. Friedrich Schlegel's *Philosophische Fragmente* thus run to over 400 pages in *Kritische Friedrich-Schlegel Ausgabe* 18: *Philosophische Lehrjahre 1796–1806*, I, ed. by Ernst Behler (München, Paderborn, Wien: Ferdinand Schöningh, 1963), pp. 1–422.

6 Franz Kafka's Gregor Samsa appears in the story "Die Verwandlung" [Metamorphosis] (1915), where he is transformed in the opening sentence into a giant vermin.

stranger's arrival thus divides Heinrich's life in two, into before and after; our little world of dynamic equilibrium may easily be upended by the arrival of a catalyst, which is what this stranger is. Heinrich thus opens his story by separating himself from the world of prose; the whole novel is written under the sign of poetry, as a sort of *Gesamtkunstwerk* in which poetry and prose cohabit, and in this, it is both typically German and quite different from the contemporary prose novels of the British and the French.

What are we to make of the stranger here? His role as wanderer was, as we have noted, still quite possible in German lands. His air of magic, remoteness, and story may remind us of a contemporary German preoccupation with supernatural deals—Goethe's *Faust* (1790–1829), Chamisso's *Peter Schlemihl* (1814), Weber's *Der Freischütz* (1821), or Hauff's *Das kalte Herz* (1827), for instance. He is a sort of spirit guide for Heinrich, who will forever leave the home life that was his for a new life of adventure and discovery in art. As Heinrich remarks, not all who listen will hear; he alone hears the call in the stranger's words, though he cannot yet express it himself. Genius was topical in 1800, and Novalis here offers a fruitful view of it.[7] First, Heinrich is more akin to the mysterious stranger than to his townsfolk, and even than to his parents, who on the next page greet his sleepless quest with prosaic, if loving, responses. Their routine does not equip them for poetry, a common enough Romantic theme. There is something strange and magical about *genius* for Novalis—"close your eyes with holy dread," writes Coleridge in the same vein in 1797.[8] Second, this genius is isolated. Novalis underlines how Heinrich separates both physically and mentally from those around him, even before he leaves his home and village to wander. Third, he remains fundamentally a *national* figure, indeed a folk figure in a way that the folk themselves can only manage with difficulty. Heinrich will wander across Germany in this novel; it is speech that calls him; he is a sort of everyman, equally at ease with king and peasant and creator, and with the words to express the inner soul of each. Finally, beyond Heinrich's anchoring in, and communion with, the real, the national,

7 On genius, compare Logan Pearsall Smith, "Four Romantic Words," in *Words and Idioms: Studies in the English Language* (London: Constable & Co., 1925) pp. 66–134.

8 "Kubla Khan" in *The Poems of Samuel Taylor Coleridge*, ed. by Ernest Hartley Coleridge (London: Oxford University Press, 1931), p. 298.

and the true, stands his bridge to a world that lies beyond. He is *vatic*, like Vigny's or Baudelaire's poet figures; his inspiration is otherworldly, and his thinking is both clear and yet unintelligible to the voiceless masses. Some might think him mad, as Goethe's Torquato Tasso appeared mad; in reality, he has acquired "superior knowledge on all subjects."[9]

To conclude: how does Heinrich in 1800 square with the Romantic hero—and artist—figures in German lands and elsewhere in Europe, contemporary and subsequent? After all, he is quite early. Well, he has many successors. We've mentioned Vigny and Baudelaire, nor are they alone in France, while the Germans Brentano, Heine, and Eichendorff inherit and complicate this legacy as they come to lyric poetry.[10] Indeed, studies of the Romantic Poet are not in short supply, from Russia to Poland to the United States or Argentina. It is perhaps worth repeating that this figure, as described by Novalis, is, at the end of the day, a sort of outcast. He is not, and cannot be, understood by the nation he represents. He communes instead like the sibyl, the oracle, the prophet, with a world unlike ours and apparently superior to it. He is *unacknowledged*. This emphatically separates Novalis's hero Heinrich and his successors from the engaged and nationally beloved figure of Corinne, which Staël offers the world in our next section. And Staël will have her own successors in poetry, Victor Hugo among them. German and French Romanticism part company from the outset, they are quite independent national traditions.

9 Compare Alfred de Vigny, "Moïse" [Moses] and Charles Baudelaire, "L'Albatros" [The Albatross]. Also, Goethe's play *Torquato Tasso* (1790).

10 Clemens Wenzeslaus Brentano, Heinrich Heine, and Joseph von Eichendorff were arguably Germany's three leading lyric poets after the loss of Goethe and Friedrich Hölderlin.

2. France, 1807
Germaine de Staël, *Corinne ou l'Italie*

Après ce qui s'était passé dans la galerie de Bologne, Oswald comprit que Lucile en savait plus sur ses relations avec Corinne qu'il ne l'avait imaginé, et il eut enfin l'idée que sa froideur et son silence venaient peut-être de quelques peines secrètes; cette fois néanmoins ce fut lui qui craignit l'explication que jusqu'alors Lucile avait redoutée. Le premier mot étant dit, elle aurait tout révélé si lord Nelvil l 'avait voulu; mais il lui en coûtait trop de parler de Corinne au moment de la revoir, de s'engager par une promesse, enfin de traiter un sujet si propre à l'émouvoir, avec une personne qui lui causait toujours un sentiment de gêne, et dont il ne connaissait le caractère qu'imparfaitement.

Ils traversèrent les Apennins, et trouvèrent par-delà le beau climat d'Italie. Le vent de mer, qui est si étouffant pendant l'été, répandait alors une douce chaleur; les gazons étaient verts; l'automne finissait à peine, et déjà le printemps semblait s'annoncer. On voyait dans les marchés des fruits de toute espèce, des oranges, des grenades. Le langage toscan commençait à se faire entendre; enfin tous les souvenirs de la belle Italie rentraient dans l'âme d'Oswald; mais aucune espérance ne venait s'y mêler: il n'y avait que du passé dans toutes ses impressions. L'air suave du Midi agissait aussi sur la disposition de Lucile: elle eût été plus confiante, plus animée, si lord Nelvil l'eût encouragée; mais ils étaient tous les deux retenus par une timidité pareille, inquiets de leur disposition mutuelle, et n'osant se communiquer ce qui les occupait. Corinne, dans une telle situation, eût bien vite obtenu le secret d'Oswald comme celui de Lucile; mais ils avaient l'un et l'autre le même genre de réserve, et plus ils se ressemblaient à cet égard, plus il était difficile qu'ils sortissent de la situation contrainte où ils se trouvaient.

After what had happened in the Bologna art gallery, Oswald realized that Lucile knew more about his relationship with Corinne than he had thought. He had, at last, thought that her cold silence was perhaps the result of some secret grief. This time, however, it was he who was afraid of the explanation that, till then, Lucile had dreaded. Now that the first words had been said, she would have disclosed everything if Lord Nelvil had so wished, but it was too painful for him to talk about Corinne just when he was going to see her again; he could not bear to commit himself by a promise to talk about a subject which still touched him nearly, to someone with whom he always felt ill at ease and whose character he only partly knew.

They crossed the Apennines and on the other side they found Italy's beautiful climate. The wind from the sea, so stifling in the summer,

> brought a gentle warmth at that time. The grass was green; autumn was barely over and already there were signs of spring. In the markets you could see all kinds of fruit, oranges, pomegranates. They began to hear the Tuscan language. In short, all his memories of beautiful Italy returned to Oswald, but unmixed with any hope. All his feelings were connected only with the past. The gentle southern breeze also affected Lucile's frame of mind. She would have been more confident, more lively, if Lord Nelvil had encouraged her; both equally constrained, however, by shyness, and uneasy about each other's attitude, they did not dare talk to each other about what was on their minds. In such circumstances Corinne would have discovered Oswald's secret very quickly and Lucile's as well. But they both had the same kind of reserve, and the more they were like each other in this respect, the more difficult it was for them to emerge from their constrained situation.[11]

Anne Louise Germaine Necker, baronne de Staël-Holstein (22 April 1766–14 July 1817). **Works**: theater—tragedies, comedies, dramas; pamphlets; moral treatises; criticism—*Lettres sur Jean-Jacques Rousseau, De la littérature, De l'Allemagne*; novels—*Delphine, Corinne ou l'Italie*; short stories; political treatises—*Des circonstances actuelles, Considérations sur les principaux événements de la révolution française*; autobiography—the *Dix années d'exil*. Staël's father Necker was the Director-General of Finance under Louis XVI. As a child, Staël met Diderot and other Enlightenment thinkers in her mother's salon. She married the Swedish Ambassador in 1786, and was present at the Convocation of the Estates General and the Declaration of the Rights of Man. On 11 July 1789, her father was dismissed. Three days later, Parisians stormed the Bastille. Staël left Paris on 2 September 1792, day of the September Massacres, after a meeting with Robespierre. Following liaisons with two noblemen—Narbonne and the Swedish exile Ribbing—she met the brilliant Benjamin Constant in 1794, her companion until 1810. Exiled from Paris in 1795, Staël restarted her Parisian salon and met Bonaparte in 1797. He exiled her once more in 1803—the topic of *Dix années d'exil*. Her work in exile brought her European fame. Beyond her Coppet group, she befriended Europe's Romantics, and also statesmen from Tsar Alexander, in a Moscow as yet unburnt by Kutuzov, and Bernadotte in Sweden, to the Duke of Wellington in occupied Paris. A.W. Schlegel

11 Madame de Staël, *Corinne, or Italy*, trans. by Sylvia Raphaël (Oxford: Oxford University Press, 1998), p. 387.

joined her as her children's tutor, and Lord Byron rowed across Lake Geneva in 1816 to pay her visits. She died in 1817 on the anniversary of the Bastille's fall, much as her friend Jefferson later died on the 4th of July.

Quite a lot has happened at this point in Staël's novel. Over the course of some four hundred pages—or two volumes of a three-volume octavo edition—a love triangle has emerged, binding Oswald, a Scottish peer, to two half-sisters, fair Lucile and dark Corinne. We are near the end of this prose novel or romance—a newish form in 1807, not wholly canonical, often gendered as feminine, and already emerging as a major genre. What then separates Staël's book from any romance of the age, from her contemporaries the Gothic Ann Radcliffe or the sentimental Fanny Burney, the astute Jane Austen or the delicate Mme de Genlis? What in short does Staël offer posterity? Perhaps above all, she offers a Romantic focus on nationhood. What is a nation, after all, and how do we perceive it? Ossianic Scotland separates imperfectly from England in this text, but Italy and the broader United Kingdom, in particular, appear in sharp relief, bracketing absent France.

In our extract—which is in fact a complete chapter—Oswald returns to Italy with his English bride, Lucile. Chapter lengths vary in *Corinne ou l'Italie*, and this one is unusually short. But markers of Italy abound, and a national contrast to Britain appears and drives our plot. It is a pivotal moment, and past and future loom in this tight space—memory "unmixed with any hope," Staël writes. The door of the future is shutting, which may surprise; 1807 seems early from a French historical perspective, a national tradition which defines this text as liminal or 'Preromantic,' since the pivotal 1830 *bataille d'Hernani* between Classics and Romantics in France is still two decades ahead. But from various, perhaps more universal angles, *Corinne ou l'Italie* is late.

Lateness is a Romantic characteristic. If Newtonian revolution in science heralded a new belief in human progress—with new talk of perfectibility, to which Staël herself was party, after Turgot in 1750—then every Romantic artist in the West confronts the weight of the past, a past which may perhaps be superseded as they look to create new art.[12] A.W. Schlegel's famous Vienna lectures on drama are devoted to the past,

12 Anne Robert Jacques Turgot, *Tableau philosophique des progrès de l'esprit humain* [A Philosophical Illustration of the Advances of the Human Spirit] (1750).

and end with two pages on the future; from Moscow to Montevideo, Romantics look to shape the future by reworking the past they inherit.[13] Furthermore, key Romantic touchstones—Rousseau, Ossian, Percy—date from the 1760s, while the world that most Romantic artists live in postdates two major revolutions; the American one of 1776 and the French one of 1789.[14] Those are definitional moments, as is the French armies' sweep across Europe, 1794–1815—weighing more in the balance than Britain's *Lyrical Ballads* or Germany's literary magazine *Athenäum*, two much-cited, if somewhat less-read, epochs in national myth and each dating as it happens from 1798–1800. Finally, Staël herself, famous before the Revolution, was no neophyte by 1807, that Empire year; there is a reason for Oswald's weariness. Europe's Romantic movements are a disparate bunch, with wildly different founding moments, and one could do worse than refocus on 1789–1815 and how those startling years of Empire and Revolution redrew the map of the West.

"Destinies of women," one fine study of Staël's work is titled.[15] 1789 meant not only the Rights of Man, it meant Olympe de Gouges and the Rights of Woman; it meant Charlotte Corday, Mme Roland, and Marie Antoinette. All four women went to the guillotine.[16] Much excellent work has retraced the considerable pressure exerted in France to return Frenchwomen to the private sphere, post-1789, and here stands another fundamental contribution of Staël's *Corinne ou l'Italie*, that wildly successful novel, to the century that followed: the gap between

13 August Wilhelm Schlegel, *Vorlesungen über dramatische Kunst und Literatur* [Lectures on Dramatic Art and Literature] (1809–1811).

14 Jean-Jacques Rousseau wrote several texts fundamental to later Romantic authors, among them *Julie, ou La Nouvelle Héloïse* [Julie or The New Heloise] (1761). James Macpherson's *The Works of Ossian*, based apparently on fragments of Scottish oral poetry, appeared in 1765, and Bishop Thomas Percy's *The Reliques of Ancient English Poetry* the same year.

15 Simone Balayé, "Destins de femmes dans *Delphine*," *Cahiers staëliens*, XXXV (1984), pp. 41–59.

16 Olympe de Gouges wrote a declaration of the rights of women; Charlotte Corday assassinated Jean-Paul Marat; Marie-Jeanne Roland, like Corday a Girondin, hosted a salon for her Revolutionary husband; Marie-Antoinette was Queen of France. On French pressure on public women after 1789, there is now considerable published work, for instance Olwen H. Hufton, *Women and the Limits of Citizenship in the French Revolution* (Toronto: University of Toronto Press, 1992), *Rebel Daughters. Women and the French Revolution*, ed. by Sara E. Melzer and Leslie W. Rabine (Oxford: Oxford University Press, 1992), and Marilyn Yalom, *Blood Sisters. The French Revolution in Women's Memory* (New York: HarperCollins, 1993).

the public Corinne and the private Lucile. Both sisters are sensitive to others, but Corinne chooses speech and action, whereas Lucile—from England, where men remain at the table while women retire to wonder if the tea is hot—chooses silence and reserve. Paradoxically, England's well-established public sphere seems less open to women than Italy's narrower one. In Rome, Corinne can triumph at the Capitol, while Lucile cannot even tell her husband she knows his heart. Staël had seen first-hand how the public sphere closed for Frenchwomen after 1789. The topic is a constant in her various treatises and fictions, and Corinne in turn shapes her successors, from George Eliot's Maggie Tulliver—explicitly—in *The Mill on the Floss* (1860) to Edgar Allan Poe's "Ligeia" (1838), that dark-haired bride who returns from beyond the grave to possess her successor. Corinne in dying instructs Lucile in how to make her daughter resemble Corinne.

Lucile has secrets. She knows more than she says, as Oswald discovers, and this is a characteristic of the voiceless and the disenfranchised. Their respective information and silence produces a sort of hall of mirrors for them, a strange married *gavotte* which Corinne would have ended, as Staël writes. Not only would Corinne have seen the truth, she would also have spoken it, as Saint-Preux speaks the truth in *La Nouvelle Héloïse* (1761), that touchstone text for early Romantic Europe. This is a tribute to Corinne's genius, but also to her authenticity. Meanwhile, Lucile and Oswald choose silence to avoid inflicting pain. "Transparence and obstacle," Starobinski called his Rousseau study, and that is precisely Staël's erotics.[17] Staël lived this debate in her relations with Benjamin Constant, who put their biography into his short novel *Adolphe* (1816); there's a moment in the movie *Blood Simple* where the hero can't kill another man, but he can bury him alive, and similarly, Oswald and Lucile pay a price for their compunction. It is ironic that this silence plays out amid Italy's openness and its appeals to pleasure—oranges, pomegranates. This is the land where Goethe's lemon trees bloom, "wo die Zitronen blühen," as Mignon sang.[18] And we, as readers, know every

17 Jean Starobinski, *Jean-Jacques Rousseau, La Transparence et l'obstacle* (Paris: Plon, 1957).

18 Johann Wolfgang von Goethe, "Mignons Gesang" [Mignon's Song], in *Goethes Sämtliche Werke*, 20 vols (Leipzig: Insel, [n.d.]), II, p. 141. The song, famously set to music by Franz Schubert, opens Book Three of *Wilhelm Meisters Lehrjahre* (1796).

secret by this point, we know the plot. Strangers have their secrets, but these two tourists are no strangers to us. We all enter the conclusion with shared baggage, and that is part of how story endings work.

Italy in our extract shows us how life could be. It is a land passing directly from autumn to spring and thus bypassing winter—this just as Staël's conclusion gets underway, under the sign of a slow death. History is a curious thing, mixing past, present, and future, and any return is fraught with difficulty. That is the kernel of Hegel's dialectics: in history, thesis and antithesis will yield a difficult synthesis at the end, as novelty and repetition play out.[19] Oswald has a wound which reopens earlier in the novel; he thereby resembles the medieval Tristan or the Guigemar of Marie de France, in an age when medieval texts were being rediscovered and revalued. That wound is the tangible mark of the past on Oswald's body, a sign that he is compromised. Oswald and Corinne each have a pathology, like us all—they each have their cross to bear, or as Racine's Phèdre neatly puts it, "mon mal vient de plus loin," my hurt comes from further away.[20] Oswald is not the first—one thinks of Goethe's *Werther* (1774)—but he is early in a long line of brooding Romantic heroes later exemplified by Byron's equally successful verse romance "Childe Harold", in 1812–1818.

If *Corinne* is a machine for reading, how has that machine operated in the two centuries from 1807 to the present day? This seems a fair question. What is the quality of its art? Well, genre theory here plays its role. From a modern perspective, Staël might have benefited from an editor, she might have tightened her focus; but the same could indisputably be said of Melville's sprawling *Moby-Dick* (1851), that mid-century American classic. What then makes Staël appear so diffuse? The answer is in part that Staël has so much she wants to say. Her novel is not *Corinne*—a romance title—but instead *Corinne ou l'Italie*, and in the nineteenth century it was shelved with guidebooks. Staël has, as a British journal put it, "created the art of analyzing the spirit of nations and the springs which move them."[21] As with Melville then, her global vision is not a bug, but a feature. This returns us to the question of novels, quite

19 See Georg Wilhelm Friedrich Hegel, *Vorlesungen über die Philosophie der Weltgeschichte* [Lectures on the Philosophy of World History] (1837).

20 Jean Racine, *Phèdre*, Act I sc. iii, l.269, in *Oeuvres complètes* (Paris: Seuil, 1962), p. 250.

21 *Blackwood's Edinburgh Magazine*, 4 (December 1818), p. 278.

topical in 1807—because novels seem uniquely suited to this enterprise; they are, in that sense, a uniquely modern genre.

Finally, we face some geopolitical questions. When *De l'Allemagne* reached the censors in 1810, Napoleon's Minister of Police told Staël her work "n'était pas français" [was not French].[22] In that age of French exceptionalism, it matters that Staël in *Corinne* chose to celebrate the United Kingdom and Italy with France occluded between them. Her novel contains no mention of Napoleon's political transformation of the peninsula, while the many Italian artworks Napoleon carted off to Paris are here silently restored to their owners. Staël was born Genevan and Protestant, like Rousseau, and she spent her career liminal from a French national perspective, with a good portion of that time in exile. She is less French, in the end, than European, as her early European fame confirmed. Among the Romantics, such international success is unusual. And looking, like Napoleon, at the Italian peninsula, Staël makes some pertinent choices. First, she unites it in the person of Corinne. Second, she visits the length and breadth of it—Venice, Milan, Florence, Rome, Naples. She is comprehensive. Third, she removes from the peninsula its oppressors and occupiers, be they French, Spanish, or Austrian. Italy is given over to the disenfranchised Italians. Fourth, and last, Staël proposes a contract built on credit, between the individual genius—in politics, thought, or art—and the silent people or nation they represent. This is Corinne's role, from the book's title onward. The idea was new when Staël wrote in 1807, though fundamental to her thought, and it was later borrowed by generations of Romantics around the globe in founding their national literatures. It doubtless helped make Italy possible.

Come 1816, with her article on translation in Milan's *Biblioteca italiana*, Staël played a pivotal role in the emergence of an Italian Romantic movement.[23] This role was political as much as it was esthetic. By and large, the Italian Romantics admired her, from Leopardi to Pellico to Manzoni, though none features in 1807's *Corinne ou l'Italie*. Staël, like

---

22 "quoique le général Savary m'ait déclaré [...] que mon ouvrage *n'était pas français*" [although General Savary declared to me ... that my last work *was not French*], in Madame de Staël, *De l'Allemagne* (1958–1960), I, p. 10.

23 On Staël's 1816 article, see John Claiborne Isbell, "The Italian Romantics and Madame de Staël: Art, Society and Nationhood," in *Rivista di letterature moderne e comparate* L.4 (1997), 355–369 [henceforth "Staël and the Italians"].

Corinne, traveled Italy in search of a national identity. What Oswald hears in fact is Tuscan, not Italian, speech, just as Farinata degli Uberti does in Canto Ten of Dante's "Inferno."[24] Manzoni, after all, wrote *I promessi sposi* in 1825–1826 in Lombard dialect, and as Staël observes, the Apennines split the peninsula down the middle. 'Italy' in 1807 was not a given; Staël did her part to create it, and that work earned her credit with American and European readers, and Italians to begin with. Staël may be early by French standards, captured as she is amid Napoleonic Europe, but she is by no means 'Preromantic,' if anyone ever was that convenient teleological fiction. She is instead building a new art, one made for the new world of stereotype printing, wood-pulp paper (a little later), and an international mass market. She does so to good effect.

24 Farinata greets Dante as a Tuscan: "O tosco che per la città del foco / Vivo ten vai cosí parlando onesto" [O Tuscan who through the city of fire / Goes by alive, thus speaking honestly]—"Inferno," Canto X, ll. 22–23, in Dante Alighieri, *La Divina Commedia* [The Divine Comedy], ed. by Natalino Sapegno, 3 vols (Florence: La Nuova Italia, 1982–1984), I, p. 111.

3. Spain, 1814–1815
Francisco Goya, *Tres de mayo 1808*

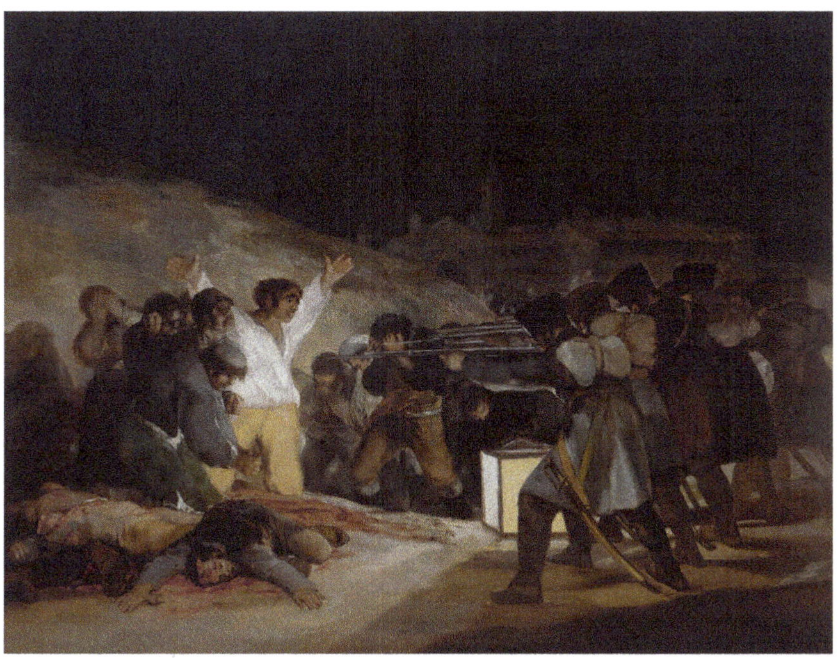

Francisco de Goya, *El Tres de Mayo* (1814), oil on canvas, Museo del Prado. Photograph by Papa Lima Whiskey 2 (2012), Wikimedia, Public domain, https://commons.wikimedia.org/wiki/File:El_Tres_de_Mayo,_by_Francisco_de_Goya,_from_Prado_thin_black_margin.jpg.

Francisco José de Goya y Lucientes (30 March 1746–16 April 1828). **Works**: portraits—*Caprichos; Los desastres de la guerra; Dos de mayo 1808* and *Tres de mayo 1808; Pinturas negras*. Goya was born into a middle-class family. He studied painting under Anton Raphael Mengs, then in Rome, being appointed court painter in 1789 and Director of the Royal Academy in 1795. Goya married in 1773, before suffering an illness in 1793 which left him deaf. In 1807, Napoleon entered Spain to begin the Peninsular War. Goya remained in Madrid, and a physical and mental breakdown followed. The extent of Goya's involvement with the court of Napoleon's brother Joseph I is not known. The Bourbon Ferdinand VII returned to Spain in 1814, but relations with Goya were not cordial. Goya's *Los desastres de la guerra* comment both on the Peninsular War and on Ferdinand VII's move to crush liberalism after his return. His fourteen *Pinturas negras* were executed in oil directly onto the plaster walls of his house. He moved to Bordeaux in 1824—the year of the new French invasion—dying there in 1828. His body was re-interred in Madrid.

What is the meaning of this wash of darkness? Well, to begin with, like Picasso's *Guernica,* it is among the great anti-war paintings of all time. It is a companion piece to Goya's *Dos de mayo 1808,* hanging like that canvas in the Prado Museum in Madrid. The two paintings chronicle then-recent Spanish history: on 2 May 1808, after Napoleon installed his older brother Joseph on the throne of Spain, the citizens of Madrid rose up against the occupying French in the person of the Emperor's mamelukes, slaughtering many. French reprisals followed on 3 May, as shown in Figure 1. Goya witnessed both uprising and reprisals, and with final French defeat after six years of Peninsular War, he came in 1814–1815 to paint these two canvases. We might add that the paintings also mark a pivotal moment in the history of Europe, one in which France's grand Revolutionary dream, as lived by the subjects—not citizens—of Europe's various kingdoms and principalities, ended. Beethoven wrote his third—or *Eroica*—symphony "for a great man," that man being Bonaparte. He then learned the man had crowned himself emperor, and so rededicated the piece "to the memory of a great man," because Bonaparte was dead to him.[25] The infant French Republic's war of survival, waged after 1792 against Europe's various invading sovereigns, turned offensive in 1794 after the battle of Fleurus, as France's citizen armies, with superior gunpowder (thanks to Lavoisier) and tactics, began their sweep across the continent.[26] At first, they created republics as they went—in the Low Countries, in Switzerland, and in the Italian peninsula—but as Bonaparte became Napoleon, so he began installing new sovereigns in their stead, often from among his

25 A copy of Beethoven's score bears the deleted, hand-written subtitle, *Intitolata Bonaparte* [Titled Bonaparte]. In 1806, the score was published under the title *Sinfonia Eroica, composta per festeggiare il sovvenire di un grande Uomo* [Heroic Symphony, Composed to celebrate the memory of a great man]. See Carl Dalhaus, *Ludwig van Beethoven: Approaches to His Music* (Oxford: Clarendon Press, 1991), pp. 23–25.

26 Lavoisier: Seymour H. Mauskopf, "Lavoisier and the improvement of gunpowder production," in *Revue d'histoire des sciences* 48.1–2 (1995), 96–122.

family. Not many would support the French invaders for the purpose of replacing their local ruler with a French one, and it is this turn in history that Goya records. In 1789, as in 1792 at the birth of the Republic, France had stood for the voiceless—for the millions, the downtrodden and disenfranchised. By 3 May 1808, the French citizen army had been reduced to literally faceless cogs in the Emperor's arsenal of war and conquest. Facing them were the people of Madrid, those proud but humble members of the Spanish nation. The new national ideal of liberation had crossed over in a sort of *translatio imperii* from the citizens of France to those countries they were occupying.

So, the French. In Goya's companion piece, *Dos de mayo 1808*, the mamelukes are individuals full of life and independent agency. Not here, where the citizen-army, the *levée en masse*, is a bare faceless diagonal, cutting through the sweep of the canvas behind leveled bayonets. Its troops are following orders, quite visibly lacking free will or independent volition. Standing for France, they have come to represent a great, unending war machine and nothing else. All the life and volition in this canvas is to the left, where the Spanish stand awaiting death. The French here exemplify a singular military virtue, that of discipline, a virtue which does not meaningfully define citizenship. They are superbly trained to execute orders, as shown by their discipline in slaughtering unarmed civilians: not one soldier questions the orders they have been given. The light in this scene, as often in Baroque paintings—say, by Georges de La Tour—comes from a lantern at their feet, which their bodies partly obscure. It lights them from behind, leaving them largely in shadow while falling starkly on the Spanish facing them, both those standing and those stretched out dead in a pool of their own blood. The sky above—the entire top third of the canvas—is black, as it is in, say, Caravaggio's *Martyrdom of St Peter*, a martyrdom where the Lord is nowhere to be seen.

For this is martyrdom. The frontmost Spaniard standing and awaiting execution is a tonsured priest, hands clasped in prayer. This shows Imperial France in action, as seen by Goya from Catholic Spain. Just behind the priest and dominating the canvas is a standing Christ figure, arms outstretched as if for crucifixion. Like Jesus in Palestine, the man is no big fish; he is an anonymous and simple man, in linen shirt and trousers like any citizen of Madrid. At the feet of these Spaniards there is no lantern, there are only the dead—the French are bringing up captives in batches and executing them by firing squad. And behind this group, head in hand, stand those who await their turn for execution. Looming up into the black nighttime sky is a church spire, a mere detail of architecture in this scene where the only priest we see is about to be shot. Finally, it seems worth noting that the Spanish display a total lack of military discipline. They are not even in uniform. This is because the French are slaughtering civilians, but it also heralds the war that was to come, the world's first *guerilla* war—a new mode of warfare which here found its Spanish name. All over Spain, after Napoleon's crowning of his brother Joseph and the massacres of 3 May, citizens rose up against the French. For six years, Spanish *guerilleros* pinned down an entire French army, to Napoleon's cost, and they had largely defeated the French in Spain by 1814. This Peninsular War was Wellington's focus before Waterloo, and it helped to shape the history of Europe.

Europe in 1808 looked very different from Europe in 1814–1815, when Goya returned to this bloody incident to create his two masterpieces. All of Spain was liberated by then; across Europe, the kings were coming back. Napoleon was in Elba, then Cannes, then St Helena. The pressing need to respond that Goya—like the Spanish people—may have felt in 1808, had surely dwindled by 1814, given Napoleon's retreat from Moscow in 1812 and France's ensuing and total defeat. With Metternich and the Congress of Vienna, the twenty-five-year dream launched by the French Revolution in 1789–1815 was at an end. What was its aftermath? Ironically, in 1824, the restored French Crown marched into Spain again, in order to suppress liberal ferment. The period 1776–1826 saw independence for every colony on the American mainland south of Canada, as France, Portugal, Spain, and the United Kingdom lost the territories they held, in part in consequence of Napoleon's continental plans for Europe. Simón Bolívar plotted his New World wars of liberation from there.[27] Spain by 1826 was a different and smaller country than Spain in 1789, or even than occupied Spain in 1808; Goya's paintings in these terms, from a Spanish perspective, mark less a turning point or pivot than a frail interlude of foreign ideals caught between long periods of Bourbon repression.

27 Simón Bolívar, in Europe 1800–1807, returned then to Venezuela to launch his revolution.

It matters perhaps that Goya's art seems closer to that of his French contemporaries—David, Géricault, Delacroix—than to the British—Turner, Constable—or to German painters like Friedrich or Runge. *Tres de mayo 1808* might easily be a Géricault painting, like, say, 1819's *The Raft of the Medusa*. This is not the British world of Turner's *The Fighting Temeraire* or Constable's *The Haywain*, or indeed the German world of Friedrich's 1818 *Wanderer above the Sea of Fog*. What does it mean, then, to call Goya a Romantic? We review in Chapter Two how very few of Europe's and America's canonical Romantics admit the term in describing their own art. The term Romantic began in Germany as a term of abuse. We might remember both that the term was highly charged for contemporaries both *pro* and *con*, and that as we contemplate the shape of Europe and the Americas, 1776–1848, it becomes rather difficult to pretend that no great international watershed in thought, art, and society is underway. This book argues that it is, and that its nature is anchored in the double revolution of 1776–1789, as in the people's voice celebrated in the opening words— "We, the people"—to the Constitution of the new United States.[28] It matters that Europe's and America's various subject peoples, as constituted back in 1700, could view themselves as citizens by 1800. This is the world of Goya's painting. It matters that Beethoven—whom musicologists name Classical—wrote the *Eroica* for Bonaparte, and that his fellow Classical composer, Mozart, produced his opera *Die Zauberflöte* in homespun and national German, like Weber's later *Der Freischütz*, not in the courtly Italian of his own *Don Giovanni*.[29] Was there in fact an international Romantic civilization? I believe there was, irrespective of any local division in time or place or topic that academic disciplines may find convenient. It stretches from Moscow to Montevideo; it has its role in architecture, in furniture, in landscaping, and in costume, as it does in literature and music, in painting, and even sculpture—Canova, Thorvaldsen—and in the thought of Kant or Hegel, Rousseau or Emerson, Jefferson or Hume. It is, in fact, by the standards of history's innumerable esthetic movements, unusually universal in scope. It is marked by the new technologies of the Industrial Revolution,

28 The Constitution of the United States, written in 1787, opens "We, the People of the United States, in Order to form a more perfect Union [...]."

29 Wolfgang Amadeus Mozart, *Die Zauberflöte* [The Magic Flute] (1791), libretto by Emanuel Schikaneder.

which started in the United Kingdom, and is shaped in politics by French and American revolution and empire, retraced in daily life by the troubled period's international Regency or Empire Style. It is a new age, one of stereotype printing and wood-pulp paper; the mass markets thus made possible; and concomitant market-driven thickening of line in art: a Romantic triangle of production.

Spain, too, matters in this broad story, as do the events of 1808. Regardless of later Spanish history, this moment marked both an end to French pretensions to be liberating Europe's subject peoples—as the French had alleged since 1794—and a start to the moment when those European subjects began liberating themselves; often, as in Spain, in a bid to eject the French, those occupiers, from their national soil. This theme would play out among the Italian Romantics after 1816, engaged with Metternich's Austrians, and among the Romantics of Eastern Europe in the following decades, dealing as they did with foreigners speaking mostly German or Russian, with Austria, Prussia, and Russia in particular. It is why Goya may matter more to European and American Romanticism than the Spanish Romantics who followed him in the narrower days of the Bourbon Restoration—Rivas, Larra, Espronceda, Zorrilla—and why Bolívar or San Martín may matter more to Western Romanticism, when all is said and done, than Argentina's Romantic poets like Echeverría or Hernández. It turns out that Spain, as seen here by Goya, was as much of a dream as France was. The return of the Bourbons established that.

4. The British Isles (England), 1818
Mary Shelley, *Frankenstein; or, The Modern Prometheus*

> "Farewell! I leave you, and in you the last of humankind whom these eyes will ever behold. Farewell, Frankenstein! If thou wert yet alive and yet cherished a desire of revenge against me, it would be better satiated in my life than in my destruction. But it was not so; thou didst seek my extinction, that I might not cause greater wretchedness; and if yet, in some mode unknown to me, thou hadst not ceased to think and feel, thou wouldst not desire against me a vengeance greater than that which I feel. Blasted as thou wert, my agony was still superior to thine, for the bitter sting of remorse will not cease to rankle in my wounds until death shall close them for ever.
>
> "But soon," he cried with sad and solemn enthusiasm, "I shall die, and what I now feel be no longer felt. Soon these burning miseries will be extinct. I shall ascend my funeral pile triumphantly and exult in the agony of the torturing flames. The light of that conflagration will fade away; my ashes will be swept into the sea by the winds. My spirit will sleep in peace, or if it thinks, it will not surely think thus. Farewell."
>
> He sprang from the cabin-window as he said this, upon the ice raft which lay close to the vessel. He was soon borne away by the waves and lost in darkness and distance.[30]

Mary Wollstonecraft Shelley; *née* Godwin (30 August 1797–1 February 1851). **Works**: novels—*The Fortunes of Perkin Warbeck, Lodore, Falkner, Valperga, The Last Man*; travel writing—*Rambles in Germany and Italy*; biographical articles. Mary also edited the works of Percy Bysshe Shelley. Mary's father was the radical philosopher William Godwin; her mother, the feminist Mary Wollstonecraft, died after giving birth to her. She was raised by her father, meeting Coleridge and others. In 1814, she met the young Percy Shelley, who was already married. She, Percy, and her stepsister, Claire Clairmont, left for France that year; Mary returned pregnant and Godwin refused to see her. Mary lost that child. Percy's first wife, like Mary's half-sister Fanny Imlay, committed suicide; Percy was ruled morally unfit for custody of his children. He and Mary married in December 1816. The couple had spent that summer in Geneva with Clairmont, Lord Byron, and Byron's physician Polidori. Byron proposed that all tell a ghost story, and Mary at last thought of *Frankenstein*. She later

30 Mary Shelley, *Frankenstein or The Modern Prometheus* (Oxford: Oxford University Press, 2015), p. 207.

wrote that the preface was Percy's, who also provided help in editing. Facing legal threats—loss of custody, debtors' prison—the couple left Britain for Italy in 1818. Mary lost two more babies before giving birth to her only surviving child, a son. In 1822, her husband drowned when his boat sank during a storm off Viareggio. Mary returned to England, meeting Washington Irving and Prosper Mérimée, raising her son on a stipend from his grandfather, editing Percy's work, and writing until her death in 1851. It seems likely that she remained a political radical throughout. At her death, the family found in her desk a copy of Percy's *Adonaïs*, folded round the remains of his heart.

Given her parents—William Godwin and Mary Wollstonecraft—Mary Shelley was, during her lifetime, almost certainly better-known than her husband Percy, whose poetry, by and large, went unread. That may not be the case today, but the monster she created is better-known to millions than its author is; an odd case of a creation eclipsing its creator, but then, Romanticism itself long ago took on a life of its own in which it has co-opted the various artists and thinkers with whom it came into contact. Fame too has a life of its own, and Mary Shelley, like Staël before her, was defined by her parents' fame from childhood on. Across Romantic Europe, Godwin in particular was a symbol of free-thinking and anarchism, while Wollstonecraft's 1792 *Vindication of the Rights of Women* stands her alongside Olympe de Gouges in a struggle for women's rights shaped by the French Revolutionary dream of 1789.

It is in this context that Mary Shelley, aged eighteen and staying by Lake Geneva with Shelley and the notorious Byron, conceived her novel, which she published anonymously two years later. It is, like *Faust* or *Don Giovanni*, one of the great Romantic myths.[31] Mary died in 1851, long outliving her doomed husband, and wrote more novels— *The Last Man* (1826), *Lodore* (1835)—but none approached her early success. Few authors—Rimbaud, perhaps—have been this good this young.

In this extract, we find ourselves on her novel's closing page, and the monster—the creature—is speaking. A good deal has happened already; Victor Frankenstein has conceived, in youthful enthusiasm and pride in science, his galvanic and Promethean experiment, and the monster he thus creates—bringing the dead to life—has committed a string of

31 Mozart, *Don Giovanni* (1787), libretto by Lorenzo Da Ponte.

murders for which Victor has been both blamed and pursued by justice. Meanwhile, Victor has himself been pursuing it, a chase that ends in the frozen Arctic with Victor dead as his creation weeps. The creature has been a sort of *Doppelgänger* for Victor, and now, as in posterity, it stands and speaks while Victor has fallen by the wayside. It speaks in a found text, which was a common eighteenth-century novelistic device, lending both a framing narrative and a plausible back story to the tale we read. The eighteenth century particularly favored epistolary novels—for instance those of Richardson, Rousseau, Montesquieu, or Goethe—in a society where people wrote long and frequent letters and where prose fictions *per se* were generically and ethically compromised.[32] Letters to structure a fiction, to advance a plot, addressed concerns that the eighteenth century's novel writers found important, and such epistolary fictions sold without difficulty. We have here, then, the creature's reported speech, in Walton's continuation of his dead friend Victor's story, as set forth in letters home from the Arctic. And as in Novalis's *Heinrich von Ofterdingen*, we never leave that closing frame. We are left, in these closing words, on the ice where the creature vanishes into the darkness. It makes for a compelling ending, one without an exit, where we finish up trapped in the Arctic and the heart is crushed. This is a composite narrative, like Laclos's 1782 *Les Liaisons dangereuses*—a kaleidoscopic array of first-person speech.[33]

As for the plot, it somewhat resembles her father Godwin's own brilliant Jacobin novel *Caleb Williams* (1794), in which Caleb is framed for crimes he did not commit: "My life," Caleb begins, "has for several years been a theatre of calamity."[34] Shelley's novel can fairly be called Gothic, a genre in vogue enough at this turn of the nineteenth century, in Britain and Germany in particular, for Jane Austen to parody it in *Northanger Abbey* (1817). The genre starts perhaps with Horace Walpole's *The Castle*

32 Samuel Richardson wrote the wildly popular *Pamela; or Virtue rewarded* (1740) and *Clarissa: Or the History of a Young Lady* (1747). Jean-Jacques Rousseau, *Julie, ou La Nouvelle Héloïse* (1761). Charles de Secondat de Montesquieu, *Lettres persanes* (1721). Goethe, *Die Leiden des jungen Werther* (1774).

33 On first-person discourse in the British Jacobin novel of the 1790s, to which Mary Shelley has a clear debt, see Gary Kelly, "Romantic Fiction," in *The Cambridge Companion to British Romanticism*, ed. by Stuart Curran, 2nd edition (Cambridge: Cambridge University Press, 2010), pp. 187–208.

34 William Godwin, *Things as They Are; or The Adventures of Caleb Williams* (1794), ed. Maurice Hindle (London: Penguin Books, 1988), p. 5.

of Otranto (1764), and some British high points include Ann Radcliffe's *The Mysteries of Udolpho* (1794), Matthew Lewis's *The Monk* (1796), and Charles Maturin's *Melmoth the Wanderer* (1820). John Polidori, with the group on Lake Geneva, published *The Vampyre* in 1819, the first modern vampire story. There is also some parallel between the accursed creature, lost in the Arctic, and the figure of the Wandering Jew: Eugène Sue's eponymous 1844 potboiler thus opens at the Bering Strait. This was a great age of exploration; witness the voyages of Captain Cook or Bougainville in the Pacific, of Alexander von Humboldt through Latin America, of Lewis and Clark crossing the new Louisiana Territory.[35] By 1818, the Russians and the British were pushing into the Arctic—but reaching the two poles remained a century away.

So much for our framing and our scene. The creature's words also echo various contemporary vogues, starting with that of Prometheus. George Cruikshank published his anti-Napoleonic engraving, *The Modern Prometheus*—Mary's subtitle—in 1814. Promethean revolt runs like a red thread through Romantic thought; it is central to *Faust* and *Don Giovanni*; it is the theme of Percy Bysshe Shelley's splendid 1820 verse drama *Prometheus Unbound*. "Pain is my element, as hate is thine," Percy there writes.[36] Just as Victor Frankenstein is Promethean, in revolt against God's ordering of life and death, so too is Victor's creature Promethean, and in revolt against its personal demiurge. This accursed world of suffering, pride, and madness is also the world of outcasts like Cain. The creature, who is a murderer, exults in suffering and revolt, somewhat as Matthew Lewis's monk exults in evil. Its death will be by fire, on a pagan funeral pyre, and as for an afterlife, the creature— "if it thinks"— is agnostic. After all, its whole existence has been an afterlife, from the moment of its creation on Victor's laboratory slab. Horror, which frames the creature's narrative, is the *raison d'être* of the Gothic genre. Here, that appears newly anchored in the sublime, which mattered a good deal to recent theorists, from Edmund Burke's 1757 *A Philosophical Enquiry into*

35 Captain James Cook made three voyages to the Pacific: 1768–1771, 1772–1775, and 1776–1780. Louis-Antoine, Comte de Bougainville circumnavigated the globe in 1763. Alexander von Humboldt traveled in Latin America from 1799–1804. Meriwether Lewis and William Clark crossed the new Louisiana Territory to the Pacific at President Jefferson's direction from 1803–1806.

36 "Prometheus Unbound," in *The Complete Poetical Works of Percy Bysshe Shelley*, ed. by Thomas Hutchinson (Oxford: Oxford University Press, 1952), p. 218: Act I, l.477.

the Origin of Our Ideas of the Sublime and Beautiful to Immanuel Kant's 1790 *Critik der Urtheilskraft*. For these theorists, nature is a key locus of the sublime, as it is in the Arctic setting of this extract. Nature and solitude, as seen here, are also curious reworkings of Rousseau's preoccupations in his 1782 *Rêveries du promeneur solitaire*. They are two themes destined for great success throughout the nineteenth century, both in the vatic figure of the poet and in the nature this vatic figure embraces. Just as nature and solitude, horror and the sublime, are here reworked, so too are the Romantic topoi of enthusiasm and melancholy.

The very existence of the creature is predicated on Luigi Galvani's 1780 experiment, which ran an electric current through a dead frog's leg to make it twitch. Just as eighteenth-century Britain had seen its share of sea journeys, so again in Galvani sociohistorical context has impact. In what world is this text conceived and published? It bears mention, for instance, that Frankenstein has assumed the female prerogative of birth; he bypasses love in marriage to embark on a sterile journey of the mind, like Dante's damned Ulysses, Coleridge's Ancient Mariner, or the scientists behind mustard gas or the atomic bomb.[37] Like her mother's *Vindication*, Mary Shelley's novel *Frankenstein* thus matters in the history of women. Facing the displacements of Britain's Industrial Revolution—the brave new world of Whitney and Arkwright, the spinning Jenny and the cotton gin, of enclosures, the railroad, Adam Smith, and industrial production—was Britain's Luddite movement of textile workers in open revolt throughout Nottinghamshire, 1811–1816.[38] In 1819, a local magistrate sent cavalry after a peaceful Manchester crowd calling for parliamentary reform, an incident known forever after as Peterloo. Mary Shelley tells her tale of science gone haywire, the first mad scientist story, against this backdrop of British progress and its discontents. As for Europe—Shelley wrote her text in the new Switzerland—the continent had, in 1816, just seen the French nation's international revolution,

37 Dante, who did not read Greek, was unaware that Ulysses returned home. He puts him near the bottom of the *Inferno* after Ulysses summons his crew to the "mondo sanza gente" [world without people]—in *Dante Alighieri* (1982–1984), I, p. 294: Canto XXVI, l.117. "The Rime of the Ancient Mariner" (1798) in *Coleridge* (1931), p. 187.

38 Eli Whitney invented the cotton gin and Richard Arkwright the spinning frame, two inventions which in fact prolonged the slavery-based cotton economy in the antebellum American South.

dear to both Shelleys' hearts, crash to an end with Napoleon's final defeat at Waterloo in 1815, and the return of the kings to the thrones of Europe. The Shelleys left in 1818 for subjugated Italy, and Mary did not return to England until after her husband's death in 1822. Their friend Byron, meanwhile, died young in 1824, fighting for Greek freedom at Missolonghi.

Today, Mary Shelley's creature has stolen Victor's name. The creature argues in this closing speech that remorse makes its agony "superior" to Victor's, much as Percy's Prometheus in his suffering is superior to Zeus. Then it departs across the ice, and this jagged text, as composite a thing as the creature itself, comes to an end. We bid farewell. And what does this ending mean, for the creature, for readers, for the author? Well, for the creature, it means it gets the last word. Its creator, enemy, and rival is now as dead as the creature was when lying on that slab. The creature is accursed, a scapegoat and outcast, but not voiceless at the close; it can say, like Shakespeare's Caliban in *The Tempest* (1611), "You taught me language; / and my profit on't, is, I know how to curse."[39] Indeed, one might see the legacy of William Wilberforce's long campaign against the Atlantic slave trade in filigree behind this figure who is, after all, "a Man and a Brother," as Wedgwood's famous anti-slavery medallion then had it.[40] As for the readers, we are left stranded in the Arctic, and our last companion is this monster and murderer. Its departure into the wastes is in turn not without recalling the last line of Percy's epochal sonnet, "Ozymandias" (1818)— "The lone and level sands stretch far away."[41] The vision that ends Frankenstein was, in short, a shared vision for the Shelley marriage, in the years 1816–1822, and one they cared a good deal about.

Finally, what did this ending mean for Mary Shelley herself? At the end of the day, as life and history played out—Percy's death by drowning, the emergence and consolidation of the Metternich Restoration in Europe, the continuing advance in Britain, Europe, and the Americas of the Industrial Revolution—it meant a retreat of sorts

39 William Shakespeare, *The Tempest*, Act I sc. ii, ll. 363–364, in *The Riverside Shakespeare* (Boston: Houghton Mifflin, 1974), p. 1616.

40 William Wilberforce helped inspire Josiah *Wedgwood's* anti-slavery medallion of 1787, in white with a black figure, which reads "Am I not a Man and a Brother?"

41 "Ozymandias" (1818) in *Shelley* (1952), p. 550.

from being a Regency author into being a Victorian one, a shift which entailed a variety of choices and obligations. It is some way from the explosive revolt that ends Mary Shelley's first novel to the more settled meditations of *Lodore* and *The Last Man*. That new environment is perhaps safer, but it loses the dream of revolution, it loses mythic weight. And with this arc, as the widowed Mary Shelley advanced through the years, came a certain respectability. That was perhaps hard to imagine in 1816, for this daughter of Godwin and Wollstonecraft, but it was increasingly common for many Englishwomen in particular—George Eliot, say—in the consolidating universe of the long-lived Queen Victoria and of her German consort. As we rediscover Britain's women Romantics—and they are not few in number—Mary Shelley's trajectory from youth to widowhood becomes, in some ways, exemplary. Britain's various women Romantics overlap in theme and biography with its six canonical male poets, those "happy few"—Wordsworth, Coleridge, Byron, Shelley, Keats, and these days, Blake—but like those other, often better-selling contemporary British poets Thomas Moore, or George Crabbe, or Sir Walter Scott for that matter, they also have their own life and their own cross to bear.[42] Our grasp of Romanticism in the West, like our grasp of the history of women, will only gain from our focus on this essential and foundational complexity.

42 Broadview has re-edited some of Mary Shelley's later novels: *The Last Man* (1826), ed. by Anne McWhir, 1996, and *Lodore* (1835), ed. by Lisa Vargo, 1997. "We few, we happy few, we band of brothers"—*Henry V*, Act IV, sc. iii, l.60, in *Shakespeare* (1974), p. 960. Stendhal dedicated his writing to "the happy few" (quoted in English).

5. Russia, 1825–1832
Alexander Pushkin, *Evgenii Onegin*

«Мой дядя самых честных правил,	'My uncle always was respected,
Когда не в шутку занемог,	But his grave illness, I confess,
Он уважать себя заставил	Is more than could have been expected:
И лучше выдумать не мог.	A stroke of genius, nothing less!
Его пример другим наука;	He offers all a fine example.
Но, боже мой, какая скука	But God, such boredom who would sample
С больным сидеть и день и ночь,	As day and night to have to sit
Не отходя ни шагу прочь!	Beside a sick-bed – think of it!
Какое низкое коварство	Low cunning must assist devotion
Полуживого забавлять,	To one who is but half-alive;
Ему подушки поправлять,	You puff his pillow and contrive
Печально подносить лекарство,	Amusement while you mix his potion;
Вздыхать и думать про себя:	You sigh and think with furrowed brow:
Когда же чёрт возьмёт тебя!»	"Why can't the devil take you now?"'
Так думал молодой повеса,	'Tis thus the gay dog's thoughts are freighted,
Летя в пыли на почтовых,	As through the dust his horses fare,
Всевышней волею Зевеса	Who by the high gods' will is fated
Наследник всех своих родных. —	To be his relatives' sole heir.
Друзья Людмилы и Руслана!	Friends of Ruslan and fair Ludmila,
С героем моего романа	For my new hero prithee feel a
Без предисловий, сей же час	Like kinship, as he takes his bow;
Позвольте познакомить вас:	Become acquainted with him now:
Онегин, добрый мой приятель,	Eugene Onegin, born and nourished
Родился на брегах Невы,	Where old Neva's grey waters flow,
Где, может быть, родились вы	Where you were born or as a beau,
Или блистали, мой читатель;	It may be, in your glory flourished,
Там некогда гулял и я:	I too strolled there – not recently:
Но вреден север для меня.	The north does not agree with me.[43]

43 Alexander Pushkin, *Eugene Onegin. A Novel in Verse*, trans. by Babette Deutsch (Harmondsworth: Penguin, 1964), pp. 19–20.

Alexander Sergeevich Pushkin (6 June 1799–10 February 1837). **Works**: long poems—*Ruslan and Liudmila, The Captive of the Caucasus, Evgenii Onegin*; plays—*Boris Godunov;* prose—*The Queen of Spades*. Pushkin was born into Russian nobility; his maternal great-grandfather, Abram Petrovich Gannibal, born, it appears, in what is now Cameroon, was kidnapped, made a page boy to the Ottoman Sultan, and then presented as a gift to Tsar Peter the Great. He rose to be *Général en Chef*, in charge of sea forts and canals in all Russia. Alexander spoke mostly French until the age of ten; he became acquainted with Russian through speaking with household serfs and his nanny. At the Lyceum, Pushkin was influenced by Kant and by the French Enlightenment, particularly Diderot and Voltaire. He became committed to social reform and emerged as a spokesman for reformers, resulting after 1820 in time away from the capital in the Caucasus, Crimea, and Moldavia. There he joined an organization working, like Byron, to overthrow Ottoman rule in Greece, and wrote two poems which brought him acclaim: 'The "Captive of the Caucasus" (1822) and "The Fountain of Bakhchisaray" (1824). In 1823, Pushkin again clashed with the government, which exiled him to his mother's rural estate from 1824 to 1826, though he was summoned to Moscow after his "Ode to Liberty" was found among the belongings of the Decembrist rebels. Around this time, he met and befriended Adam Mickiewicz during the latter's own exile, and also married the sixteen-year-old Natalia Goncharova, one of Moscow's most celebrated beauties. He met and supported the writer Nikolai Gogol after 1831. In 1837, Pushkin was killed in a duel with his brother-in-law, Georges-Charles de Heeckeren d'Anthès, a French officer serving in Russia who had attempted to seduce the poet's wife.

By common consent, Russian literature takes flight with Pushkin, and this is not unusual in the history of European Romanticism. Across Eastern Europe in particular, Romantic authors are foundational. What is perhaps unusual in this tradition is Pushkin's wit, sophistication, and polish; he stands comparison with any nation's preeminent Romantic poet, be it Goethe or Hölderlin, Wordsworth or Keats, Hugo, Lamartine, or Leopardi. In Russia, he is a national hero. His is also the first verse romance here, though Northern and Eastern Europe saw others, from Tegnér's Swedish *Frithiofs Saga* in 1825, through to Mickiewicz's Polish *Pan Tadeusz* in 1834 and Shevchenko's Ukrainian *Haidamaky* in 1841, to Petöfi's Hungarian *János vitéz* (John the Valiant), in 1845. Curiously, the form cannot be called central to French, German, or Italian Romantic production, but it did play an outsize role in shaping Europe's Romantic movements after Byron used it for *Childe Harold*—a European success—in 1812–1818. Byron returned to it in his rather funnier *Don Juan*, a touchstone text for *Onegin* (1825–1832). Across the British Isles, in fact, Southey, Scott, and Thomas Moore showed the form's staying power; it covers Eastern Europe; and Longfellow helped found American poetry with it, in *The Song of Hiawatha* (1855) in particular. It is a fitting pendant to the undoubted and lasting success of the novel during Europe's Romantic era.

There is a fine line between verse romance and the epic. A.W. Schlegel might argue that epic ended with the Classical world, and that Chaucer, Tasso, and Camoëns are working in a new form, the romance, bequeathed to them by the Christian Middle Ages. In romance, for instance, the divine tends to yield to the popular and magical as an agent of the plot. The new interest in romance that typified the later eighteenth century is marked by the success of Ossian as a counterweight to Homer, and by parodies like William Combe's now-neglected *Three Tours of Dr. Syntax* (1809–1821), the first of them in search of the picturesque—Hudibrastic fun serialized in Britain from 1809 to 1811. It is also fair to say that heroes of romance may be ironized in a way impossible for Virgil or Homer, which is emphatically Onegin's case.

One irony of Onegin's lasting popularity in Russia is that he is, like the title characters of Byron's *Don Juan* or Lermontov's *Hero of Our Time* (1840), very much an anti-hero.[44] Reading *Onegin* is a bittersweet experience, to some extent unique in European Romantic literature, though one thinks of Heine. Romantic irony is common enough, but giving us empathy for our hero while making him fundamentally compromised is less common. Alfred de Musset has that knack in *On ne badine pas avec l'amour* (1834). Pushkin opens his love story—for it is a love story—with Onegin awaiting his wealthy uncle's death. Mid-romance, Onegin will duel with and kill his best friend Lensky for, after all, no reason, and that moment is dropped into the narrative like a pebble into a stream without interrupting its onward flow. From the opening lines, Onegin is an entitled young man—an heir, an inheritor—somewhat

44 Mikhail Lermontov, *Geroi nashego vremeni* [A Hero of Our Time] (1840).

along the lines of Dickens's Pip in *Great Expectations* (1860), or Balzac's Eugène de Rastignac in *Le Père Goriot* (1834), or for that matter, Pierre Bezukhov in Tolstoy's later *War and Peace* (1867).[45] Onegin is, in short, a 'superfluous person,' as the Russian saying had it, one of European Romanticism's young minor nobles. From the outset, Onegin is disabused and *blasé*. He is, like Oswald or Frankenstein but unlike, say, Heinrich von Ofterdingen, very modern. Europe's Romantics were equally ready to dive into the Christian Middle Ages or to remain in the chaotic present, relying on a dialectic that divided post-Classical Christian Europe and its productions from the Greek and Roman art that had shaped European output since the Renaissance. Victor Hugo for instance is equally comfortable, in his prose fictions, in medieval Paris or the Paris of 1793 or 1830.[46] This book argues that the agendas of Romantic Neoclassicism on the one hand, and Romantic medievalism on the other, work in tandem and coexist in the minds of more than one author of the era. Certainly, Pushkin combines Romantic and Neoclassical elements.

Onegin strikes a Byronic pose. He is belated—which may surprise, as Russian literature here commences. Topical, modern, witty, he is not a man for enthusiasm, and in that, he contrasts markedly with the Tatiana who falls in love with him. Like his narrator— "The north does not agree with me"—he is a child of pleasure and ease. He is after all very young. And what does it mean to be young, not old, in this world? Well, it means to be lovable. To see possibility stretch out before you, as Lensky does before his death. It means perhaps to be *authentic*, in contrast to the trimming and hypocrisy to which the old are often reduced. To be poor, though one may have expectations, and to depend on uncles for our inheritance. It may mean to have solidarity with those who will later die poor—as heirs like these will, in theory, not—and thus to see value in revolution, like Julien, who has nothing, or the aristocratic Mathilde who loves him in Stendhal's *Le Rouge et le Noir* (1830).[47] That is how *Evgenii Onegin* opens.

45 Lev Tolstoy, *Voina i mir* [War and Peace] (1867).

46 Compare Victor Hugo, *Notre-Dame de Paris* (1831), *Les Misérables* [The Wretched] (1862), *Quatrevingt-treize* [Ninety-Three] (1874).

47 Stendhal [Marie-Henri Beyle], *Le Rouge et le Noir: Chronique du XIXe siècle* [The Red and the Black: Chronicle of the 19th Century] (1830).

Testaments mattered to the Romantics as they do to anyone. They separate families from strangers. Within families, they separate old and young along hierarchical lines. They bring the weight of societal inertia, of impersonal structuring principles, to bear on the Promethean individual. They compromise free will and independence, as in the case of Jarndyce v. Jarndyce in Dickens's 1852 *Bleak House*. Onegin will live his life representing the family name, and aristocratic honor matters enough to him to fight a duel with his best friend over it. It is worth remembering that peasant heroes are not common in the Romantic era; Stendhal's Julien Sorel is one. It is instead common for this art which is focused on the folk—on recording the people's voice—to do so via the minor nobility; indeed, kings and queens are not rare in Romantic pages. Here, we might turn a moment to Pushkin's own life, and the story of Russia in the years leading up to 1825–1832, when this poem was published. Pushkin fought more than one duel, and that is how he died. He ran afoul of the new tsar, Nicholas I, in the 1825 Decembrist uprising, and was exiled from St Petersburg in consequence. The liberal dreams that had attached to Tsar Alexander I, around 1813 as he founded the Holy Alliance, had dissipated as he consolidated power. Serfdom remained unreformed throughout the empire. That is the backdrop to Onegin's feckless adventuring.

The text is not short of Romantic baggage. Big Romantic themes are handled lightly, as in Byron's *Don Juan*, in Stendhal's epigraphs to *Le Rouge et le Noir*, and in Almeida Garrett's chapter rubrics for his *Viagens na minha terra* (1846). Pushkin combines name-dropping with wit—*Ruslan and Liudmila* was his own poem, published in 1820. This lightness of touch, this humor in narrative, is the world laid out by Laurence Sterne in his novel *Tristram Shandy* (1759–1767). From the opening words of a book, both reader and author form an implicit contract, and it is worth asking how that contract looks in Pushkin. What do we know of our hero? What do we know of the author and narrator? Are they, for instance, Russian like ourselves? Onegin, the protagonist, we have discussed. The young Pushkin was well enough known by 1825 that the Decembrists viewed him as their inspiration, and fame and its specific mechanics have their role in Pushkin's storytelling. Let us mention that like Alexandre Dumas, Alexander Pushkin had African ancestors, but unlike Dumas, he did not find himself excluded from the canon on that basis. As for Pushkin's narrator, he (or she) is complex. To begin with, he speaks in a fluent stanza form, which again has its debt to Byron's *Don Juan* and the poem's brisk and elegant *ottava rima*. This is a novel in verse, as Pushkin announces on his title page, thereby complicating genre theory. Prose fiction is not typically the home of the lyric moment, but Pushkin has found a genre which allows the two to be combined. The narrator is, if not omniscient, then certainly well-informed, hence the topical name dropping. He is an educated man addressing the educated—not always a priority in Eastern European verse romance. He is *blasé* and tends to report Onegin's behavior without undue commentary or judgment. He is easily bored, as in the story's final line: "As, my Onegin, I drop you" (214). In short, he is very civilized, a fine companion for our journey through Onegin's adventures.

Let us return for a moment to the opening extract. Our own reader's contract with Pushkin and this book takes shape quickly. The young author, in 1825–1832, was already famous, with liberal leanings that had seen him exiled from St Petersburg. The narrator is *comme il faut*, a suitable and entertaining companion for our reading. Our protagonist is, from the opening stanza, not a hero in the traditional sense, but compromised, if not an anti-hero. The opening, like any opening, is a tuning fork that will determine the tone of every page thereafter, and Pushkin hits that note with aplomb. Every page of Onegin's subsequent thought and action is informed by these opening stanzas. Openings are tricky things, but Pushkin makes the difficult look easy. This entire 'novel in verse' is never heavy-handed or slow; even Lensky's death, as noted, goes by like a breath of air in this light plotting. And yet, that is Onegin's best friend, and he won't be coming back. It is not easy to look this easy, and that is what Pushkin does. It seems all the more worth recognizing that Pushkin has contrived to be entirely Russian and national—to speak to generations of Russians—in a text full of echoes of his broad European reading; that he has opened a national literature with a tone notable for its world-weariness; that he is polished and elegant where you might expect earnest simplicity, if not mediocre art; that he is, at the end of the day, really very old, like his narrator, where you might expect him to be young. There is a certain miracle to it all, a certain magic and wonder. It might make Pushkin smile from beyond the grave.

6. The United States, 1826
James Fenimore Cooper, *The Last of the Mohicans*

> Chingachgook grasped the hand that, in the warmth of feeling, the scout had stretched across the fresh earth, and in an attitude of friendship these two sturdy and intrepid woodsmen bowed their heads together, while scalding tears fell to their feet, watering the grave of Uncas like drops of falling rain.
>
> In the midst of the awful stillness with which such a burst of feeling, coming as it did, from the two most renowned warriors of that region, was received, Tamenund lifted his voice to disperse the multitude.
>
> "It is enough," he said. "Go, children of the Lenape, the anger of the Manitou is not done. Why should Tamenund stay? The pale faces are masters of the earth, and the time of the red men has not yet come again. My day has been too long. In the morning I saw the sons of Unamis happy and strong; and yet, before the night has come, have I lived to see the last warrior of the wise race of the Mohicans."[48]

James Fenimore Cooper (September 15, 1789-September 14, 1851). **Works**: novels, notably the Leatherstocking series; political tracts—*A Letter to My Countrymen*; naval writings—*History of the Navy of the United States of America*. Cooper spent his boyhood and old age in Cooperstown, New York, a town founded by his father. He attended Yale University but was expelled for pranks—a donkey on campus, an exploding door. In 1806, Cooper joined the merchant marine and saw an American crewmate impressed into the British Royal Navy. He joined the United States Navy as an officer in 1811, marrying into a Loyalist family the same year. Cooper published *The Spy* in 1821—America's first bestseller—before moving on to the Leatherstocking series from 1823 to 1841, featuring Natty Bumppo, a woodsman at home with the Delaware Indians. Cooper moved his family to Europe in 1826, befriending the Marquis de La Fayette, though he was no fan of aristocracy in politics. He returned to the United States in 1833 and published the broadside "A Letter to My Countrymen." Cooper admired Jefferson and Jackson; Whig editors attacked anything he wrote. Cooper's death was followed by a memorial service in New York led by the writers Daniel Webster, Washington Irving, and William Cullen Bryant.

48 James Fenimore Cooper, *The Last of the Mohicans* (New York, NY: Penguin Books, 1986), pp. 349–350.

By the 1820s, a new European vogue for prose historical romances, launched by Sir Walter Scott in 1814 when he switched from verse to prose with *Waverley* (1814), had crossed the Atlantic. Cooper became famous with *The Spy* (1821), but he pivoted his five *Leatherstocking Tales* around *The Last of the Mohicans* in 1826, and indeed the book anchors his fame today. Just as Scott spoke for a junior partner in the British enterprise—Scotland has played second fiddle to England since the Act of Union in 1707—so Cooper gave voice to a junior partner in the emerging Anglosphere, the new United States. In 1826, the Declaration of Independence was just fifty years in the past; the constitution dated only from 1787, and in the War of 1812—that sidebar to Europe's titanic Napoleonic struggle—the British had taken the new nation's capital and burned its White House. America was not yet the world power it became after the Civil War; it remained federal, agricultural, provincial, frontiersy. It is against this backdrop that Cooper chose to place his scout Natty Bumppo—Hawkeye—in late Colonial days, the time of the French and Indian War. That was North America's piece of the Seven Years' War between France and the United Kingdom, which played out between 1756–1763 from the Caribbean to India. One could imagine, after independence and the War of 1812, that Cooper might be anti-British, and the sentiment is common enough in American history. His villains are instead the French, who gave determinative support to the War of Independence, along with the Hurons, their former Indian allies. New nations sometimes align unexpectedly within existing power dynamics.

The short paragraphs above close Cooper's novel. Tamenund, the speaker, is an indigenous tribal leader—though European settlers and Indian tribes were to fight and kill each other for another century on the nation's Western frontier. Cooper's decision to make Uncas a hero, and to give Tamenund the last word, may be gauged in its radicalism by Echeverría's contemporary and pivotal Argentine verse romance, "La Cautiva" (1837), whose heroine's capture by bloodthirsty Indians shapes his plot and title. The two nations have their differences, reflecting their different stories: boasting to an Argentine friend of my Native American ancestry, I was—to my surprise—commiserated with. It was not entirely apparent, in 1826, that American Indian power in North America would forever end, but in fact The Prophet's defeat at Tippecanoe in 1811, combined with the Creek War in 1813–1814, had ended all organized indigenous resistance east of the Mississippi. Furthermore, Lewis and Clark had, in 1804–1806, crossed the entire new Louisiana Territory—Indian Territory—with their guide Sacagawea and, like Keats's Cortez of 1816, reached the Pacific.[49] The whole breadth of North America was within the new colonial nation's grasp. This is the context for Cooper's pregnant title—*The Last of the Mohicans*—and for Tamenund's closing words.

How might one expect Europeans and non-Europeans, in 1826, to interact? Cooper's novel is focused on this topic. Technology plays its part here. The first successful steamboats appeared in the 1780s, opening up the great rivers of the planet—the Yangtze, the Congo, the Mississippi, the Orinoco—to navigation and thus launching the era of gunboat diplomacy.[50] The world's continental interiors became accessible to European firepower and, indeed, the European powers spent much of the nineteenth century acquiring as much of the globe as they could manage, primarily in competition with each other. Local populations, in their varying states of economic, sociopolitical, and military development, were subjugated or wiped out. If the eighteenth century was a great age of exploration—the British Captain Cook was murdered in 1779 on the remote Hawaiian archipelago—the nineteenth was an age for imperialism, in which the new United States took part: annexing Hawaii from its last queen, for instance, in 1898. It is nostalgic, not to say sentimental, for Cooper to set his novel during the Seven Years War, a time when colonizing powers and Native American tribes could negotiate on an almost equal footing. Such was not the case in 1826. We might also note that America's then-ongoing pillage of the West African coast—the Atlantic slave trade—is effectively invisible in this novel. It would be another forty years before the young, slave-owning American republic came to address that issue, after 1861, and at the cost of some 600,000 dead. The story of these interactions played out differently in Latin America, for various reasons. It was a region which

---

49 "On First Looking into Chapman's Homer," in *The Poetical Works of John Keats*, ed. by Harry Buxton Forman (Oxford: Oxford University Press, 1944), p. 39: "Or like stout Cortez when with eagle eyes / He star'd at the Pacific [...]"

50 On steamboats and gunboat diplomacy, see Paul Johnson, *The Birth of the Modern. World Society 1815–1830* (New York: HarperCollins, 1991).

saw comparatively less genocide than the United States, though indeed it saw its share, as well as more assimilation and cohabitation. The Western frontier in the United States was a place of slaughter.

Cooper is, then, offering his readers something exotic, a native exoticism which would very likely have been less apparent to readers in any other of the Americas' new nations. As Uncas represents a sort of noble savage, in Rousseau's tradition, so too does he represent a lost civilization, much like those Mayan step pyramids—notably Chichén-Itzá—revealed to the world by Stephens and Catherwood in 1842–1843.[51] *Who gets to speak*?—one might ask of Romantic texts featuring non-European characters. Here, as in Mary Shelley's *Frankenstein*, the last word is given to a speaker standing outside of Eurocentric civilization, that European project to which these two novels' authors and audiences belong. This leap into otherness, only hinted at in the eighteenth century, is a central Romantic preoccupation, and indeed a fundamental contribution of the Romantic period to the world. We see it early in Ossian, Percy, or Herder, in the era's calls for compilations of texts from sources alien to their authors—the Grimms' fairy tale collections or A.W. Schlegel's Sanskrit critical editions.[52] This is a new value system, focused on authenticity and on the recognition of human diversity, on a desire to preserve the complexity of what exists before it is lost in the march of progress and revolution. It is anchored in a certain vision of history, one where new things replace old ones, not always for the better, and old ones can be mourned. We see it in the great historians of the age, from Michelet to Niebuhr or Ranke; we see it in the historical sweep of novelists like Manzoni, Hugo or Thomas Hardy, Tolstoy or Melville. It continues to shape modern thought. It is, at the end of the day, why Scott's and Cooper's contemporaries so loved historical novels.

It matters too that Cooper's main character—the hero of the *Leatherstocking Tales*—is not Native American but European. Natty Bumppo is a woodsman, at ease in the Native American universe, but remaining a colonist at the same time. It seems perhaps unlikely

51 Frederick Catherwood and John Lloyd Stephens, *Incidents of Travel in Central America, Chiapas and Yucatán* (1842) and *Incidents of Travel in Yucatán* (1843).

52 Jacob and Wilhelm Grimm, *Kinder- und Hausmärchen* [Children's and House Fairy Tales] (1812–1815); on August Wilhelm Schlegel's scholarly work, see Roger Paulin, *The Life of August Wilhelm Schlegel. Cosmopolitan of Art and Poetry* (Cambridge, UK: Open Book Publishers, 2016), https://doi.org/10.11647/OBP.0069.

that Cooper's readers in 1826 would have been ready for the Apache hero, Winnetou, who earned Karl May 200 million readers a century or so later, though Longfellow's providential *Hiawatha* (1855) matters a great deal here.[53] The United States were taking shape, in literature as in politics and society; Thoreau, Irving, Emerson, Poe, Longfellow, and Hawthorne all began the American project around this time. Amid this early group, Cooper stands out for an epic scope largely unrivalled until Melville's 1851 *Moby-Dick*; he is indeed at work creating the American epic. And this returns us to that thorny Romantic question: is a modern epic possible? One answer might be: does it matter, if romance will perform that genre's traditional function? And the case can be made that it does just that. A way to achieve this goal is to produce novel cycles, like Cooper here or Balzac in *La Comédie humaine*. The new genre's values and esthetics may yet differ from those of Homer and Virgil, but its sweep and weight may be equivalent.

What has happened, then, as this particular novel closes? Well, an intrigue has played out, involving heroism, treachery, and romance, against a backdrop of war, loss, and a shifting in human alliances. Individuals with their virtues, their foibles, and their free will appear on society's vast chessboard, which they can only partly grasp and only begin to influence. The impersonal forces of history operate, leaving participants to be remembered for good or ill by posterity. It is grand Romantic stuff, well-conceived and well-executed, like Scott's wildly successful Waverley novels, like the Romantic tragedies—*Egmont* (1789), *Don Karlos* (1787), *Die Jungfrau von Orleans* (1801)—of a Goethe or a Schiller, like the novels of Balzac. And now, Tamenund will speak. First, Chingachgook and Hawkeye shake hands over the grave of Uncas. These two representatives of two very different civilizations weep together in a moment of friendship, male bonding, and mutual loss. Now Tamenund breaks his silence, as we have seen, to say, "It is enough." He doesn't say a lot—echoing an old Native American trope—but his words are to the point. He speaks of the Manitou, his world spirit or god. "The pale faces," he says, "are masters of the earth." "My day has been too long," he goes on to remark. This is 1757, a time that was by 1826 vanishing into the past, as Irving's 1819 *Rip van Winkle* pointedly reminds us. But

53 Karl May found immense international success in a series of novels starring his Apache hero Winnetou, despite having never visited America.

already, American Indian power has been broken. There is in history a path to extinction in which some things die while others flourish, and it is not always the bad which dies, as we have said, and the good or noble which triumphs. Tamenund has seen, in his last words to the gathering, "the last warrior of the wise race of the Mohicans."

Why, finally, does Cooper write? A variety of themes emerge in this closing extract. It matters that men bond here and women are not foregrounded; that Natty Bumppo is a crack shot; that two men weep. It matters that Tamenund is laconic; that he speaks of his alien god or spirit; that the pale faces do not end the novel, but he does. And it matters that the United States was a new republic in 1826, yet Tamenund is old; that these provincial, if not semi-barbaric figures have the dignity of epic, since the United States, after all, saw itself as provincial, indeed minor, in art until the 1960s. Or, indeed, that this ending walks a fine line between melodrama and the sublime; that it is good writing, but also simple writing; that some here have bursts of feeling, while others remain poised. It matters, finally, that in this New World with its new republics, the tale is one of old and young, of old and new. That the reader has made this journey with Cooper, despite, say, the prominent French role in American independence, despite the War of 1812, the burning of the White House, and the Battle of New Orleans. It matters that all this history is recent and local, and that American literature starts like this.

7. Eastern Europe (Poland), 1834 Adam Mickiewicz, *Pan Tadeusz*

Razem ze strun wiela	He lifts his hands, then both together fall
Buchnął dźwięk, jakby cała janczarska kapela	And smite at once, astonishing them all.
Ozwała się z dzwonkami, z zelami, z bębenki:	A sudden crash bursts forth from many strings
Brzmi Polonez Trzeciego Maja! — Skoczne dźwięki	As when a band of janissaries rings
Radością oddychają, radością słuch poją;	With cymbals, bells, and drums. And now resounds
Dziewki chcą tańczyć, chłopcy w miejscu nie dostoją —	The Polonaise of May the 3rd! It bounds
Lecz starców myśli z dźwiękiem w przeszłość się unlosły,	And breathes with joy, its notes with gladness fill;
W owe lata szczęśliwe, gdy senat i posły,	Girls long to dance and boys can scarce keep still.
Po dniu Trzeciego Maja, w ratuszowej sali,	But of the old men every one remembers
Zgodzonego z narodem króla fetowali,	That Third of May, when Senators and Members
Gdy przy tańcu śpiewano: «Wiwat Król kochany!	in the assembly hall with joy went wild,
Wiwat Sejm, wiwat Naród, wiwat wszystkie Stany!»	That king and Nation had been reconciled;
	"Long live the King, long live the Sejm!" they sang,
	"Long live the Nation!" through the concourse rang.
Mistrz coraz takty nagli i tony natęża;	The music ever louder grew and faster,
A wtem puścił fałszywy akord jak syk węża,	Then suddenly a false chord—from the master!
Jak zgrzyt żelaza po szkle: przejął wszystkich dreszczem	Like hissing snakes or shattering glass, that chilled
I wesołość pomięszał przeczuciem złowieszczem.	Their hearts and with a dire foreboding filled.

Zasmuceni, strwożeni, słuchacze zwątpili,	Dismayed and wondering the audience heard:
Czy instrument niestrojny? czy się muzyk myli?	Was the instrument ill-tuned? Or had he erred?
Nie zmylił się mistrz taki! On umyślnie trąca	He had not erred! he struck repeatedly
Wciąż tę zdradziecką strunę, melodyję zmąca,	That treacherous string and broke the melody,
Coraz głośniej targając akord rozdąsany,	And ever louder smote that sullen wire,
Przeciwko zgodzie tonów skonfederowany:	That dared against the melody conspire,
Aż Klucznik pojął mistrza, zakrył ręką lica	Until the Warden, hiding face in hand,
I krzyknął: «Znam! znam głos ten! to jest Targowica!»	Cried out, "I know that sound, I understand;
I wnet pękła ze świstem struna złowróżąca;	It's Targowica! Suddenly, as he speaks,
Muzyk bieży do prymów, urywa takt, zmaca,	The string with evil-omened hissing breaks;
Porzuca prymy, bieży z drążkami do basów.	At once the hammers to the treble race,
	Confuse the rhythm, hurry to the bass.[54]

Adam Bernard Mickiewicz (24 December 1798–26 November 1855). **Works**: drama—*Dziady* [Forefathers' Eve]; epic—*Pan Tadeusz, Konrad Wallenrod;* newspaper articles. Mickiewicz was born in or near Navahrudak, now in Belarus. The region lay within the Grand Duchy of Lithuania until the third and final partition of Poland in 1795, when it became Russian: Mickiewicz is thus a national poet in three countries. He attended university in Vilnius. In 1817, Mickiewicz and his friends created an organization with ties to a pro-independence group. In 1822–1823, as Mickiewicz published his first poetry collections, a government

54 Adam Mickiewicz, *Pan Tadeusz,* trans. by Kenneth R. MacKenzie (New York: Hippocrene Books, 1992), pp. 564–566.

search for secret student organizations led to arrests. These included Mickiewicz, who was banished further into Russia. In five years there, he published *Konrad Wallenrod* (1828) and befriended Pushkin. Mickiewicz left Russian soil in 1829 for Berlin, where he attended Hegel's lectures, then for Prague and Weimar where he met Goethe. After a stay in Rome, Mickiewicz journeyed to German-occupied Poland (Poznań), Geneva, and Paris in 1832. There he published *Pan Tadeusz* (1834), married, and worked from 1840–1844 as chair of Slavic Languages and Literatures at the Collège de France. In 1848, Mickiewicz organized a military unit to support the Polish insurgents—which saw no action—and was visited at home by the ailing Frédéric Chopin. In 1849, he founded a newspaper, writing over seventy articles for it in order to promote democracy, socialism, and other Revolutionary and Napoleonic ideals. Mickiewicz supported France's Second Empire and also the Crimean War, hoping it would lead to a restored Poland. His last composition was a Latin ode in praise of Napoleon III. He traveled to Constantinople in 1855, looking to organize Polish and Jewish forces to fight against Russia, and died there that year, likely of cholera. His works served as inspiration for Polish uprisings against the powers that had partitioned his nation out of existence.

Simply put, Poland in 1834 did not exist. It had ceased to exist with the Third Partition of Poland, carried out by the Russian and Austrian Emperors and the King of Prussia. The new French Emperor, Napoleon Bonaparte, briefly created a ghost of Poland, the Grand-Duchy of Warsaw, from 1807 until 1815, when that territory was again partitioned between Prussia and the Russian tsar. Not until 1918 did Poland reappear on the map. This is why Adam Mickiewicz, born in Russia, wrote and published *Pan Tadeusz* in Paris. Nationalism, if not downright tribalism, tends to shape canon formation, and nowhere more so than in nations' foundational Romantic texts. The Russians have spent generations overlooking Pushkin's cosmopolitanism in favor of his 'Russian soul.' In the Mickiewicz Museum in Warsaw, staff speak only Polish; the man's internationalism has fallen by the wayside, just as in Prague's Kafka Museum, where Kafka's own native German is not understood. An old saying holds that a dialect is a language without an army. Compare Ján Kóllar's German title for his 1836 pan-Slavic study, *Reciprocity between the Various Tribes and Dialects of the Slavic Nation,* where the lack of available referents seems to have prompted Kóllar's odd lexical choices—tribes, dialects—to frame his argument. Eastern Europe raises issues for nation-builders that were less prevalent in those Western regions—the United Kingdom, German lands—where these ideas were first elaborated. The nation-states of Eastern Europe were largely created *ex nihilo*, unlike their languages, by *fiat* of the Allied Powers in 1918. Slovakia and the Czech Republic, like the states of the former Yugoslavia, have redrawn their borders since 1991. In Ukraine, Taras Shevchenko founded a national literature in the 1840s, though Ukraine only attained nationhood briefly between 1917–1921, and then again after 1991. Meanwhile, in Western Europe, Hendrik Conscience's Flemish-language historical novel, *De Leeuw van Vlaanderen* (The Lion of Flanders, 1838), records a nation that existed as a dynastic county from 862 to 1795, and has not existed since. The Flemish independence movement splits the modern state of Belgium down the middle, a small echo of nationalism's toxic potential—as exemplified in Hitler's expanded German Reich or, for instance, those irredentist postcards for sale in Budapest's National Gallery in 2010, showing borders as they might be, with all Magyars in Europe part of one Hungary. This is the background to Mickiewicz's achievement, and to his place with *Pan Tadeusz* in the canon of Polish authors. Romanticism and nationalism go hand in hand across the nations of the West; it is, in a real sense, the people's voice.

In our extract, Jankiel plays patriotic songs on his dulcimer to an assembled crowd: "The Polonaise of May the 3rd" and "Targowica." It helps here to be Polish; on 3 May 1791, a truncated Poland ratified its liberal constitution, and then at Targowica on 27 April 1792, in one of Poland's many betrayals, a group of Polish-Lithuanian nobles formed a confederacy to reject that document. These are references destined to be tribal, and that is broadly true of Mickiewicz's entire verse romance. It is difficult to overstate such works' national prestige, but foreign readers face confusion, even tedium in such moments, and that in turn risks leaving foundational Romantic authors like, say, Petöfi, Shevchenko, Conscience, or Echeverría relegated to the narrow national boundaries they themselves promoted.[55] For nationalism is a two-edged sword.

55 For Sandór Petöfi, see the English/Hungarian edition of *John the Valiant* (London: Hesperus, 2004); for Taras Shevchenko, see *Selected Poetry* (Kiev: Dnipro, 1977), also bilingual.

Poland is a nation much-betrayed; in 1834, Polish memories remained fresh of the country's renewed deletion from the map at the Congress of Vienna in 1815. Mickiewicz understandably, even rightly, chooses instead to recall an earlier moment of national betrayal, elegantly putting the reminder into music and leaving a Jewish musician to recall it. The story of the Jews in Poland is painful and complex, but Mickiewicz gives space to Jankiel in his narrative. This plot unfolds during the Napoleonic Wars, a time for Poland's last brief and compromised independence prior to 1918. It was at least possible to dream. Poland's ties to France are thus worth a mention. Chopin, like Mickiewicz, died in Paris, and it was Napoleon who bought a partitioned Poland those eight years of partial independence. The man is a hero in *Pan Tadeusz*.

Our scene is a people's gathering, and Jankiel's music—suitably, a *polonaise*—is not courtly or complex. Romantic composers—Chopin, Liszt—borrowed folk elements for inspiration.[56] One might call Jankiel's music limited, as one might call *Pan Tadeusz* less witty than *Evgenii Onegin*, but such a statement would to an extent be beside the point. First, I am no judge of Polish-language folk epic, though the choice of fourteener couplets may seem less than ideal. Second, as with the above composers, Mickiewicz is to an extent consciously rejecting courtly norms of elegance, although his heroes belong once again to the minor nobility, as is so often the case in Europe's Romantic texts. Third, as we have seen, creating a national art involves a certain amount of hermetic referencing; there are tribal flags needing to be planted, and Mickiewicz does that, like countless Romantics. This art is not courtly and cosmopolitan, it is popular and local. The man also wrote edgier work—*Konrad Wallenrod* (1828), say, or the fine drama *Dziady* (1822). His short national epic about the Teutonic Knights—*Konrad Wallenrod*—is interspersed, interestingly, with songs that serve to advance the plot. But *Pan Tadeusz* is his *Iliad*.

What role does music have in this extract, or indeed in literature in general? Here, it is martial, designed to rouse its listeners to resistance against the occupier, and is effective in so doing, as Mickiewicz relates. It creates enthusiasm, that quintessential Romantic emotion. It readies people to fight, to resist, to create an army. This aim—to stir

56 On folk influence in Frédéric Chopin and Franz Liszt, critics cite Chopin's mazurkas and Liszt's *Hungarian Rhapsodies*.

up passion through music—is not alien to the German Wagner in his near-contemporaneous theory of the *Gesamtkunstwerk*.[57] It is a non-Aristotelian view of art, in its lack of interest in catharsis. More broadly, Romantic authors had considerable interest in music, and folk music in particular. We see this play out in Britain and in German lands, places where, after Bishop Percy, the ballad tradition is collected in anthologies and revived in lyric poetry, and also, as noted, in the works of Europe's Romantic composers.[58] Traditional musical forms—symphony, concerto, sonata—make space in this period for new forms—*étude, nocturne, ballade*. Chopin, that other Pole in exile, is a master of this redefinition. Lastly, music since the Greeks has been fundamental to poetry. This is true in lyric verse, but it is also true in epic and verse romance, which are of course separated from their sister, prose, by their musical structural elements, such as meter and rhyme. *Pan Tadeusz* lingers in the mind as prose can do only with the greatest difficulty.

Finally, what is to be major, after all, and what is to be minor in our canons? One might say that Mickiewicz is major in Poland and minor—indeed, largely unread—outside its borders. This is part of Eastern Europe's importance in the story of Romantic civilization. Its recurrent and explicit nation-building exercise exposes some of the fault lines of the Romantic project— "We, the people"—which were simply less apparent in the nations further West. Eastern Europe has its own history of silencing and oppression. It is telling, indeed fitting, that Mickiewicz in his nation-building project gives that dulcimer to Jankiel the Jew. Poland was in 1834 a nation of outcasts, and Mickiewicz has no interest in further dividing the citizens of a country which then lacked an army, a capital, or even borders to be policed. Its citizens were subjugated: this tale first published in Paris is that Polish voice returned. It is impossible, of course, to know which countries may rise, and which ones fall, in the course of human history. Mickiewicz had seen cosmopolitanism; he wrote this work in Parisian exile and after earlier exile in Russia. But unlike, say, Pushkin or Almeida Garrett, he chose

57 Richard Wagner developed his *Gesamtkunstwerk* theory in two 1849 essays, "Das Kunstwerk der Zukunft" [The Art Work of the Future] and "Die Kunst und die Revolution" [Art and Revolution].

58 On ballads, see Bishop Thomas Percy, *The Reliques of Ancient English Poetry* (1765) and Clemens Brentano and Ludwig Achim von Arnim, *Des Knaben Wunderhorn Alte deutsche Lieder* [The Boy's Magic Horn Old German Songs] (1805–1808).

to pass that cosmopolitan knowledge over silently in his plot. He may seem unphilosophical here, even a little folksy, when compared with the worldly elegance of a Pushkin, a Heine, a Leopardi. He may indeed seem over-sincere in his nationalist intensity. But Mickiewicz wrote this work in exile from a country that did not exist. In his museum today, in a Warsaw rebuilt after the great Russo-German betrayal of 1944, the staff still speak only Polish.

8. Northern Europe (Denmark), 1835–1837 Hans Christian Andersen, *Eventyr, fortalt for Børn*

Snedronningen. Syvende historie. Hvad der skete i snedronningens slot, og hvad der siden skete

Lille Kay var ganske blå af kulde, ja næsten sort, men han mærkede det dog ikke, for hun havde jo kysset kuldegyset af ham, og hans hjerte var så godt som en isklump. Han gik og slæbte på nogle skarpe flade isstykker, som han lagde på alle mulige måder, for han ville have noget ud deraf; det var ligesom når vi andre har små træplader og lægger disse i figurer, der kaldes det kinesiske spil. Kay gik også og lagde figurer, de allerkunstigste, det var forstands-isspillet; for hans øjne var figurerne ganske udmærkede og af den allerhøjeste vigtighed; Det gjorde det glaskorn, der sad ham i øjet! han lagde hele figurer, der var et skrevet ord, men aldrig kunne han finde på at lægge det ord, som han just ville, det ord: Evigheden, og snedronningen havde sagt: "Kan du udfinde mig den figur, så skal du være din egen herre, og jeg forærer dig hele verden og et par nye skøjter." Men han kunne ikke.

The Snow Queen. Seventh Story. Of the Palace of the Snow Queen and What Happened There at Last

Little Kay was quite blue with cold, indeed almost black, but he did not feel it; for the Snow Queen had kissed away the icy shiverings, and his heart was already a lump of ice. He dragged some sharp, flat pieces of ice to and fro, and placed them together in all kinds of positions, as if he wished to make something out of them; just as we try to form various figures with little tablets of wood which we call "a Chinese puzzle." Kay's fingers were very artistic; it was the icy game of reason at which he played, and in his eyes the figures were very remarkable, and of the highest importance; this opinion was owing to the piece of glass still sticking in his eye. He composed many complete figures, forming different words, but there was one word he never could manage to form, although he wished it very much. It was the word "Eternity." The Snow Queen had said to him, "When you can find out this, you shall be your own master, and I will give you the whole world and a new pair of skates." But he could not accomplish it.[59]

59 H.C. Andersen, *Hans Andersen's Fairy Tales. A New Translation*, trans. by H.B. Paull (New York: Scribner, 1867), pp. 116–117.

Hans Christian Andersen (2 April 1805–4 August 1875). **Works**: plays; travelogues; novels; poems; fairy tales—*Eventyr, fortalt for Børn*. Andersen's father received an elementary school education, while his mother was a washerwoman who remarried after her husband's death and sent Andersen, aged eleven, to a school for the poor. Andersen's short story of 1829 featuring Saint Peter and a talking cat earned him a small royal grant which took him to Italy, a trip he fictionalized in his first novel, published in 1835 to instant acclaim. Andersen went on to publish nine fairy tales in three installments, from 1835–1837. Reviews of the first two condemned his informal style and lack of moral lessons for children. The third booklet contained "The Little Mermaid"—Andersen's creation, though influenced like Staël's *Corinne ou l'Italie* by La Motte Fouqué's *Undine* (1811)—and "The Emperor's New Clothes." These established Andersen's international reputation; his eventual 156 tales have been translated into more than 125 languages. In 1847, Andersen met Dickens in England, who like him was preoccupied by the victims of poverty and the Industrial Revolution. In 1857, he stayed at Dickens's home for five weeks until asked to leave. Dickens gradually stopped all correspondence between them, which confused and disappointed Andersen. Andersen often fell in love with unattainable women; thus, his story "The Nightingale" was written for Jenny Lind. He evidently experienced same-sex attraction as well, though apparently without acting on it.

It would seem a little odd for a survey on Romanticism to contain no mention of fairy tales. Here we are, then, amid the stories for all ages that Andersen wrote in Danish, but for the whole world. Denmark had shrunk somewhat after the Napoleonic Wars, as it was to shrink again after 1860. After siding with France, Denmark had seen its capital twice shelled by the British fleet, and at the Congress of Vienna, Norway was passed from Denmark to Sweden, though Denmark retained Greenland. For Denmark, the Restoration period was nevertheless a golden age, that of Kierkegaard and the sculptor Thorvaldsen, as well as of Andersen in literature. In 1848, Denmark became a constitutional monarchy, whereas most of Europe saw that particular year's liberal revolutions crushed. We may then ask, as we contemplate contemporary Scandinavia—Sweden's much-translated writer Tegnér, for instance—whether Denmark was a major or a minor European power; whether Scandinavia matters; about the Baltic and the North Sea. Denmark is a pleasant and civilized place, but how does it, and the Baltic, weigh in Europe's balance? It seems worth suggesting that Europe, as we understand it, consists of more than its Great Powers. The European continent is a mix of large and small nation-states and languages; its fabric contains metropolises and forests just as it contains mountains, rivers, and plains. Without that complexity, Europe would be some other place. It deserves celebration, or at the very least presentation exactly as its complex history has made it. It matters, then, that Denmark today is smaller than it was, and that in this small land, Andersen wrote these tales for little people.

There is a statue of the Little Mermaid in Copenhagen harbor, and Andersen himself is the subject of a national myth, in which a popular artist creates almost independently of book learning, relying instead on the simple but resonant genius of the folk. This myth is quite Romantic. But as folklorists will tell you, folk art tends to form top-down instead of bottom-up; and in point of fact, Andersen's Little Mermaid has her debts to Friedrich de La Motte-Fouqué's German *Undine* of 1811, just as Kai's distorted vision in *The Snow Queen* has its debts to Kant's vision of the *noumenon*—ultimately unknowable—in 1781's *Critik der reinen Vernunft*. Andersen's sources can, in short, sometimes be highbrow and foreign, a fact which may seem the antithesis of the myth he inhabits. This is not an obvious topic for Danish pride, contrasting as it does top-down and bottom-up, home and abroad, truth and fiction. But Denmark is, after all and unavoidably, part of the Europe amid which it sits, and Andersen in his internationalism reflects that simple truth. So, we may well ask: is Andersen *authentic* in the end? Is this writing folk art, or is it refined? German scholars have shown that the Grimms' fairy tale collections of 1812–1815, presented to Romantic readers as a compilation of authentic popular speech, were in fact the product of art and careful editing. We might expect an artist to want to craft their work, and Wordsworth's talk of a "spontaneous overflow of powerful feelings," for instance, should not obscure that simple truth.[60] Authentic folk art may ultimately be as unknowable as the *noumenon* itself.

60 *Lyrical Ballads*, preface to the second edition (1800) in William Wordsworth, *The Poetical Works of Wordsworth*, ed. by Thomas Hutchinson and Ernest de Selincourt (Oxford: Oxford University Press, 1964), p. 740: "poetry is the spontaneous overflow of powerful feelings; it takes its origin from emotion recollected in tranquillity [...]"

Andersen has read more widely than is sometimes credited. But it may be that his speech is popular in a way that his sources are not. He has an ear for the *sermo humilis*, the speech actual people on Copenhagen's actual streets might use. And this, more than Andersen's use of Kant, may help explain Andersen's fame abroad, one unmatched by any other Romantic author writing in Europe's less-spoken and less-studied languages. Almeida Garrett, Mickiewicz, Shevchenko, or Conscience, for instance, cannot begin to rival Andersen's international prestige. Simplicity is hard, and Andersen remains simple. Andersen is also writing a kind of wisdom literature; his tales tilt toward morals much as a preacher might. And this, once again, is hard when writing a text for all ages of people, as Andersen must make his points lightly. It's worth noting, then, that *fairy tales* is only one meaning of his Danish title *Eventyr*, which also means *adventures*. His is a world of dream, wishing, and magic; the ground may shift beneath our feet, but the heart is true. It is a world, put simply, which has a point.

What games does Andersen play with us? Byron, Pushkin, Garrett, Sterne, Diderot, or Stendhal are all full of games. Much of that scope for play is unavailable to Andersen, but his tales remain playful; they are indeed adventures, and we advance through them on a voyage of discovery and surprise. Andersen may seem very Danish, but he was a keen traveler, and his tales remain open at all times to novel things, alien things, to the magical and the unknown. A key gift of Andersen's is to present his novelties, his surprises, in the simplest and humblest terms; in words that make immediate sense. Indeed, he knows how to tell a story. In our extract, for instance, we are almost at the end of the story of *The Snow Queen*. Gerda and Kai, friends from infancy, have been separated, and Gerda has come on an exhausting quest to find and rescue her dear friend. Now she has found him at last, in the extreme North, sitting in the Snow Queen's palace. The tale has a certain grandeur to it. And Kai is playing a game. Play, almost by definition, involves a leap of imagination. As Gombrich notes in *Meditations on a Hobby Horse* (1985), this leap is the definitional moment around which art is constituted; we take a stick and call it a horse.[61] Play involves the creation of a reality parallel to

61 E.H. Gombrich, *Meditations on a Hobby Horse and other essays on the theory of art* (Oxford: Phaidon, 1985), p. 4: "The 'first' hobby horse [...] was probably no image at all. Just a stick which qualified as a horse because one could ride on it."

our own, and yet independent of it; we play at war, but no actual war takes place. Children play—hopscotch, baseball, tic-tac-toe—to discover how to process the world. The stakes in play are only make-believe; they mimic actual stakes but are not actual. And so, Kai plays. What is he doing? He is assembling ice shards into patterns. Games are, by definition, futile, and Kai's occupation here certainly qualifies. For ice is a sterile thing, like the *isklump* that is now Kai's heart, while the ice on this palace floor has no structural, ornamental, or Utilitarian function. At the same time, the Snow Queen's promise to Kai— "the whole world and a new pair of skates"—shows she is not to be trusted. It is, after all, Satan's promise to Christ in Matthew 4: 8–9, with that new pair of skates to show how little she expects common sense or logic in response.[62] And Kai calls this the game of reason.

Now, various nineteenth-century thinkers, including many Romantics, devoted real effort to rejecting the somewhat monochrome Enlightenment that the eighteenth century had bequeathed them. Keats, for instance, remarked that Isaac Newton "had destroyed all the Poetry of the rainbow by reducing it to a prism."[63] It was, similarly, a cliché in Restoration thinking to attribute the French Revolution to the writings of the *philosophes*, which is why the child Gavroche in Victor Hugo's *Les Misérables* (1862), just before he is shot dead by the forces of order, sings "Je suis tombé par terre, / C'est la faute à Voltaire."[64] Andersen is working within that tradition, which makes it all the more curious that Kai's inability to see things as they are, thanks to the shard of glass stuck in his eye, directly echoes Kant's observation that our senses allow us knowledge of the *phenomenon* alone, leaving the *noumenon*—the thing in itself—unknowable. Andersen has rather neatly borrowed Kant's *Critique of Pure Reason* (1781) to offer his own critique of reason in the young person of Kai. It is, though, precisely the unchecked use of the intellect that Andersen is cautioning against, somewhat as Mary Shelley

62 *Holy Bible*, Authorized King James Version (1611), Matthew 4: 8–9: "the devil [...] showeth him all the kingdoms of the world [...] And saith unto him, All these things will I give thee [...]."

63 Robert Gittings, *John Keats* (Boston & Toronto: Little, Brown & Co., 1968), p. 177: Lamb and Keats told Wordsworth at a gathering in 1817 that Newton "had destroyed all the Poetry of the rainbow, by reducing it to a prism," and then drank "Newton's health, and confusion to mathematics."

64 *Les Misérables*, "Jean Valjean," I, ch. 15, in Victor Hugo, *Romans*, 3 vols (Paris: Seuil, 1963), II, p. 468.

did in the person of Victor Frankenstein. And Kai is working on a puzzle, struggling like Frankenstein to build a composite, if not organic whole, out of the icy fragments available to him. Fragments are curious things—as Friedrich Schlegel had shown—but in the end, Kai has only fragments to work with. This is perhaps a male proclivity. Certainly, Gerda seems immune to the Snow Queen and to the appeal of the ice shards at Kai's feet. She is the hero of this story, as the Snow Queen is the villain. If Kai's world is sterile, Gerda's is not; it is anchored in the heart and reflects a value system unimpressed by the Snow Queen and all her trappings. Unlike Kai, Gerda is not playing; she instead has a job to do.

Kai wants to write the word *eternity* in order to earn the Snow Queen's promised reward. This is not explicitly Christian, but it leans towards it. Eternity is many things, and one of them is a Christian afterlife, the nature of the dwelling-place of God. Kai's own stake here is clear—to get that promise—but it is unclear what the Snow Queen might get out of this. Is she simply amusing herself at Kai's expense? Or would success open some door for her, grant her some needful thing? Perhaps it would, much as Satan sought to profit from tempting Jesus in the Synoptic Gospels. This is a dystopian scene, and Kai appears already marked for death in its opening sentence; Gerda will arrive like a breath of spring. There will be no mystical unveiling, only a homespun, if fraught, reunion of two dear friends, and a return from the Snow Queen's palace to a land where it is summer once again. Andersen has evidently read Kant and La Motte-Fouqué—or at least read of them—just as he has read the Bible. But his ethics in art and storytelling, with its focus on what is popular and what is childlike, propels Andersen along a path designed to reshape both his actual body of work into a mythical one, and Andersen himself into something he only partly was: a simple man, more interested in telling stories on his own behalf, and for his listeners, than in reading the various books that others around the world had already written. Andersen emerges from this process as homespun as his young heroine Gerda. And he seems, in the end, to have found a sort of eternity, without journeying through the Snow Queen's palace of ice.

9. The Italian Peninsula, 1835 Giacomo Leopardi, *Canti*, *L'infinito*

Sempre caro mi fu quest'ermo colle,	This lonely hill was always dear to me,
E questa siepe, che da tanta parte	and this hedgerow, which cuts off the view
Dell'ultimo orizzonte il guardo esclude.	of so much of the last horizon.
Ma sedendo e mirando, interminati	But sitting here and gazing, I can see
Spazi di là da quella, e sovrumani	beyond, in my mind's eye, unending spaces,
Silenzi, e profondissima quiete	and superhuman silences, and depthless calm,
Io nel pensier mi fingo; ove per poco	till what I feel
Il cor non si spaura. E come il vento	is almost fear. And when I hear
Odo stormir tra queste piante, io quello	the wind stir in these branches, I begin
Infinito silenzio a questa voce	comparing that endless stillness with this noise:
Vo comparando: e mi sovvien l'eterno,	and the eternal comes to mind,
E le morte stagioni, e la presente	and the dead seasons, and the present
E viva, e il suon di lei. Così tra questa	living one, and how it sounds.
Immensità s'annega il pensier mio:	So my mind sinks in this immensity:
E il naufragar m'è dolce in questo mare.	and foundering is sweet in such a sea.[65]

Giacomo Taldegardo Francesco di Sales Saverio Pietro Leopardi (29 June 1798–14 June 1837). **Works**: poems—*Canti, Canzoni*; philosophical works—*Pensieri*, the *Zibaldone*; prose—*Operette morali*. Leopardi was born into minor nobility in Recanati in Italy's Papal States, where his father gambled while his mother focused on rebuilding the family's finances destroyed by that habit. Leopardi was taught by two priests,

65 Giacomo Leopardi, *Canti: Poems*, trans. by Jonathan Galassi (New York: Farrar, Straus, and Giroux, 2010), pp. 106–107.

but mostly taught himself in his father's library. He read and wrote Italian, Latin, ancient Greek, and Hebrew. Leopardi suffered for years from ankylosing spondylitis. In 1816, he sent a letter to the *Biblioteca Italiana*, which put him on the map, arguing against Staël's article in that journal inviting Italians to turn from the past to foreign literature to reinvigorate their writing. Leopardi maintained that Italians should not allow themselves to be contaminated by modern literature, but instead look to the Greek and Latin classics. A poet must be original, Leopardi wrote, not suffocated by study and imitation. Meanwhile, he spent much of 1816 translating the second book of the *Aeneid* and the first book of the *Odyssey*. Leopardi returned to Europe's Classic-Romantic debate in his *Discorso di un Italiano attorno alla poesia romantica*, and in 1817, his influential correspondent Giordani visited and became a lifelong friend. In 1822, Leopardi visited Rome and in 1824 he was called to Milan as an author. In Florence, in 1827, he met Manzoni, though they disagreed, and he returned to Recanati in 1828. He left again from 1830–1832, finding company among the liberals and republicans seeking to liberate Italy from Austria. Leopardi moved to Naples hoping to benefit from the climate but died there during the cholera epidemic of 1837. A friend kept him from a common grave.

This small, brilliant, multifaceted gem is the work of Giacomo Leopardi, a man who lived, like the poet Heine in his Parisian exile, an invalid and in considerable pain.[66] His spinal deformation indirectly contributed to his early death. Leopardi was born in Recanati, a small city-state—until Italian unification in 1860—in the Marche on Italy's Adriatic Coast. We may feel, with Klemens von Metternich, that Italy then was "a geographical expression," but the Italian language had subsisted since Dante, in its Tuscan *lingua franca* and local dialects.[67] Leopardi published his short volume of *Canti*, or *Odes*, shortly before his death in 1837, but he had been working on them since 1818, for almost twenty years. And those years had seen a good deal. The Austrians had held Milan since 1707; the Venetian Republic also became Austrian in 1797, after an independent millennium, and Austria in fact took the

66 Heine was bedridden for his last eight years, on what he called his *Matratzengruft* or 'mattress-grave.'

67 *Mémoires [...] laissés par le Prince de Metternich*, ed. Richard de Metternich, 4th edn, 8 vols (Paris: Plon, 1883–1886), VII 415: 6 August 1847.

entire Italian North in 1815 when Napoleon's short-lived Kingdom of Italy was dissolved. After Waterloo, Austria in Italy fiercely suppressed any liberal or national agitation, and Italy's leading Romantics were brought to heel. In 1816, the year Staël's Milan article on translation crystallized a northern Italian Romantic movement, the somewhat older Foscolo chose English exile. In 1821, the Austrians imprisoned the leading Romantics Borsieri and Pellico—who wrote *Le mie prigioni* (1832) about those prison years—and they exiled Berchet, author of the *Lettera semiseria* (1816). In 1827, Manzoni published his great historical novel *I promessi sposi* in Lombard dialect, about a plague-ridden Lombardy occupied by Spanish troops. Leopardi continued to work at his art. In central Italy, where the Marche lie, the Papal States survived until Italian unification. In the South, the Kingdom of the Two Sicilies lasted until Garibaldi conquered it, also in 1860, for Cavour's new Kingdom of Italy. Leopardi, like a good number of Europe's Romantic authors, was writing for a nation which did not exist.

This ode "L'infinito" is in part about difficulty and τέχνη or craft. "Que ton rêve flottant / Se scelle / Dans le bloc résistant," [May your floating dream / Seal itself / Into the resisting block], writes Théophile Gautier, and Leopardi has done just that, much as Michelangelo removed from his block of marble all the stone that was not David.[68] The resulting art is perhaps as miniature in the end as one of Gautier's own 1852 "Émaux et camées", but it is chiseled and arguably perfect. It is, as art, antithetical to the prolixity of a Boiardo, an Ariosto, a Tasso, to the verbosity of the countless Italian *improvvisatori* Staël points to in *Corinne ou l'Italie*.[69] This work of Leopardi's is hard, including for the reader, and that has made his art travel poorly. Leopardi deserves better of posterity; he has, like Hölderlin in the 1790s, few sculptural rivals in lyric on Europe's Romantic stage.[70] There are great Romantic lyric poets—Pushkin, Heine, Wordsworth, Keats, Hugo—but it seems to me

68 "L'Art" [Art], in Théophile Gautier, *Emaux et camées* (Geneva: Droz, 1947), p. 132.

69 Matteo Maria *Boiardo, Orlando innamorato* [Orlando in Love] (1483–1495), Ludovico *Ariosto, Orlando Furioso* [Orlando Mad] (1516), Torquato Tasso, *Gerusalemme liberata* [Jerusalem Delivered] (1581).

70 Friedrich Hölderlin, *Poems and Fragments*, trans. by Michael Hamburger (London: Anvil, 2004) presents Hölderlin's difficult lyric in bilingual format, as the bilingual *Leopardi* (2010) makes Leopardi accessible to non-Italian speakers.

that the British or French Romantics, for instance, tend not to chisel in this fashion.

What is Leopardi up to? For one thing, he is making a Horatian claim about brevity and discipline. "Less is more," we have been told. "Put your poems away for nine years," Horace wrote, and Leopardi put his odes away for twenty.[71] This labor may be described as a neoclassical priority, one that bows to the poets of Greece and Rome. Passion is perhaps central to Leopardi's vision, but he will not let it shape his craft. His "spontaneous overflow of powerful feelings" is, as Wordsworth had prescribed in 1800, instead "recollected in tranquillity."[72] Yet, in point of fact, Leopardi is at work explaining how art matters, and in that, if not in his timeless craft, he rejoins all Europe's Romantics. Because Leopardi has a crystalline vision of the lyric moment, a crisp awareness of what is organic to his poem and what is not. As his brevity attests, he knows how to leave things out. This combination of intense emotion with perfect craft is not typical of eighteenth-century poetry. A Voltaire, for instance, lacks it, though Voltaire could certainly versify, and here the Romantics perhaps add to their forebears.[73] Leopardi's vision of the lyric moment sees in it a springboard for open-ended thought; he does not need to put it all on the page, the readers' minds will do that for him. This insight gives Leopardi's work a strange tension, just as Pushkin's bittersweetness gives Pushkin a tension of his own. This new tension also lets Leopardi redefine what is minor and what is not. The Romantic period, like others before it, saw much talk in favor of big poems versus little poems; Leopardi chooses the little and sets out to make it infinite. Starting from the lyric moment, what is local becomes universal; this focus on the small to show the big is typical, as it happens, of biblical thought, but not of Greek or Roman thinking, and it separates Leopardi from his Horatian model. He is unique and weird—which is, to an extent, a Romantic dream. Pope in England, that great Augustan, called wit

---

71 "Nonumque prematur in annum", *Ars poetica*, l.389, in Horace, *Satires and Epistles* (Oxford: Oxford University Press, 2011), p. 116.

72 *Lyrical Ballads*, preface to the second edition (1800) in William Wordsworth, *The Poetical Works of Wordsworth*, ed. by Thomas Hutchinson and Ernest de Selincourt (Oxford: Oxford University Press, 1964), p. 740.

73 Voltaire wrote lyric, dramatic, and epic poetry, all with more apparent elegance than passion.

"What oft was thought, but ne'er so well express'd."[74] Such familiarity for readers is emphatically not Leopardi's goal in art. Romanticism, in its international outline, made Leopardi's weirdness possible; it's there in *Frankenstein*, it's there in *Onegin*, it's there in *Heinrich von Ofterdingen*. It is a reminder of why Leopardi matters today.

In these terms, it is perhaps worth looking at Leopardi's last line and its weight. The whole poem is in a sense an Archimedean lever to reach that point. Why does this poem exist, we might ask? What is Leopardi's place in the Romantic or Neoclassical enterprise, what is his legacy? "E il naufragar m'è dolce in questo mare," Leopardi writes, *Shipwreck is sweet to me in such an ocean*. Leopardi is making a claim about dissolution; that into life's humdrum to-and-fro, epiphany may fall, bringing a glimpse of infinite or absolute order. And we as humans may feel the tug of that infinity, as if in a trance, calling us from this warm bath into some other reality, a world that lies athwart our own, like the world Heinrich glimpses to open Novalis's novel. This is a Romantic insight, at home in the nineteenth century and alien to the eighteenth. It is the world of German yearning, of what is unspeakable and unknowable in the end. And Leopardi's trigger, as we have noted, is minor enough that another eye might overlook it; it is a hedgerow blocking his view. Leopardi's eye, in short, is unique and privileged. It has seen what is difficult of seeing: it notices. "To see a World in a Grain of Sand," writes Blake in England a little earlier, and that is Leopardi's program.[75] It is Leopardi's great and personal insight that the fundamental Romantic search for the sublime—that characteristic nineteenth-century activity—could be answered in a hedgerow blocking our view. What is a poet after all? Can modern poetry be written, and if it can, what use will it have? Shelley's vision of poets as "the unacknowledged legislators of the world" is not alien to Leopardi on his Adriatic Coast. Leopardi has seemingly chosen an ivory tower—like Nerval—in the twenty years of silence he elected, in order to focus on the minor, the little, the overlooked; he does not appear to be at work creating the Italy for which Garibaldi worked so

74 Alexander Pope, "An Essay on Criticism" (1711) in *Pope. Poetical Works* (Oxford: Oxford University Press, 1966), p. 72.

75 "Auguries of Innocence," in *Poetry and Prose of William Blake*, ed. by Geoffrey Keynes (Bloomsbury: Nonesuch, 1927), p. 118.

hard.[76] And yet, Leopardi is indeed shaping Italy in 1835. He is giving that peninsula new meaning and purpose, giving the nation, so to speak, the backbone it had lacked or neglected for all these years. Ten thousand hours, they say, will make a master, and Leopardi is a man who put in those hours. He is a different kind of patriot, chiseling away at the language and our thought in order, in T.S. Eliot's words, to "purify the dialect of the tribe."[77] The year 1835, that midpoint in peninsular history between post-Napoleonic repression and Garibaldian unification, was a perfectly good moment to redefine what being Italian means. Being Italian may have seemed easy in Staël's eyes, but it is, says Leopardi with his crippling spinal deformity and his forty short years on Earth, as difficult as you would like it to be. It is chiseled and laconic, it has a Roman weight. Poetry is good for such a task; there is a reason Primo Levi heard Dante "like the voice of God" on his Auschwitz work detail, as he recited the speech of Ulysses in Hell to Pikolo who wanted to learn Italian. "Fatti non foste a viver come bruti," Levi declaims to Pikolo, "ma per seguir virtute e canoscenza" [You were not made to live as brutes, but to follow virtue and knowledge].[78] Poetry is a little thing, and Leopardi, in his *Canti*, is certainly portable. But if we take our time over these short pieces, as Leopardi clearly did, we too may come to a point where a hedgerow opens onto the infinite; we may readjust our priorities; we may be patriots of a different sort. These reasons are as good as any for reading Leopardi—and indeed, for taking our sweet time in doing so, though it may be years.

76 *Sylvie. Souvenirs du Valois* [Sylvie. Memories of the Valois] (1853) in Gérard de Nerval, *Œuvres*, ed. By H. Lemaitre (Paris: Garnier, 1966), p. 591: "Il ne nous restait pour asile que cette tour d'ivoire des poètes, où nous montions toujours plus haut pour nous isoler de la foule." [Our only remaining shelter was that poets' ivory tower where we climbed ever higher to isolate ourselves from the crowd.]

77 "Little Gidding" in *Collected Poems 1909–1962 by T.S. Eliot* (London: Faber & Faber, 1963), p. 218.

78 Primo Levi, *If This Is a Man and The Truce* (London: Penguin/Sphere, 1979), p. 119.

10. Latin America (Argentina), 1838/1871 Esteban Echeverría, *El Matadero*

Los federales habian dado fin á una de sus innumerables proesas.

En aquel tiempo los carniceros degolladores del Matadero eran los apóstoles que propagaban á verga y puñal la federacion rosina, y no es dificil imaginarse qué federacion saldria de sus cabezas y cuchillas. Llamaban ellos savaje unitario, conforme á la jerga inventada por el Restaurador, patron de la cofradia, á todo el que no era degollador, carnicero, ni salvage, ni ladron; á todo hombre decente y de corazon bien puesto, á todo patriota ilustrado amigo de las luces y de la libertad; y por el suceso anterior puede verse á las claras que el foco de la federacion estaba en el Matadero.

The Federalists had carried out another of their many deeds of heroism. At that period, the cut-throats of the slaughter yard were the apostles who by rod and fist spread the gospel of the rosy federation, and it is not hard to imagine the sort of federation that would spring from these butchers' heads and knives. In accordance with the cant invented by the Restorer, patron of their brotherhood, they dubbed 'barbarous Unitarian' anyone who was not a barbarian, a butcher, a cut-throat, or a thief; anyone who was decent or whose heart was in the right place; every illustrious patriot or friend of enlightenment and freedom. From the events related above, it can clearly be seen that the hotbed of the Federation was in the slaughter yard.[79]

José Esteban Antonio Echeverría (September 2, 1805-January 19, 1851). **Works**: poems—*Los Consuelos, Rimas, La Insurrección del Sur, Elvira o la novia del Plata*; short stories—*El Matadero*. Echeverría was an Argentine poet, fiction writer, and liberal political activist. Early on, he spent five years in Paris, 1825–1830, where he discovered the Romantic movement, and he became one of its promoters on his return to Argentina. In Buenos Aires, he joined a group of young intellectuals who organized the *Asociación de Mayo* (named after Argentina's May 1810 Revolution), aspiring to develop a national literature. Echeverría also worked for the overthrow of the *caudillo* of Buenos Aires, Juan Manuel de Rosas. In 1840, he was forced to go into exile in nearby Uruguay, where he died in

79 Esteban Echeverría, *The Slaughter Yard*, trans. by Norman Thomas Di Giovanni and Susan Ashe (London: Friday Project, 2010), p. 32. *Unitarian* here refers to one of Argentina's two warring early parties, opposing the Federalist *caudillo* Rosas and seeking greater central authority from Buenos Aires.

1851—just before the fall of Rosas, whose Federalist supporters are the topic of this story.

We have already seen in Europe how often emergent national literatures, in this time of Romanticism in art and revolution in politics, encountered a native speaker—a Mickiewicz—ready to bring out a substantial new text in their neglected idiom, often a national epic or a historical novel, designed to give that idiom's speakers a foundational national moment. The moment is there in Polish, Ukrainian, Hungarian, Croatian, and Swedish; it is there in Flemish, Finnish, and Estonian; it is there in Russian with Pushkin. And so, Europe's various nations and ethnicities—its language communities—to this day often return to touchstone canonical texts produced in that brief Romantic period and with those priorities. Crossing the Atlantic, this project shapes the art of Longfellow and Cooper, and we might anticipate finding it across Latin America and the Caribbean as well. But curiously, at first it seems thin on the ground. Just as Spain's and Portugal's Romantic authors mostly come late, so too, throughout Latin America, as in the islands of the Caribbean, do foundational Romantic authors cluster post-1850—delayed perhaps because these new nation-states mostly shared Spanish as the language of government and empire, amid a tapestry of indigenous idioms, though that seems impossible to determine.

Caribbean literature pre-1850 centers on Cuba and Haiti, and it has a strong anti-slavery element. Cuban anti-slavery works include Gertrudis Gómez de Avellaneda's *Sab* in 1841—first published in Cuba in 1914—a love story about a slave (Sab) in love with his mistress, and Anselmo Suárez y Romero's *Francisco*, again abolitionist, written in 1839–1840 though also published much later. José María Heredia y Heredia, a Cuban exile who lived in the United States and Mexico, fills Neoclassical form with a Romantic focus on nature—a hurricane, Niagara Falls—and on Cuban independence. After 1826, Spain had lost all her American colonies but Cuba and Puerto Rico, and chose severe repression, including torture, to prevent further losses, as Heredia also chronicles. In Mexico and throughout Central America, I have yet to find foundational Romantic authors before 1850, while South America's new nations offer few early names: Venezuela's Andrés Bello is Virgilian, and Ecuador's José Joaquín de Olmedo writes odes to South American independence, like the 1825 "La victoria de Junín: canto a Bolívar." Outside Cuba and perhaps francophone Haiti, early Caribbean or Latin American Romantics seem then mostly to be found in Brazil and Argentina.

A Brazilian Romantic movement began in 1836, a decade after independence from Portugal, through the efforts of the expatriate poet Gonçalves de Magalhães. Several young poets, such as Casimiro de Abreu, began using Romantic topoi, stressing passion, nature, the nation, and colloquial speech. Novelists like Joaquim Manuel de Macedo, Manuel Antônio de Almeida, and José de Alencar became famous after 1840. Meanwhile in Argentina, Esteban Echeverría returned from Paris in 1830 promoting democracy and Romantic literature. The poems in his *Los Consuelos* (1834) introduced Romantic art to Latin America, while in his *Rimas* (1837) the long centerpiece, "La Cautiva," was among the first Latin American poems anchored in local color (the Andes and the pampas). In 1845, Domingo Faustino Sarmiento, future president of Argentina, published *Civilización y barbarie: Vida de Juan Facundo Quiroga*. Written during exile in Chile, it is another vehement attack on the cult of the strong man exemplified by Rosas. The dearth of early Latin American Romantics is particularly pointed, in that almost the entirety of the Americas won independence from Europe in the half-century 1776–1826, which is quite specifically the Romantic era. Why did the region's authors not mirror the political achievements of Bolívar and San Martín? The question seems worth asking. After all, those liberators' focus was, precisely, to empower the people's democratic voice, as happened in North America's Thirteen Colonies in 1776 and in France in 1789. Several Latin American writers in the ensuing century—Octavio Paz, Mario Vargas Llosa, Pablo Neruda, Gabriel García Marquez—won Nobel Prizes, which only deepens the mystery.

In any case, here is Echeverría's *El Matadero* from 1838, a tad late alongside Europe's foundational Romantics, but early in Latin American terms. Echeverría died in exile and the story was unpublished until 1871; it is allegedly the most-studied story in South American school classrooms. Its plot is simple: a crowd at the Buenos Aires slaughter yard torture and murder a passer-by, whom they accuse of being a political Unitarian, since he is not wearing the Federalist insignia worn in support of the *caudillo* Rosas. Literary precedents for such mob violence seem somewhat thin on the ground in Romantic Europe and the Americas. Murder and even cannibalism appear in the Gothic tradition, in Byron's *Don Juan*, in Géricault's *Le Radeau de la Méduse*, but few Romantic texts show mob violence—Louvet de Couvray, *L'Amour traqué* (1793); stories of Heinrich von Kleist like *Das Erdbeben in Chili* (1807); perhaps Zacharias Werner's tragedy of fate, *Der vierundzwanzigste Februar* (1808); Hendrik Conscience's novel *De Leeuw van Vlaanderen* (1838); Edgar Allan Poe's tale *Hop Frog* (1849); Staël's lost play *Jean de Witt*; perhaps Victor Hugo's novel *Notre Dame de Paris* (1831); on occasion, Dickens and Balzac. It seems odd to note the dearth of mob violence in narratives across Europe by those so close in time to France's Reign of Terror; perhaps the topic seemed unsuited to their various objectives. Earlier, there are elements of such violence in, say, Voltaire's *Candide* (1759), before they disappear from plots.

And what are Echeverría's objectives in putting this violence front and center? To begin with, Echeverría anchors his story in the grotesque. That is not to say that it is grotesquerie gratuitous and purely to shock, as sometimes in the Gothic tradition after Horace Walpole's *The Castle of Otranto*. It instead serves a double social purpose: paradoxically, it suggests both that the slaughter yard's frequenters are depraved, and that the suffocating milieu they inhabit is the reason for it, as in Victor Hugo's *Cour des miracles* in *Notre Dame de Paris*. Because, in fact, Echeverría believed in, and worked hard for, the transformation of the urban poor. In France, 1825–1830, he read avidly, including French socialist religious thinkers like the Lamennais who wrote *Essai sur l'indifférence en matière religieuse* (1817–1823) and *Paroles d'un croyant* (1834). Bowman traces French ferment about such ideas in *Le Christ des barricades, 1789–1848*, reviewing the role of Saint-Simon, Fourier, and over time, Hugo.[80] Echeverría's May Association published its 1838 manifesto as the *Dogma socialista de la asociación Mayo*, where that term's closeness to, say, a Lamennais matters. Thus, this short story stresses the extreme poverty on show in the slaughter yard, alongside the grotesque struggles of the poor to obtain food to eat. It also heavily ironizes the actions of the Catholic Church during the flooding that frames the narrative, though these esthetic choices seem local and not equivalent to, say, Marx in the *Communist Manifesto* of 1848. Second, Echeverría focuses on the lawlessness of these supporters of Rosas—as in his closing paragraph—and the violence makes this graphic. A judge appears who

80 Frank Paul Bowman, *Le Christ des barricades 1789–1848* (Paris: Editions du Cerf, 1987).

is at ease with torture; proposals trade between judge and mob; a man is tortured and suddenly dies. This, Echeverría suggests, is the world of the dictators, which may have contributed to the text's enduring South American popularity. Third, this mob seems a demonic variant of the people or nation so fundamental to Romantic thought. We may ask where, under Rosas, does the Argentinian nation reside? In answer, it seems reduced to scrambling in the mud for bull's testicles to feed spouse or children. It is participatory, if not complicit, in the equalizing mud. This is a world—and the Nazi death camps repeated this lesson—where the only organizing is by the goons. How can an Echeverría, or a young Unitarian, hope to reach through the veil of brutality and terror to those scrabbling in the mud? It matters perhaps that this 1838 story was left in the manuscript when Echeverría fled for Uruguay, and that, in the words of its first editor, "the shakiness in the handwriting [...] may be the result of rage rather than fear."[81] That is the very phrase the Unitarian offered his torturers and killers.

To conclude: I know nothing quite like this text, or with quite its urgency, in the Romantic literature of the Western world. The scene is unremittingly brutal; the irony, as in our extract, is savage. Echeverría focuses intensely on the mud, the filth, the obscenities, the casual violence and crime, and the system of oppression and degradation that underlies, as it undercuts, the bourgeois niceties of, say, the established church in the city of Buenos Aires. A bull is slaughtered as its testicles preoccupy the crowd; a passing stranger is caught, stripped, tortured, and murdered by the mob. Few other Romantic texts have such a plot. It is also, almost by definition, intensely local in its descriptions and its Argentine narrative. Echeverría has taken the local color that distinguishes his previous year's "La Cautiva" and gone one better. We are there on every page of his story, and right to the end, in the flood-soaked, mud-infested slaughter yard.

Lastly, this dramatic tale suggests that Latin American, or at least Argentine Romanticism, can be both characteristic and different from all the Romanticisms of the North, which seem to have produced nothing quite like this. It is brutal, it is compassionate. It engages with the poor; with oppression; with hunger; with violence and crime. It is quite modern after all. It seems worth a look.

81 Echeverría, *The Slaughter Yard*, p. xiii.

11. The Low Countries (Belgium), 1838 Hendrik Conscience, *De Leeuw Van Vlaanderen*

> Tijdens de oorlog van het jaar 1296, wanneer de Fransen gans West-Vlaanderen hadden ingenomen, bood het slot Nieuwenhove hun een hardnekkige tegenstand. Een groot getal Vlaamse ridders hadden zich onder Robrecht van Bethune erin opgesloten, en wilden het niet overgeven zolang één van hen zich kon verdedigen. Maar het groot getal vijanden maakte deze heldenmoed ten onnutte; zij sneuvelden meestal op de muren der vesting. Door de omvergeworpen wallen in het slot tredende, vonden de Fransen niets anders dan lijken; en daar zij hun woede op geen vijanden konden verzadigen, staken zij het kasteel in brand, braken de muren af en vervulden de grachten met gruis.

> At the time of the conquest of West Flanders by the French, in the year 1296, the castle of Nieuwenhove had offered them an especially obstinate resistance. A great number of Flemish knights had shut themselves up within it under Robert de Bethune, fully resolved to listen to no proposals of surrender so long as a single man remained in a condition to defend himself. But their valor was in vain against the overpowering force of their assailants; most of them perished, fighting desperately on the ramparts. The French, on entering through the breach effected by their engines, found not a living soul within the walls; and for want of living beings upon whom to wreak their vengeance, they fired the castle, and afterward deliberately battered down what the flames had spared, and filled up the moat with the rubbish.[82]

Henri (Hendrik) Conscience (3 December 1812–10 September 1883). **Works**: novels—*In't Wonderjaar* [In the Year of Miracles], *De Leeuw van Vlaanderen* [The Lion of Flanders], *The Conscript;* history—*History of Belgium.* Conscience's father was a French Napoleonic veteran who married an illiterate Fleming. She died in 1820, leaving two boys for their father to raise. The young Hendrik fought in the Belgian revolution of 1830 and was a pioneer of writing in Flemish. His father thought it so vulgar of his son to write a book in Flemish that he evicted him. In Antwerp, Conscience met King Leopold I, who ordered *In't Wonderjaar* to be presented to every Belgian school. In 1838, he had great success with his novel *De Leeuw van Vlaanderen*—it inspired "De Vlaamse Leeuw" or *The Flemish Lion*, long the unofficial and now the official

82 Hendrik Conscience, *The Lion of Flanders*, trans. by A. Schade van Westrum (New York: Collier, 1906), p. 278.

anthem of Flanders. He published over a hundred novels and novellas and achieved considerable success. After 1855, translations of his books began to appear in English, French, German, Czech, and Italian. He was given various official positions. The French writer Alexandre Dumas plagiarized two chapters of Conscience's book *The Conscript* to produce a novel of his own, appropriately called *Conscience*.

In this novel, Henri "Hendrik" Conscience writes about a political unit—this was in the days before there were nations—which ceased to exist in 1795. It had a long run, close to a millennium from 862 CE, but has yet to return to the map. Aptly enough, Conscience sets his novel in the thirteenth century, a golden age for the unit in question: Flanders. A dynastic county until 1795, Flanders has, since 1830, constituted one half of the bilingual nation-state of Belgium, which covers roughly the territory of the old Austrian Netherlands. So, what defines Flemish identity today? It seems a question worth asking. Is it that lost thousand-year history? Drawing modern borders based on past European boundaries might seem self-evidently catastrophic. Is it the Flemish language? That is, in essence, Dutch, as spoken by millions to Flanders's north. Is it the region's Catholicism? Faith does little to distinguish Flemings from Walloons (or from the French for that matter), though making just that distinction seems the driving force behind Flemish agitation for splitting Belgium down the middle. In short, this Flemish Romantic text raises problematic, indeed foundational questions about popular national movements—the West's Romantic dream, after all—and their legacy today.

After the French victory at Fleurus in 1794, the former Austrian Netherlands became four new *départements* of, first, the expanding French Republic, and then the expanding Napoleonic Empire. Opposition to French Revolutionary policies did much to unite the area's bilingual population, and Hendrik Conscience shows traces of that fraught period in this book. In 1815, these lowland territories were joined to the new Dutch Crown, until the 1830 Revolution brought the new Belgian republic a progressive constitution—then in 1831, after a hasty congress in London, the throne that Europe's Restoration politics demanded, in the royal person of a Protestant German nobleman, Leopold I of Saxe-Coburg, who unlike his new Catholic subjects was not given to speaking Flemish around the house. Belgium's 1830 revolution had been liberal and popular—it began, curiously, at a performance of Auber's 1828 opera *La Muette de Portici*—but like France's 1830 July Revolution, it simply brought the Belgian nation a new boss when the dust cleared, and one whose descendants still reign. Subsequent years were to oppose liberal and reactionary hopes among Flemings and Walloons alike.

In Conscience's 1838 historical novel, the Dutch—those foreign overlords of 1815–1830, who tried more than once before 1839 to recapture their lost southern territories—are not mentioned. This is perhaps logical, since the northern Netherlands were, in the thirteenth century, both behind Flanders in economic and cultural development, and also utterly lacking in the political autonomy or army needed to threaten one's neighbors. But Conscience finds a villain necessary, and the French serve that purpose. This makes for an interesting story. When Mickiewicz writes in 1834 of Poland's various betrayals, those were quite recent, and the betraying powers, namely Russia, Prussia, and Austria, still controlled all of Poland. None of those neighbors is popular in Poland today. But when Conscience vilifies the French—they are, in his plot, deceitful, brutal, and alien, and they rely as occupiers on a fifth column of traitors to Flanders—he is appealing to a past which was by then centuries old, in order to stir up new and fresh animosities. This approach is not without precedent in Romantic Europe—Sir Walter Scott writes of long-ago English betrayals of the Scots—but that man's Scottish homeland remained effectively under English rule, whereas 1795's invading French had left Belgium in 1815 and not returned. What then is Conscience's agenda? Does he see the rather different Orleanist France of 1838 as a clear and present danger? Are the French a stand-in for the Dutch Crown, which was quite literally at work trying to recapture Belgium until 1839? Is Conscience wildly swinging at all comers, blaming any neighbor who ever entered Flanders for shaping that land's compromised fate? Any of these ideas is possible, and they would be in keeping with the work of many a Romantic author—a Mickiewicz, for instance—looking to build a nation-state in the face of external threats. The task has its merits. But finally, all these explanations seem inadequate. This is, perhaps, intended as nothing more than a rollicking good yarn. But it also seems possible that Conscience has a specific Flemish agenda, one still available today; namely to focus, via the French, inside Belgium's borders on that fifth column he singles out for vituperation, the Lilyards, those medieval Flemings who allied themselves with them. Conscience finds room to treat the King of France as noble, but the Lilyards are allowed no such room, as Conscience leaves a clear space for contemporary and factional intra-Belgian debate within his picturesque thirteenth-century plot. The 1830s were a period of considerable Flemish agitation in Belgium: societies were founded, appeals made for the use of Flemish in government, and books published in Flemish. That is the backdrop to Conscience's work.[83]

Conscience invites us to know our own distant Middle Ages: dates, architecture, heraldry, and so forth. Details are fictionalized, but the plot focuses on real events: the situation in occupied Flanders leading up to 1302's Battle of Courtrai or of The Golden Spurs, a crushing defeat for France. The Flemish burghers—clothworkers, for instance—did in fact play their part in this story, and that data point dovetails with Romantic populist priorities. But like Romantics across Europe, Conscience declines to anchor his plot in non-noble protagonists. Nobles are praised and play major roles, a fact which would have horrified the Revolutionary French, but which made perfect sense, across Europe, with the crushing of the Revolutionary enterprise after 1815. It is also worth noting that Conscience's hero, Robert of Bethune, spoke no Flemish and was absent at the battle. A French war machine is on display in this passage, as in Goya's *Tres de mayo 1808*. And Conscience makes room for brutality; here, the French raze the castle of Nieuwenhove, much as the Romans razed Carthage then salted its earth to end the Punic Wars. I've seen an eighteenth-century print of this castle, and it was visibly not in ruins. Thus, I have no evidence for Conscience's storyline. Today, the place is a hotel. But perceived atrocities are powerful motivators when you want to rile up a crowd— "Remember the Alamo," went the cry that parted slave-holding Texas from free Mexico after 1836. Conscience is creating a mythic past for the unrepresented Flemish nation, and such myths are powerful things. For the book's Flemish readers, one may argue French rule had not ceased even by 1838; it continued on under the united Belgian national government. Compare for instance the linguistic status of French in Quebec before the 1960s, a language looked down on and even banned in public spaces: thus around 1960, an American colleague

83 Sir Walter Scott's novels set in Scotland include *The Monastery* (1820) and *Kenilworth* (1821), both set in the 1500s.

of mine in a Montreal department store spoke French and was told to "Speak white." Language politics around the globe is rarely as self-evident as it might appear, or as it might have appeared to Europe's and America's various Romantic authors.

In closing, what is Belgium, after all? Is it a *nation* in the Romantic sense? One thinks of those irredentist postcards—*Hungaria irredenta*—still unashamedly for sale in 2010 in Budapest's National Gallery. Nationalism is a toxic thing, or at least, it has toxic potential; it also has a life of its own that, like Frankenstein's creation, will escape the grip of those who wield it. What nation exactly is Ukraine? Or Germany? Where are their borders? National myths are important, but they deserve caution; the brave little Belgium that the second German *Reich* marched over in 1914 was also the colonizer of the Belgian Congo, that vast swathe of Africa where nationhood visibly played out in other terms. People need heroes just as they need scapegoats, but in reality, things are rarely so convenient. Who are our scapegoats here to be? The French? The Dutch? The Walloons? And who then are to be our heroes? Let us swear an oath to Flanders, that vanished state. Let us embrace its proud yet humble people—who are, after all, much like people everywhere—in Romantic enthusiasm, be they citizens or subjects. The ins and outs of history—its vicissitudes—are, as the Kurds or the Irish might tell us, in the end no basis on which to draw a nation's borders, to determine a people's autonomy or self-rule. Perhaps that old Romantic dream—the one in which each nation on Earth gets to speak for itself—is not such a terrible dream after all, when seen *sub specie aeternitatis* and freed, if need be, of its local agents. Perhaps the West's Romantics were, in their own way, right.

12. Portugal, 1846
João de Almeida Garrett, *Viagens na minha terra*

Prova-se como o velho Camões não teve outro remédio senão misturar o maravilhoso da mitologia com o do cristianismo. — Dá-se razão, e tira-se depois, ao padre José Agostinho. — No meio destas disceptações académico-literárias, vem o A. a descobrir que para tudo é preciso ter fé neste mundo. Diz-se neste mundo, porque, quanto ao outro, já era sabido. — Os Lusíadas, o Fausto e a Divina Comédia. — Desgraça do Camões em ter nascido antes do romantismo. — Mostra-se como a Estige e o Cocito sempre são melhores sítios que o Inferno e o Purgatório. — Vai o A. em procura do marquês de Pombal, e dá com ele nas ilhas Beatas do poeta Alceu. — Partida de whist entre os ilustres finados. — Compaixão do marquês pelos pobres homens de Ricardo Smith e J. B. Say. — Resposta dele e da sua luneta às perguntas peralvilhas do A. — Chegada a este mundo e ao Cartaxo.

It is shown that old Camoens had no choice but to mingle the legends of classical mythology with those of Christianity. — Father José Agostinho is first considered right then wrong. — In the midst of these academic-literary disceptations the author comes to discover that one needs faith for everything in this world. — This world, because, as far as the other is concerned, he knew it already. — The Lusiads, Faust and the Divine Comedy. — Camoens's misfortune in being born before the romantic period. — The Styx and Cocytus are shown to be better places, after all, than Hell and Purgatory. — The author goes in search of the Marquis of Pombal and comes upon him in the Blessed Isles of the poet Alcaeus. — A game of whist between the illustrious deceased. — The marquis shows pity for Richard Smith and J.B. Say, poor fellows. — The marquis and his eyeglass answer the author's pretentious questions. — Return to the real world and arrival in Cartaxo.[84]

João Baptista da Silva Leitão de Almeida Garrett, 1st Viscount of Almeida Garrett (4 February 1799–9 December 1854). **Works**: poems—*O Retrato de Vénus, Hymno Constitucional, Hymno Patriótico, Camões, Dona Branca, Romanceiro e Cancioneiro Geral;* plays—*Catão;* political texts; prose fiction—*O Arco de Santana, Viagens na Minha Terra.* Garrett was born to a *fidalgo* of the Royal Household and his Irish-Italian wife. In 1809, his family fled Soult's French invasion for the Azores. There, he

84 Almeida Garrett, *Travels in My Homeland*, trans. by John M. Parker (London: Peter Owen, 1987), p. 43.

was taught by his uncle, the Bishop of Angra. In 1818, he enrolled at the Coimbra university law school, publishing "O Retrato de Vénus," a work prosecuted as immoral. Although Garrett did not take an active part in the 1820 Liberal Revolution, he contributed two poems, the "Hymno Constitucional" and the "Hymno Patriótico." A coup led by the Infante Dom Miguel in 1823 forced him to seek exile in England. He had just married his friend's twelve-year-old sister. In England, he began his association with Romanticism, discovering Shakespeare and Scott. Garrett left for France in 1825 where he wrote "Camões" and "Dona Branca," poems often considered the first Romantic works in Portuguese. In 1826, he returned to Portugal, but in 1828 was again forced to settle in England. He took part in the liberal Landing of Mindelo in 1832, and under the new constitutional monarchy briefly served as Consul General to Brussels. In 1843, Garrett published *Romanceiro e Cancioneiro Geral*, a mixture of his own lyrics with folk lyrics and ballads somewhat in the vein of Percy's 1765 *Reliques of Ancient English Poetry*, and then his 1846 *Viagens na Minha Terra*. He divorced his first wife in 1835 to marry a seventeen-year-old. He died in 1854 and was buried beside Luís Vaz de Camões.

And so, we come to Portugal, where the Romantic enterprise seems to have arrived a tad late. It is, we may argue, a liminal country, perched as it is alongside Spain on the Atlantic edge of the Iberian Peninsula. The territory achieved independence around 1100 and has maintained it, almost unbroken, ever since. Portugal was, with Spain, a major figure in early European exploration, colonialism, and the Atlantic slave trade, acquiring an empire stretching from Brazil to Angola, Mozambique, and various trading outposts on the coasts of Asia—Goa, Macau. The French invasion of the peninsula after 1807, when Portugal refused to accede to Napoleon's Continental System, broke peninsular links with the colonies for Spain and Portugal alike. With British aid, the Portuguese expelled the French after 1812, but from 1807 to 1821, Rio de Janeiro was Portugal's capital. 1820's constitutionalist insurrections across Portugal, and Brazil's declaration of independence in 1822, were followed by Lisbon's reinstatement. At the death of King John VI in 1826, his son Pedro I left Portugal for the Empire of Brazil, an empire perched amid America's new republics. Briefly King of Portugal as well, he soon bowed to popular pressure and abdicated the Portuguese throne in favor of his seven-year-old daughter Maria. Dissatisfaction at Pedro's constitutional reforms led the 'absolutist' faction to proclaim his brother Miguel King of Portugal in a second coup in 1828. In the ensuing Liberal Wars, Pedro forced his brother Miguel to abdicate and go into exile in 1834, placing his daughter Maria back on the Portuguese throne. This political and dynastic struggle—lasting from 1820 to 1834, between Portugal's liberals and absolutists but stretching from Portugal to her former colony Brazil—is the backdrop to Almeida Garrett's work.

Let's look now at the text. To begin with, Almeida Garrett's title is an explicit homage—he names the man—to Xavier de Maistre's 1794 *Voyage autour de ma chambre* (Journey Around My Bedroom), a book written under house arrest and in good-hearted parody of such works as the French explorer Bougainville's 1771 *Voyage autour du monde*. Xavier de Maistre is the lesser-known, less political brother of Joseph de Maistre, that theorist of tsarist absolutism. Almeida Garrett was, though a peer of the realm, also a liberal, exiled to Britain and France from 1823–1826 and again from 1828–1832, a period ending with the landing at Mindelo, in which he took part, and which hastened the close of the Liberal Wars.[85] In short, Almeida Garrett seems more interested here in Maistre's tone than in his politics, and that is typical of this charming book.

Almeida Garrett opens every chapter with a long rubric, a prefacing device that shapes and redirects his more traditional narrative portions at every step. The device is both ironic and playful, and it has a certain humility to it. Nor is this framing device without precedent; it is fairly common in British eighteenth-century novels, such as Henry Fielding's influential *History of Tom Jones* (1749), whose long, witty titles serve a parallel function. Fielding's novelistic successor, Laurence Sterne's *Tristram Shandy* (1759–1767), is (along with Sterne's *Sentimental Journey* (1768)) yet more fundamental among Almeida Garrett's many sources, focused as both novels are on wit, play, charm, digression, and the unexpected.[86] To do this, Almeida Garrett requires an educated reader, one who shares his cultural baggage and is prepared to treat its inertial weight with impartial and equal lightness, much as Pushkin does. Thus,

85 Joseph de Maistre wrote the *Soirées de Saint Pétersbourg* [Evenings of Saint Petersburg], 1821.

86 Laurence Sterne, *The Life and Opinions of Tristram Shandy, Gentleman* (1759–1767); *A Sentimental Journey through France and Italy* (1768).

we might want to know that Jean-Baptiste Say was a liberal French economist, and the creator in this field of Say's Law, while "Richard Smith"—*Ricardo* in Portuguese—is likely that still more famous Scottish economist, Adam Smith of *The Wealth of Nations* (1776), combined with that other modern free trader, David Ricardo. The book has a patina of learning, lending it glamor. Camoëns and his *Lusiads* will be no surprise to Portuguese readers; but *Faust* and *The Divine Comedy*, presented in parallel, form a sort of Romantic manifesto, which the author then complicates by referring next to the ancient lyric poet Alcaeus of Mytilene.[87] Almeida Garrett is unprepared to be labeled or categorized: Romanticism informs his thinking but does not circumscribe it, he remains open to things of value from any tradition, including the Classics. This is, of course, a position common to a great number of Europe's Romantics, as I argue below, and one rare in art prior to their appearance.

Almeida Garrett is, in a word, late. And how does that shape his writing? Well, it helps to make him acutely aware of fashion, of what is *in* and what is *out*. It is Almeida Garrett's aim to leaven with pleasure any information he has to provide us; that is his contract with the reader. "Take light things seriously and serious things lightly," said the French in the run-up to 1789, a philosophy which allowed aristocrats to mount to the guillotine with a last *bon mot* for their executioner. Almeida Garrett may choose to cite foreign liberal economists in his text, Smith and Say (and perhaps Ricardo), but he will do so off-handedly— "those poor fellows." This is an ironizing approach, where the author cannot be held responsible for his learning because he refuses to take it in earnest. "Old Camoëns," he writes, to preface his Romantic argument that Camoëns inevitably mingled Classical and Christian material. The author is playing a game in which we readers are invited to participate— "A game of whist," the author writes, "between the illustrious deceased." There is a certain universal learning to which all things on Earth are of equal value and importance. It may seem that when nothing is taken seriously, we have no values left with which to form a judgment, and yet, this text has not been leveled into uniformity. It is instead individual, even unique; it has flavor. And that flavor derives from its playfulness;

87 Luís Vaz de Camões, *Os Lusíadas* [The Lusiads] (1572).

Almeida Garrett is prepared to be atypical, indeed eccentric, as is any Romantic worth their salt. We've seen how rare this position is in Europe prior to, say, Rousseau or Diderot. But this eccentricity does not in fact make the author minor; true, he has found an unusual window through which to look at the world, anchored as it is in play, but his view from there takes in the planet, or at least a good portion of Europe. And if Almeida Garrett is not prepared to be minor, neither, we may say, is the Portuguese nation, as exemplified in this text. Nor, for that matter, is Portuguese art. The author has traveled, in his years of exile, to England and to France; he has observed two of the nineteenth century's major economic, military, and cultural powers. But he has then chosen to return to Portugal. It is in this context that we might consider his self-deprecation and wit. It is not unlike that of a Pushkin or an Andersen, and it seems well suited to those who write on Europe's margins. There is poise here, a certain ease, and there is even perhaps a sort of wisdom.

To explore the world, we may as well begin just where we find ourselves. A fishing boat, goes the story, left the Portuguese Algarve—under French occupation since 1807—to inform the king in faraway Brazil that their village had been liberated from the French. Portugal, that old seafaring country, is a good place from which to observe the planet: all Europe stretches to the East, and to the West and South lie the territories of Portugal's Atlantic slave trade. Portugal was already cutting itself loose, by 1846, from its old imperial narrative, and Almeida Garrett had already risked his life in 1832 to help reform the nation. But that is not his topic in this book. His topic is, instead, everything. Art matters: Camoëns, Dante, Goethe, Alcaeus. The sciences matter: Smith, Ricardo, Say, those "poor fellows." The author had seen England in person—the Industrial Revolution, Utilitarianism, the enclosure movement, popular unrest. But for now, he tells a Portuguese story. Which sciences make our lives better, and which arts? The question would not be alien to a Mary Shelley. Which beliefs improve our existence? These are wisdom questions after all. "Father José Agostinho," writes Almeida Garrett in this extract, "is first considered right then wrong." That is perhaps not so different from Goya's position on theodicy in 1814, in his electric *Tres de mayo 1808*. Almeida Garrett has, by this time in the century, seen many things. But he is, like the young Pellico in his various Austrian prisons, not bitter about it, nor does he belabor the point.

Finally: the people's voice. Almeida Garrett is, one can argue, a sophisticate; not for nothing was he a peer of the realm, a returnee from exile in England and France. Can this book nonetheless be called a people's book, an example of popular art? I believe it fairly can. Our narrator, our pair of eyes if you like, is, as in Pushkin's *Onegin*, concerned not to bore us, full of information, playful and even ludic with the most serious things. But the world we travel through here is, in the end, that of everyday Portuguese existence. There is a little religion, a little romance. There is work being done and simple conversation being had. This vision shows us the inner life and also the autonomy of the Portuguese people; it is what defines them, their national character. This national life had perhaps, after Brazil's departure in 1822, become less world-shaping than it once was, or than that of contemporary England, France, or Germany, but it was not subordinate to anyone. It had, and has, its place in the concert of nations. The author, like Portugal, may indeed lack international prestige, but that is our loss. Portugal's liminal European position perhaps encourages the author to focus on boredom, on pleasure, on inattention—indeed on Schlegel's arabesque, that definitional aspect of comedy, governing the works of a Gozzi or a Sterne.[88] It also informs his mechanics of reading. Almeida Garrett's art opens playfully onto the world in its infinite variety, but it does so from within a self-contained, organic whole. And that organic whole is defined by the Kingdom of Portugal's national borders, and by the Romantic homeland through which Almeida Garrett journeys.

---

88 Arabesque: *Brief über den Roman*, in *Gespräch über die Poesie*, pp. 284–362, in *Friedrich Schlegel* II: *Charakteristiken und Kritiken I (1796–1801)*, ed. by Hans Eichner (1967), p. 331. Or as A.W. Schlegel says of the Greek Old Comedy, "a seeming aimlessness reigns throughout"—August Wilhelm Schlegel, *Vorlesungen über dramatische Kunst und Literatur* I, ed. by Edgar Lohner, in *Kritische Schriften und Briefe* VII (Stuttgart, Berlin, Cologne, Mainz: W. Kohlhammer, 1966), p. 133 (lecture XI): "eine scheinbare Zwecklosigkeit und Willkür herrscht darin." Carlo Gozzi was the author of *L'amore delle tre melarance* [The Love of Three Oranges] (1761) and *Turandot* (1762).

2. The Frankenstein Dilemma: Romantic Disavowals of Romanticism, 1800–1830

> The title Realist was imposed on me as the men of 1830 had the title Romantics imposed on them. At no time have titles given a just idea of things; if it were otherwise, works would be superfluous.
>
> Gustave Courbet[1]

> Now that I had finished, the beauty of the dream vanished, and breathless horror and disgust filled my heart.
>
> Mary Shelley[2]

To ask what 'Romanticism' is at the beginning of the twenty-first century may seem little different from asking how many angels can dance on the head of a pin. "When I make words work harder," argues Humpty Dumpty to Alice, "I pay them extra;" a laudable solution, but one which describing realities will not allow us.[3] This, in essence, is Lovejoy's famous position: defining the word *Romanticism,* he writes, will either require assuming the word has one accepted meaning, or will be a personal definition leading to "a vast amount of bad history." "To call these new ideas of the 1780s and 1790s 'Romanticism' [...] suggests that there was only one such idea, or, if many, that they were all implicates of one fundamental 'Romantic' idea, or, at the least, that

1 "Le titre de réaliste m'a été imposé comme on a imposé aux hommes de 1830 celui de romantiques. Les titres n'ont donné en aucun temps une idée juste des choses; s'il en était autrement, les œuvres seraient superflues" (ctd. in Barrère, "Définitions" 104).

2 Mary Shelley, *Frankenstein*, p. 56.

3 Carroll, *Looking-Glass*, p. 197.

 https://doi.org/10.11647/OBP.0302.02

they were harmonious *inter se* and formed some sort of systematic unity. None of these things are true."[4] Eichner replies that "if we are not permitted to mean more than 'organic dynamicism,' it is much simpler to say 'organic dynamicism'," and as Peckham writes, any theory of romanticism worth its salt "must show that Wordsworth and Byron, Goethe and Chateaubriand, were all part of a general European literary movement."[5] One common solution to this dilemma is empirical: if it quacks like a Romantic, then call the thing Romantic. Eichner notes that in sixty years, "some seven hundred articles and treatises have been devoted to this quest."[6] "The spirit of the age was Romanticism," states MacFarland, adding a quote from Blake, "To Generalize is to be an Idiot."[7] This chapter prefers to examine some first-hand Romantic positions on the 'Romantic movement' as such; taking Blake's advice to heart, it hopes less to map a field than to open a window for debate, and to raise more questions than answers.

Three pressures complicate its global survey. First, 'Romanticism' is a civilization. Peyre thus contrasts it with other movements: "We could hardly speak of symbolist history or even symbolist philosophy, of realist music or politics, of existentialist music, painting, criticism, and hardly more appropriately of existentialist poetry. Classicism [...] never reached, even in France, a fraction of the reading public."[8] Second, 'Romantic' works reflect a series of apparently irreconcilable antinomies: male/female; energy/*ennui*; form/chaos; art/science; public/private; group/individual; right-wing/left-wing; nation/exoticism; naïve/ironic; antique/Christian; classic/romantic/realist. Third, as Courbet notes, thing and label repeatedly blur. Behler remarks on "the amazing fact that most of the authors whom we today call Romantic poets did not consider themselves to be Romantics," citing the Schlegels, Novalis and Brentano, Staël and Chateaubriand, Coleridge, Wordsworth, Keats, Shelley, and Byron.[9] If none of these Romantics use the term, then who did? McGann, in particular, has argued that here we are the unwitting prisoners of forgotten late-nineteenth-century critics. Writing of

4 Lovejoy, "Meaning," pp. 259–261.
5 Eichner, "Genesis," p. 214. Peckham, "Theory," p. 5.
6 Eichner, "*Romantic*," p. 3.
7 MacFarland, *Cruxes*, p. 103.
8 Peyre, "Originality," p. 333.
9 Behler, "Origins," p. 110.

'Romantic irony,' Fetzer notes that "the addition of the adjective *Romantic* was apparently the arbitrary decision of a later, influential critic writing in the mid-nineteenth century;" Greene observes that "*neo-classicism* [...] had an obscure birth in uninspired manuals of literary history around the end of the nineteenth century," while Wellek remarks that 'classicisme' has never entered the dictionary of the French Academy and dates *Klassik* in Germany from 1887.[10] As Perkins notes, "The major Victorian critics [...] did not refer to an 'English Romantic Movement,' though they wrote abundantly about the poets."[11] Taine names the French school 'Romantic' in 1863, echoing Anatole France, and Pater in 1889 calls it a French and German term. That story has many fascinating aspects, and several recur here: artists show the mellowing of age and personal feuds among Classics and Romantics alike, and critics show ideology and the politics of canon formation. But this study's main focus lies elsewhere, focused on a group of facts that throw our primary sources into a new light. It argues that a common thread does indeed link Europe's major Romantics, despite religion, politics, and national boundaries: their disavowal of their own creation. Goethe, Tieck, and the Schlegels; Wordsworth and Byron; Manzoni, Leopardi, Pushkin, Chateaubriand, Hugo: their parallel remarks show more than personal feuds or late regrets, since it is their own works these romantics disown, and the doubts are there from their first manifestos.

1. German Lands

Historians may call them 'Weimar Classicists,' another term we owe to Wilhelmine scholarship, but Wieland and Herder, Goethe and Schiller, launched the adjective *romantisch* in Germany. Alert critics still struggle with "the common German view that romanticism is the creation of the Schlegels, Tieck, Novalis, and Wackenroder."[12] Wellek argued in 1949 that since Goethe in particular shapes German Romanticism, to sidestep Goethe as 'Classic' is to read the Apocrypha without the Bible, and

10 Fetzer, "Irony," p. 21. Greene, "Neo-Classicism," p. 70. Wellek, *Discriminations*, pp. 68, 74.

11 Perkins, "Construction," p. 137.

12 Wellek, "Concept," pp. 147–148; see also Eichner, "*Romantic*," pp. 60–65, 145–148 and *Period*, pp. 39–42, 48–53; and Wellek, *History*, pp. 1–2.

Eichner repeats this complaint decades later: "matters are not so simple as the reader of most German histories of literature is led to believe."[13] In 1798, Novalis uses the noun *die Romantik*, describing a science of 'Romantics' akin to physics or numismatics (*Das allgemeine Brouillon*). In 1804, Jean Paul Richter applies this noun to the art of Klopstock, Herder, Goethe, Schiller, and the Schlegels (see his *Vorschule der Ästhetik*). In Heidelberg, 1808, Voss and Baggesen use the agent noun *Romantiker* for living writers, as an insult (*Der Karfunkel oder, Klingelklingel-almanach: Ein Taschenbuch für vollendete Romantiker und angehende Mystiker*). Brentano and Arnim take the insult as a badge of honor, and Romanticists are born (*Zeitschrift für Einsiedler*). Germany's media debate runs 1801–1808, in essence; Bouterwek's monumental *Geschichte der Poesie und Beredsamkeit* already reviews German *Romantiker* in 1819.

Here also are the first to disown the term. Goethe claims that he and Schiller invented the Classic/Romantic distinction; Pushkin and Heine call Goethe "the giant of Romantic poetry."[14] Goethe's place in German Romantic lyric is fundamental; his *Märchen* launched the Romantic literary fairy tale, his *Wilhelm Meister* prompted the Romantic *Bildungsroman*, from *Heinrich von Ofterdingen*, which Novalis wrote in reply, to Tieck's *Sternbald*—not to mention *Faust's* or *Werther*'s impact, and this is a short list.[15] Yet Goethe's rejection of Romanticism is explicit. In an unpublished *Römische Elegie*, Goethe says that if Werther had been his brother, he would have killed him.[16] On the Weimar stage, he classicizes Kleist; and he refuses Brentano's *Ponce de Leon*, an 1801 competition entry, preferring Kotzebue and even Terence.[17] He talks of his "horror and loathing" [Schauder und Abscheu] at each contact with Kleist.[18] As early as 1808, he despairs of Germany's spoiled talents, listing Werner, Oehlenschläger, Jean Paul, Görres, Arnim, and Brentano whom he had praised in 1806; his attacks on "charakterlose" romantic art continue through the 1820s.[19] Expanding on his famous observation

13 Wellek, "Concept," pp. 147–148. Eichner "*Romantic*," p. 10.

14 *Pushkin on Literature*, p. 465. Heine ctd. Eichner, "*Romantic*," p. 151.

15 Eichner, "*Romantic*," p. 98. Trainer, *Märchen*, p. 98. Goethe, *Gedenkausgabe* 1: p. 585.

16 Menhennet, *Movement*, p. 122.

17 Staël, *Allemagne* 3: pp. 247–248. Burckhardt, *Repertoire*; also Balayé, *Carnets*, p. 80.

18 Goethe, *Schriften* 3: p. 141.

19 Goethe, *Briefe* 3: p. 92.

that the classic is healthy while the romantic is sick, Goethe notes that "they encounter one another in the emptiness."[20]

Germany's 'Romantics' have since Bouterwek and Heine been rather a fluid list, with many common absentees: Herder, Bürger, Klopstock, Schiller, Goethe; Hölderlin, Jean Paul, Kleist. What purpose is served, we may ask, by a history of Romantic lyric where Goethe, Bürger, and Hölderlin are unmentioned? Surely it will only be half a story? Yet the Schlegels, at least, remain Romantic shibboleths for a fastidious post-Wilhelmine tradition, making their own resistance to the term all the more surprising.

Friedrich Schlegel, that modernist, stopped calling modern art *charakterlos* after 1796, instead looking to combine Europe's old split between the ancient and medieval, classical and Romantic ages, to create the *Indifferenzpunkt* of new art, an equilibrium of the universal in the local. And indeed, Goethe is his model. By 1797 (*Über das Studium der griechischen Poesie*), Friedrich's definition of *romantisch* is "125 sheets long", and in 1800, Friedrich famously suggests that Romantic art is not dead: "the Romantic type of poetry is still becoming."[21] Yet his preceding remark in the same passage goes uncited, on "the prospect of a boundlessly growing classicism." What impulse makes us suppress half of Friedrich Schlegel's message? Wellek claims that "the Schlegels were obviously strongly anticlassicist at the time," and even Eichner deletes just this remark in his meticulous study's page-long Schlegel extract.[22] Berlin's *Athenäum* writers use *romantisch* in art, like its partner *klassisch*, almost wholly for the past, not the future or even the present. And after Paris in 1802, Friedrich drops his "highly idiosyncratic" usage, consigning the term *romantisch* to history.[23] He calls Jean Paul's novels "the only romantic products of our unromantic age," as he had said of

20 "Das Klassische nenne ich das Gesunde und das Romantische das Kranke,"in Goethe, *Gespräche mit Eckermann*, March 21 and April 2, 1829; "wodurch sie sich denn beide im Nichtigen begegnen," Goethe's *Moderne Guelfen und Ghibellinen*, in *Über Kunst und Alterthum* (Stuttgart: Cotta, 1827), VI, p. 166..

21 "Bogen lang;" in Baldensperger, "Romantique," pp. 93–95.

22 Wellek, "Concept," p. 7. Both Eichner, "*Romantic*," p. 112 and Immerwahr, "Romantisch," pp. 50–54 cite the 116 *Athenäum* Fragment's "die romantische Dichtart ist noch im Werden," but not its talk of "grenzenlos wachsende Klassizität."

23 Baldensperger, "Romantique," p. 91.

Tieck's *Sternbald* in 1799.[24] Even for Friedrich at his peak, Romantic and classical art are two old parents for a new artistic future. As Behler writes, Friedrich's aesthetic theory tries to unite "two antagonistic aesthetics, to find a synthesis of [...] the antique and the modern, the Classical and the Romantic;" a third epoch will bring "the harmony of the Classical and the Romantic," which the 1800 *Gespräch über die Poesie* [Talk About Poetry] calls the ultimate goal of all literature.[25] Moreover, Schlegel not only distrusts his own Romantic label, but also the new art that took his name: around 1800, he writes that "Tieck has no sense at all of art [...] he is absolutely *unclassic and unprogressive*."[26] In 1806, he complains to his brother Wilhelm of Goethe's "indecent and scandalous praise" for Brentano's "rabble songs," *Des Knaben Wunderhorn* (The Boy's Magic Horn, 1806): "German scholars have become a band of gypsies; thank God we are out of that!"[27] He calls all he dislikes *brentanisch*, and remarks at Kleist's suicide, in 1812, that Kleist had mistaken madness for genius.[28] Wilhelm repeats this to Staël six days later, and Staël then quotes it in her *Réflexions sur le suicide* (Reflections on Suicide).[29] Friedrich and his brother Wilhelm, meanwhile, turned to the East.

One key to Schlegel's thought may be the mistranslated term *Roman* itself. Eichner stresses three points: "The *Roman* is the dominant form both of the earliest and the most recent post-classical poetry; the central position in the history of the *Roman* is occupied by Shakespeare, [...] the *Roman* is characterized by the vast quantity of forms it can assume."[30] For Schlegel, Shakespeare mixes classical *Tragödie* with *Roman*, as does

24 "die einzigen romantischen Erzeugnisse unseres unromantischen Zeitalters;" F. Schlegel, *Kritische* 2: p. 330.

25 Behler, "Origins," pp. 117–119.

26 "Tieck hat gar keinen Sinn für Kunst sondern nur ... [für] Fantasmus und Sentimentalität ... Es fehlt ihm an Stoff, an Realismus, an Philosophie ... Er ist absolut unklassisch und unprogressiv;" F. Schlegel, *Fragmente*, 65.

27 "Goethe hat ... ein ausschweifendes und skandalöses Lob auf Brentano wegen der Pöbellieder in seinem Freimüthigen aufgestellt; die Deutschen Gelehrten ... sind jetzt ein wahres Zigeunergesindel. Gott sei Dank daß wir heraus sind!" in F. Schlegel, *Krisenjahre* 1: p. 292.

28 Brentanisch: F. Schlegel, *Krisenjahre* 1: 246. Kleist "hat also nicht bloß in Werken sondern auch im Leben Tollheit für Genie genommen;" F. Schlegel, *Krisenjahre* 2: p. 239.

29 See Pange, *Auguste-Guillaume Schlegel et Madame de Staël*. Also Staël, *Réflexions sur le suicide* in *De l'influence des passions et autres essais moraux*, ed. Florence Lotterie (Paris: Champion, 2008), pp. 378–379.

30 Eichner, "Theory," p. 1021.

Schiller in *Die Jungfrau von Orleans: Eine romantische Tragödie* (The Maid of Orleans: A Romantic Tragedy); the *Gespräch* suggests that "Dante, Petrarch, Shakespeare, and Cervantes should all be discussed in a *Theorie des Romans*."[31] These facts may illustrate the absurdity in translating *Roman* as *novel* when the term *romance* exists—*romance* will subsume Eichner's dispute with Lovejoy, where both are right, and force a fruitful rethinking for us of the links between novel and verse romance throughout European Romanticism, from Byron and Pushkin to Mickiewicz and Hugo.[32] Eichner notes that the word *Roman* had a wider range "than the English 'novel' and 'romance' combined."[33] Yes, indeed! Schlegel's antipathy is precisely the "sogenannte Roman" or *novel* of Fielding and Richardson. Revealingly, Schlegel later replaces the problem term *romantisch* by *romanartig* or 'romancy,' stressing his etymology and locating its pastness.[34]

For his part, Jean Paul prefers Kames to the Schlegels, who were hardly friends, and attacks their new Fichtean idealism as pernicious solipsism and egotism.[35] In 1792, a friend persuades him to delete the word *romantisch* in a title, since it had been "used too often and [...] had acquired a bad reputation."[36] Uhland similarly condemns "what seemed to him the selfish poetry of those blinded by introspection to their nation's agony."[37] For here is a central paradox: if Romantic art talks of people and nation, how can it ignore its public and national role? The 1803 *Reichsdeputationshauptschluß* and then Napoleon's crushing of Prussia at Jena in 1806 had left all these writers in defeated and occupied territory, and that burning concern drives many German disavowals. The disavowals also show a series of avant-garde artists finding, in succession, that their message is being distorted by rivals and imitators: Tieck finds the Brentanos histrionic and insincere, and calls Hoffmann a scribbler of grotesques. Heine's *Die romantische Schule*, 1832–1835, is no encomium. Eichendorff talks of "faded Romanticism" and "juvenile

31 Eichner, "Theory," pp. 1030, 1041.
32 Ibid., p. 1040.
33 Ibid., "Theory," p. 1019.
34 Eichner, "*Romantic*," p. 110.
35 Wellek, *History*, pp. 100–101.
36 *Jean Pauls sämtliche Werke: historisch-kritische Ausgabe*, ed. Eduard Berend, vol. IV.1, *Briefe an Jean Paul 1781–1793*, ed. Monika Meier (Berlin: Akademie Verlag, 2003), p. 258.
37 Rodger, "Lyric," p. 148.

reawakening," while Brentano himself uses *Romantismus* to Arnim in 1803 as a synonym of bad rhyming and empty lyricism.[38]

'Classic-Romantic-Realist,' runs the old chronology, and its simplicity has a certain schematic appeal, like Ptolemy's cosmogony. Yet, as epicycles multiply, a new starting point may furnish a path forward for research. As Tieck tells Friedrich Schlegel in 1813, he finds no pleasure "in all the things we have instigated," and resents being considered the "head of the *so-called Romantic school*."[39] Friedrich Schlegel himself talks of the "so-called New School" in 1812. *Trivial-, Schauer-, Afterromantik*; critics have coined many tools to keep true and false Romanticism apart. *Goethezeit* polemic is vastly complex, due in part to geography and to endless personal feuds, but when Tieck, Goethe, and the Schlegels reject their *own* creations, something more is at issue. A German scholar, told of a conference on Europe's Romantics, asked if it ran 1800–1804. In this narrow inner sanctum, our high priests will be apostates.

2. The Swiss Confederation

German Romanticism reached the world in translation after 1813, from three writers under one Swiss roof—A.W. (Wilhelm) Schlegel, Staël, and Sismondi—Coppet's *Confédération romantique* (a phrase coined by the Bonapartist *Nain jaune*).[40] These creators of the genre are again profoundly ambivalent about their romantic dawn. Wellek claimed that Wilhelm Schlegel's "scales are heavily weighted in favor of the romantic"—true only if *romantic* means the dead past, medieval and renaissance.[41] As early as 1797, Wilhelm deplored modern taste: "From Vehmic courts, mysterious compacts, and ghosts there is now absolutely

38 Matenko, *Tieck*, p. 437 cites Tieck on "Affen-Incest" and "Generationen wie die Brentanos," *ape incest* and *generations like the Brentanos*. "weil es zu verbraucht und ... schon in zu schlechten Ruf gekommen ist," ctd. Eichner, "*Romantic*" 101. "die verblichene Romantik;" "juvenile Wiedererweckung der Romantik;" "eine der Schule entwachsene Romantik," Eichendorff, *Werke*, pp. 1073–1074; "ein solch Gesinge und ein solcher Romantismus ... daß man sich schämt," Brentano, *Briefe* 1: p. 220.

39 "Ich habe überhaupt keine Freude an allen den Sachen, die wir veranlasst haben," in Lüdeke, *Tieck-Schlegel*, p. 169. "sogenannte Neue Schule;" in Eichner, "*Romantic*," p. 141. See Köpke, *Tiecks Schriften* 2: p. 173.

40 See F. Schlegel, *Botschaft* and also Isbell, "Groupe de Coppet."

41 Wellek, *History*, p. 60.

no escape."[42] Körner called Wilhelm's 1808 Vienna lectures "German Romanticism's Message to Europe"—their message is that Romanticism is over. To Wilhelm Schlegel, Spain's *siglo de oro* is "the last summit of Romantic poetry;" after 600 pages on the past, he ends with just two on the future of German theatre, lamenting the *Romantic* as "a word profaned in a hundred posters."[43] Wilhelm "gradually lost sympathy," writes Wellek, not without evidence, "with the group of which he was supposed to be a leader."[44]Furthermore, he told Staël's son in 1822, amid his Sanskrit studies, "je me moque de la littérature" [I could care less about literature], and called Görres in 1840 an "ultramontane buffoon"—yet his disavowal of Romanticism came years earlier, in the very works that defined the term.[45]

Staël's *De l'Allemagne* was decisive in bringing Romanticism to the Latin world, Britain, and America. Hugo dates the concept from this "femme de genie," *woman of genius* (in the preface of *Odes et ballades*), while the *Quarterly Review* stated that Staël "has made the British public familiar" with the classical/romantic distinction.[46] Eggli printed 500 pages of polemic Staël caused in France in three years, 1813–1816; Pushkin, Emerson, and Leopardi cited her in founding their national literatures.[47] Yet her manifesto is also famous for its silences: Wackenroder, Hölderlin; Kleist, Hoffmann, La Motte-Fouqué; the Brentanos, Görres; Runge, Friedrich, Beethoven; and her friends Arnim, Adam Müller, and Chamisso. Arnim had refused to visit the author. The space in her manuscript for Görres was deleted, while Friedrich Schlegel was indignant at his small place in her text.[48] Niebuhr and Hegel were unknown, like Chamisso; the Schlegels' feuds, and also political expediency, play some part here, but Staël's resistance runs deeper. Though Staël likes *Faust*, she writes that such productions should "not be repeated," rejecting the "singular system" of "the new German

42 "Von den Fehmgerichten, den geheimen Bündnissen und den Geistern ist vollends gar keine Rettung mehr," A.W. Schlegel, *Werke* 11: p. 26.

43 "Der letzte Gipfel der romantischen Poésie;" "auf hundert Komödienzettlen wird der Name romantisch an rohe und verfehlte Erzeugnisse verschwendet und entweiht," A.W. Schlegel, *Vorlesungen* 2: pp. 266, 290.

44 Wellek, *History*, p. 72.

45 F. Schlegel, *Krisenjahre* 2: p. 394, Solovieff, *Allemagne*, p. 50 n65.

46 *Quarterly Review*, October 1814: p. 113.

47 Isbell, *Birth*, pp. 2–3.

48 Staël, *De l'Allemagne*, p. 3: 364a, Isbell, *Birth*, p. 56.

school."[49] She finds in Germany, as Moreau remarks, "the elements of a new Classicism;" actual Romantics she then puts elsewhere, in ancillary texts.[50] Thus, Staël's *Corinne ou l'Italie* reworks La Motte-Fouqué's *Saalnixe*, and her *Sainte Geneviève de Brabant* puts onstage the heroine, though not the plot, of Tieck's seminal 1799 *Genoveva*.[51] Meanwhile, her comedy *Le Mannequin* directly parallels Hoffmann's *Der Sandmann*. In 1812, her *Réflexions sur le suicide* speaks out against Germany's 'Romantic ideology.' Seeing Kleist's double suicide as an insult to a suffering nation, Staël strongly condemns the "new school" and its effects: "genius is, in many regards, popular [...] those who torment themselves to draw the public's attention [...] imagine that what revolts the sentiments of the greater number is of a higher order than what touches them [...] Gigantic vanity!"[52] This verdict is unjust, given Kleist's passionate nationalism (*Die Hermannsschlacht*), while Staël had, in fact, appeared alongside Kleist in the literary journal *Phöbus*. But her mind is fixed on liberating Europe, and romantic egotism is, to her mind, a dangerous poison. She goes on to argue that "when one can be reborn as a nation and thus revive Europe's heart paralyzed by slavery, there must be no more talk of sickly *sentimentality*, of literary suicides."[53]

Finally, Sismondi's impact has long been neglected outside Italy, where D.M., in 1819, translated Chapter Thirty of his *De la littérature du Midi de l'Europe*, without permission, and called it *Vera definizione del Romanticismo* [True Definition of Romanticism].[54] But Sismondi himself never uses that noun, and Italy's living Romantics are as strangely missing from his history as are Germany's Romantics from Staël's and Schlegel's famously 'Romantic' surveys. His friend Foscolo appears in the third edition as a translator.[55] Sismondi's own reaction to Dalla's

---

49 "il est à désirer que de telles productions ne se renouvellent pas;" *Meister* and the "système singulier" of the "nouvelle école allemande" Staël, *De l'Allemagne* 3: pp. 127, 257.

50 "les éléments d'un classicisme nouveau ;" Moreau, *Classicisme*, p. 118.

51 Staël, *Corinne*, p. 11.

52 "Le génie est, à plusieurs égards, populaire [...] ceux qui se tourmentent pour attirer l'attention du public [...] vont jusqu'à s'imaginer que ce qui révolte les sentiments de la plupart des hommes est d'un ordre plus relevé que ce qui les touche [...] Gigantesque vanité !" Staël, *Œuvres* 1: pp. 190–191.

53 Staël, *ibid.*, p. 191: "quand on peut renaître comme nation et faire ainsi revivre le cœur de l'Europe paralysé par la servitude, il ne doit plus être question de *sentimentalité* maladive, de suicides littéraires."

54 See Pellegrini, *Storia*, pp. 138–139.

55 Gennari, *Voyage*, p. 208.

Romantic label was to rewrite the entire offending chapter, cutting five paragraphs and adding eighteen (he deletes 461–463 and 470–474 from the 1813 edition, and adds 474–484 in 1829; the rest remains untouched). We lose both his "three romantic unities" and his attack on those hamstrung by "the narrow prejudices of a fatal ignorance."[56] We gain, however, his insistence that his "desire for impartiality has not been recognized," which adds, "we will persist in not aligning ourselves beneath any banner."[57] An enemy of popes and dictators, Sismondi does not mention his antipathy to Schlegel, but a letter to the Comtesse d'Albany on 20 June 1816 was discreetly explicit: "Chateaubriand in France, Goethe, Novalis, and Werner in Germany, Lord Byron and Walter Scott in England do not imagine they belong to the same school; and yet it is in the same point that all sin against truth."[58]

3. The British Isles

In Britain, the word *romantique* dates at least from Pepys (*Diary*, 10 March 1667). The media debate dates from 1811–1831, and the *Lyrical Ballads* from 1798–1800—precisely the dates of the *Athenäum*. Scholars are unanimous in calling this the romantic period. Yet, critics repeat, "none of the English poets of the time [...] recognized himself as a romanticist or admitted the relevance of the debate."[59] Wordsworth uses the term ten times in poetry; Coleridge, five; Keats, four times in all his writings, once after the word *werry*, and even Byron just fifteen times in his verse.[60] Shelley "used [the word] thrice in his prefaces." Examining each instance, Whalley suggests that Britain's present-day 'romantic' canon avoided the term as a tiresome and vulgar nonce-word, which can only cause trouble, concluding that "the poets themselves never

56 "trois unités romantiques;" "des préjugés étroits dans une ignorance fatale," Sismondi, *Midi* [1813], 3: pp. 461–463.

57 "ce désir d'impartialité n'a point été reconnu;" "nous persisterons à ne nous ranger sous aucune bannière," Sismondi, *Midi* [1829], 3: p. 476.

58 Antipathy: Isbell, "*Confédération*," p. 309. "Chateaubriand en France, Goethe et Novalis et Werner en Allemagne, lord Byron et W. Scott en Angleterre ne se figurent point être de la même école; cependant, c'est par le même point que tous pêchent contre la vérité," Sismondi, *Epistolario* 20 June 1816.

59 Wellek, *History*, pp. 110–111, 123.

60 Whalley, "England," pp. 164, 178 (Wordsworth), p. 178 (Coleridge), pp. 194–195 (Keats, Byron), 233n (Shelley).

applied the term to themselves, nor did their enemies apply it to them."[61] Our use of the term *romantic*, he argues, "has done widespread (but probably not irreversible) damage to the precise appreciation of early nineteenth-century poets and their work," quite apart from its impact on the rest of the canon.[62] Britain's 'romantics' all knew the term and chose not to use it. So why do we?

Let us consider some authors in sequence. Whalley notes that Wordsworth "never regarded himself as a romantic at all, but took the word to mean barbaric, gothical, grotesque."[63] Wordsworth protests Jeffrey's *Lake School* coinage in 1804: "As to the school about which so much noise (I am told) has been made, [...] I do not know what is meant by it nor of whom it consists."[64] Coleridge in the *Biographia Literaria* also mentions, like Tieck or Schlegel, "this fiction of a *new school* in poetry."[65] Lockhart's *Cockney School* and Southey's *Satanic School* were modeled on Jeffrey's term. This may seem a label war, and the Lake poets—Southey, Coleridge, Wordsworth—did settle with age. Yet even in 1798, the *Lyrical Ballads'* landmark preface makes for a curious romantic revolution: "The invaluable works of our elder writers, [...] are driven into neglect by frantic novels, sickly and stupid German Tragedies, and deluges of idle and extravagant stories in verse."[66]

Byron, famously labeled one of the dangerous fifth column *Romantici* by an Austrian spy in Venice, seems another likely British romantic.[67] "We are," he writes, though, in 1817, "upon a wrong revolutionary poetical system—or systems—not worth a damn in itself—& from which none but Rogers and Crabbe are free."[68] This is intriguing since, in 1821, Shelley for his part remarks that, in *Marino Falieri*, Byron is following a false system, the "pernicious effects" of which will "cramp and limit his future efforts" if unchecked.[69] In 1821, Byron attacks Bowles, Pope's detractor, saying like Goethe that "I have been amongst the builders of this Babel," and "I am ashamed of it."[70] To Moore, he writes "As to Pope,

61 Whalley, "England," p. 159.
62 Ibid., pp. 256–257.
63 Whalley, "Literary," p. 242.
64 Perkins, "Construction," p. 131.
65 Coleridge ctd. Whalley, "England," p. 235.
66 Wordsworth, *Works*, p. 735.
67 Byron, *Letters* 4: p. 463.
68 Ibid.: p. 169.
69 P.B. Shelley, *Works* 10: p. 297.
70 Byron, *Letters* 5: p. 559.

I have always regarded him as the greatest name in our poetry. Depend on it, the rest are barbarians."[71]

It seems possible to talk of Britain's failed Classical-Romantic debate. Weisinger remarks that discussion of the debate "occurs in the work of Coleridge, Hazlitt, Scott, Robinson, and De Quincey [...] it is hard to understand why the idea was not treated more extensively."[72] Coleridge borrows this German usage in 1811; by the 1813–1814 lectures, he is reworking Wilhelm Schlegel's terms.[73] Hazlitt and the others briefly discuss Staël and the Germans, though De Quincey, who found *Endymion* vaguer "than the reveries of an oyster," claims, with less support than Coleridge, that the Germans deserve no credit.[74] As De Quincey hints, this seemed a silly European quarrel, alien to Britain: "nobody thought them worth making a sect of," says Byron.[75] For indeed, the terms arrived late: *romantic* as either a label for the modern, as opposed to its picturesque sense, or Warton's historical usage, echoed in Coleridge, Staël, and Schlegel—though the *OED*, bizarrely, cites Byron's usage of the term in his rejected epistle to Goethe on *Marino Falieri*, not published until 1896, and *Romanticism* from 1831, when Carlyle remarks that "we are troubled with no controversies on Romanticism and Classicism,—the Bowles controversy on Pope having long since evaporated without result."[76] In France, the term was common and used in analogy with Protestantism.[77]

Artists, media, and the public intersect in canon formation. Britain's 'romantic movement' as a concept is owed to late Victorian scholarship: Mrs. Oliphant's 1882 *Literary History of England* still ignores the term. Perkins cites Peter Bürger's *Theory of the Avant-Garde* (1974) in arguing that the cultural meaning of works of art—specifically those associated with romanticism—"is determined by the sociological character of the public and by the "institution of art" within which they are received."[78] Or, as Shelley puts it in the preface to *Prometheus Unbound*, "Poets [...] are, in one sense, the creators, and in another, the creations, of their age.

71 Byron, *Letters* 5: p. 274.
72 Weisinger, "Treatment," p. 479.
73 Wellek, *History*, p. 152; compare his "Concept," p. 15.
74 Lucas, *Decline*, p. 39.
75 Weisinger, "Treatment," p. 486.
76 *Oxford English Dictionary*, Classical.6.a. Carlyle, *Works* 14: p. 149.
77 See Goblot's "Les Mots *protestants* et *protestantisme* sous la Restauration."
78 Perkins, "Construction," p. 142.

From this subjection the loftiest do not escape."[79] Canons shift, and in 1985, the fourth edition of *The English Romantic Poets* brought startling news: "the inclusion of Blake."[80] Expanding that brief male canon from five to six is one thing, but calling Blake *romantic* only renews our dilemma. As Massey remarks, Blake despises *chiaroscuro* and insists on absolute clarity of line, like Ingres the classicist, yet unlike Turner or Delacroix: "the mere passage of time does not give us the right to simplify their lives in retrospect."[81] Mellor meanwhile argues that an entire female romantic tradition, including ten of the day's twelve most popular writers, disavowed basic male romantic tenets: "Mary Shelley," she notes, "was profoundly disturbed by what she saw to be a powerful egotism at the core of the romantic ideology."[82] Austen wrote *Northanger Abbey* (1817) for a reason, and Scott, "with whom, more than with anyone else, the adjective 'Romantic' was associated during their lifetime," shares Austen's ironic distance from romantic excess.[83] As David Simpson remarks of Raymond Williams, "Goldsmith, Crabbe, Cobbett, and Clare are more important to his narrative than Wordsworth or Keats or Shelley. This has surely had the effect of making Williams's work more ignorable than it deserves to be."[84] The fine poet Crabbe, "Pope in worsted stockings," still suffers from our feeling that history led elsewhere, as do Moore and Rogers, despite immense contemporary success. If we want to see what the romantic age read with pleasure, Blake, Keats, and Shelley should not head our list.

4. Italy, Russia, Sweden

Milan was, after Heidelberg, only Europe's second city to have an explicitly 'Romantic' group, with a media debate between 1816–1827.[85] Italy and Germany, as such, were geographical concepts. Critics date Italian Romantic debate from Staël's 1816 article on internationalism, which had four replies within the year: in support, Breme, Borsieri, and

79 P.B. Shelley, *Works* 2: p. 174.

80 *The English Romantic Poets: A Review of Research and Criticism*, ed. Frank Jordan (New York, NY: Modern Language Association of America, 1985), p. vii.

81 Massey, "Phrase," pp. 402, 409.

82 Mellor, "Women," p. 284.

83 Pierce, *Currents*, p. 293.

84 In Curran, *Companion*, p. 13.

85 Wilkins, *Italian*, pp. 400. 411–413.

Berchet's *Semi-Serious Letter;* vehemently against, Leopardi. Berchet wants 'popular' art, while to Leopardi, the Romantics do not see that poetry needs 'myth' or illusion.[86] In Milan, media debate was skewed by Austrian occupation, as elsewhere by other local circumstances. In the *Conciliatore,* Visconti argues that "romanticism does not consist in the lugubrious and the melancholic."[87] The age's two great poets, Leopardi and then Foscolo in 1827's *Della scuola nuova drammatica in Italia,* attack 'Romanticism,' though they fit its European profile.[88] Curiously, in Staël, Leopardi finds a firm ally against "the romantic system" and a *bellissima, solennissima* [very lovely, very solemn] "condemnation of the horrors and excess of terror so dear to the romantics."[89] Foscolo for his part ignores the Romantics in his survey of recent Italian literature appended to Byron's *Childe Harold.*[90] After 1821, Breme was dead, and as active patriots, many Italian Romanticists were in prison like Pellico or Borsieri, or in exile like Foscolo, Berchet, and Gabriele Rossetti, thus prematurely ending the movement: "It seems hardly surprising that a modern student could argue that there really was no Italian romanticism."[91]

Though Milanese, Manzoni stands apart, thanks in part to his five years in Paris, 1805–1810: Shakespeare, Goethe, Schiller, Schlegel, and Scott helped to shape his plays *Carmagnola* (1820) and *Adelchi* (1822), and his novel *I promessi sposi* (1827). Wellek calls Manzoni "the one great Italian who expressly proclaimed himself a romanticist," although begging the definition; when asked if romanticism would last, Manzoni "replied that the name was already being forgotten, but that the influence of the movement would continue."[92] Three treatises explain the views of this self-proclaimed "bon et loyal partisan du classique," or good and loyal supporter of classicism.[93] There are people, he says, who by the term *Romanticismo* understand "a hodgepodge of witches, of specters, a systematic disorder, a striving for the extravagant, a forswearing of

86 See Moget, "Milan," Pange, "Article," and Isbell, "Italian".

87 "Il romanticismo non consiste nel lugubre e nel malinconico," ctd. Ragusa, "Romantico," p. 317.

88 Wellek, *History*, pp. 264–265 ; see also Martegiani, *Non esiste.*

89 "Bellissima condanna del sistema romantico;" "una solennissima condanna degli orrori e dell'eccessivo terribile tanto caro ai romantici," Leopardi, *Opere* (1969) pp. 50, 46.

90 Foscolo, *Opere* 11.2: p. 490.

91 Wellek, *History*, p. 264.

92 Ibid., p. 261, McKenzie, "Italy," p. 33.

93 Manzoni, *Opere*, p. 1683.

common sense." If such were indeed its character, says the prince of Italian Romanticism, it would deserve oblivion.[94]

As Wellek deduces from his vast reading, "one important argument for the coherence and unity of the European romantic movement emerges from an investigation of the minor literatures—the 'predictability' of their general character."[95] Van Tieghem's equally global survey supports this view.[96] This chapter is briefer, but let us linger for a moment on two exemplary cases, Russia and Sweden. Pushkin in *Boris Godunov* (1831) lists himself in the romantic camp and calls the work a "truly romantic tragedy;" yet in 1830, he praises the poet Glinka for "not professing either ancient or French Classicism and not following either Gothic or modern Romanticism."[97] His 1831 review of *Joseph Delorme* talks once more of "the so-called *Romantic* school of French writers." Mersereau adds that "among his contemporaries only Goethe categorically qualified as a *Romantic*."[98] Gogol's 1847 history of Russian poetry simply avoids the term. In 1836, Gogol calls the romantics "desperately audacious people like those who foment social rebellions."[99] Tegnér, "traditionally the foremost romantic in Swedish literature," states similar views over two decades—writing in his *Om det Romantiska i Grekiska Poesien* (1822–1824) that "romanticism degenerates into the fantastic and marvelous through the misuse of freedom," and he condemns French taste in 1841 for "the cannibalistic style they seem to view as the principal constituent of Romanticism."[100] In both these countries, the curious stress on France and revolution is worth noting; other countries tend to stress Germany and reaction, while talk of Britain focuses on Byron, Scott, and the *Edinburgh Review*.

94 "non so qual guazzabuglio di streghe, di spettri, un disordine sistematico, una ricerca stravagante, una abiura in termini del senso commune," Manzoni, *Opere*, p. 1726.

95 Wellek, *History*, p. 170.

96 Van Tieghem, *Romantisme*.

97 Pushkin ctd. Saprynkina in Sötér, *European*, p. 106. In Wellek, *Discriminations*, p. 69.

98 Mersereau, "Pushkin," pp. 38–40.

99 Gogol quoted in Proffer, "Gogol," pp. 121–122.

100 "så urartar äfven det romantiska genom frihetens missbruk till det phantastiska och vidunderliga;" "Det [...] kannibaliska tyckas de anse för Romantikens hufvudelement," Tegnér ctd. Mitchell, "Scandinavia," pp. 380–381, 394.

5. France

French media debate runs largely from 1813–1830, but the English borrowing *romantique* as an alternative to *romanesque*— 'romancy,' perhaps—reached France in 1776–1777, in passages on gardening by Gerardin and Rousseau.[101] *Romantique* describes not only the scene, but also "the touching impression we receive from it," an epochal distinction which empowers the consumer.[102] Chateaubriand's *Essai sur les Révolutions* borrows the term early from d'Agincourt: the man later massages chronology to call Staël and Byron ungrateful imitators, though in fact he launched his career attacking Staël, and the Byron letter he alleges dates from 1802, when Byron was fourteen.[103] His famous "critique de beautés," or critique of beauties, is also silently borrowed from Staël and the Germans. "The Romantics—my sons," Chateaubriand proclaims, yet the rest of his judgments are "full of the clichés of classicism."[104] He revises his *Génie du Christianisme* to replace *mélancolique* with *sérieux*, to prefer Homer now to Milton, to praise Sophocles, and to add a *peut-être* to his praise of Dante.[105] His aim, he says, is to "put [...] the classic tongue in the mouth of my romantic characters."[106] But we cannot ignore his public impact. Chateaubriand, like Goethe, Tieck, or Byron, deplores the consequences of his early writings: "A family of poet Renés and prose-writing Renés has pullulated," he writes, dreaming of destroying *René*, which "has infested the spirit of part of our youth".[107] "If in the past we fell too short of the romantic," he argues, "now we have overshot the mark."[108]

"Je suis un romantique furieux," wrote Stendhal in 1818, *I am a furious romantic*.[109] Wellek says of Stendhal that he is "the first Frenchman

101 Baldensperger, "Romantique," p. 76.

102 Logan Pearsall Smith, "Four Romantic Words," in *Words and Idioms: Studies in the English Language* (London: Constable, 1925), p. 81.

103 Chateaubriand, *Mémoires* 1: p. 418.

104 See Chateaubriand, *Lettres*, p. 363: "O mes fils! Combien vous êtes dégénérés!".

105 Moreau, *Classicisme*, pp. 88–90.

106 "mettre [...] la langue classique dans la bouche de mes personnages romantiques," Chateaubriand, *Mémoires*, p. 452.

107 "une famille de René poètes et de René prosateurs a pullulé" (p. 462); "infesté l'esprit d'une partie de la jeunesse," Chateaubriand, *Mémoires* 1: p. 462..

108 "Si jadis on resta trop en deçà du romantique, maintenant on a passé le but," Chateaubriand, *Œuvres* 11: p. 579.

109 Stendhal, *Correspondance* 1: p. 909.

who called himself a romantic."[110] Van Tieghem prefers, as many do, to group Stendhal among writers "still"—rather tellingly—classic by taste or temperament, who toyed with some aspects of Romanticism while belonging in another box: "restés classiques," remaining classic, he calls them.[111] He adds that the generation of 1840's "réaction contre l'ère romantique est systématique," its reaction against the romantic era is systematic, which is more teleology.[112] But is there not some sleight of hand involved in refusing the term to those who claim it, while forcing it on those who resist? The term, after all, is theirs, not ours. By 1823, Stendhal sharply divides his liberal Italianate *romanticisme*, a *hapax legomenon* in France, from *émigré* reaction and "the German gibberish many people today call *romantic*."[113] He despises Chateaubriand and Schlegel and rejects Vigny, Lamartine, and Hugo, whose *Han d'Islande* (1823) disgusts him.[114] Stendhal seems Italian much as Coleridge the critic seems German, standing apart from his national contemporaries.

What then of the great romantics, Hugo, Vigny, Musset, and Lamartine? In 1824, Lamartine remarks, "I am neither classic as you understand it, nor romantic as they understand it," adding, "the two rival absurdities, in tumbling, will make way for truth in literature."[115] The ever-subtle Musset, often presented as naïve, detests writing "three words when two will do."[116] Musset parodies his much-cited *Confession d'un enfant du siècle* (1836) in his less-quoted *Histoire d'un merle blanc* (1851), proud to be white among blackbirds. Flaubert the ironist took *Bouvard et Pécuchet* (1881), as it happens, from Musset's earlier *Dupuis et Cotonet* (1836–1837), dogged provincial catalogers of romantic's bizarre semantics in the 1830s: "From 1833 to 1834, we thought romanticism consisted in not shaving, and in wearing large-breasted starched waistcoats."[117] The arch-romantic Hugo later suppressed his

110 Wellek, "Concept," p. 10.
111 Van Tieghem, *Romantisme*, p. 461.
112 Ibid., p. 463.
113 "Le galimatias allemand, que beaucoup de gens appellent *romantique* aujourd'hui," Stendhal, *Racine*, p. 75.
114 Wellek, *History*, pp. 245–251.
115 "Je ne suis ni classique comme vous l'entendez, ni romantique comme ils l'entendent;" "les deux absurdités rivales, en s'écroulant, feront place à la vérité en littérature," Lamartine, *Correspondance* 2: pp. 276, 266.
116 "Trois mots quand il n'en faut que deux," in Moreau, *Classicisme*, p. 317.
117 "de 1833 à 1834 nous crûmes que le romantisme consistait à ne pas se raser, et à porter des gilets à larges revers, très empesés," Musset, *Œuvres*, p. 876.

1820 remark about having never "understood this difference between the classic genre and the romantic genre."[118] Barrère notes that Hugo "stood himself in 1824 outside the two camps among the 'conciliators' and repudiated 'all these conventional terms that the two parties toss about reciprocally like empty balloons.'"[119] Hugo uses the term with caution after 1824—qualified by *dit* or 'so-called' in 1826, for instance—and almost never after 1830. His revised *Littérature et Philosophies mêlées* (1834), at the height of the textbook romantic period, would instead talk of terms that he "always refused to pronounce seriously;" in 1864, he even claims that "he who writes these lines never used the words *romanticism* or *romantic*."[120] In 1827, his famous preface to *Cromwell* seeks to change tradition safely, unlike "some unenlightened partisans of *romanticism*," and calls precisely like Deschamps for "powerful dikes against the irruption of the common."[121] Thus, Deschamps's "War in peace-time" in *La Muse française* of 1824 had demanded a "powerful dike" against modern "adventurous innovation."[122] Moreau has brilliantly shown echoes of Molière and fragments of Corneille in *Cromwell*'s verse, as indeed in Constant's *Wallstein*. Once again, our touchstone romantic manifestoes are ambivalent; or rather, they simply refuse the pat all-or-nothing teleology encouraged by literary historians.[123]

Moreau talks of Nodier's "duplicité souriante," his *smiling duplicity*.[124] Despite his romantic *cénacle*, Nodier, in his turn, rejects the label, talking of "this often ridiculous and sometimes revolting genre," and adding: "the romantic genre is a false invention."[125] Nodier's 1822 preface to

118 "Nous n'avons jamais compris cette différence entre le genre classique et le genre romantique," Hugo, *Conservateur* 25.III.1820.

119 "se rangeait en 1824 en dehors des deux 'camps' parmi les 'conciliateurs' et répudiait 'tous ces termes de convention que les deux partis se rejettent réciproquement comme des ballons vides'," Barrère, "Définitions," pp. 94–95.

120 "s'est toujours refusé à prononcer sérieusement," Hugo, *Littérature* 1: p. 191. "Celui qui écrit ces lignes n'a jamais employé les mots *romantisme* ou *romantique*," Hugo, *Œuvres* 2: p. 208.

121 "quelques partisans peu avancés du romantisme;" "des digues plus puissantes contre l'irruption du commun," Hugo, *Préface*, pp. 260, 267.

122 Deschamps, "La Guerre en temps de paix": "digue puissante;" "innovation aventureuse," Deschamps, *Œuvres* 4: p. 13.

123 . See Moreau, *Classicisme*, pp. 175–176 and Constant, *Wallstein*, p. 109.

124 Moreau, *Classicisme*, pp. 166–167.

125 "le genre souvent ridicule et quelquefois révoltant qu'on appelle en France romantique," Nodier, *Bertram*, p. 70. "Le genre romantique est une invention fausse," in Moreau, *Classicisme*, pp. 166–167.

Trilby calls the *romantique* "un fort mauvais genre" [a very bad genre][126] Saintine remarks that in 1820 the Romantics included Guiraud, Lebrun, and Soumet, the latter of whom authored the *Scrupules littéraires de Mme de Staël*, yet by 1830 they were Classicists, changed by the excess around them. Gautier's *Grotesques* mock the *barbouilleurs* or "daubers" of local color; his *Les Jeunes France* mock the young who no longer find Chateaubriand romantic enough, as does Sand's *Histoire de ma vie* (1855), which also smiles at Hugo's dealings with these *marmots*, or "brats from his own school."[127] Perhaps most frustrating, as Sismondi found, is to see discretion ignored by one's readers. Bizet makes *Carmen* romantic simply by discarding Mérimée's ironic frame, while Mérimée's *Colomba* says of *couleur locale*: "Let whoever wishes explain the sense of these words which I understood very well some years ago."[128] In short, this first-generation *romantisme mitigé* is not some 'Preromantic' failure of nerve or vision: since Schlegel invented the term, romanticism was never more than half a pole, except to fools and historians. When Barante talks of classic and romantic genius meeting, that is not neoclassical reaction, but an echo of Berlin; when the *Globe*, on the other hand, praises the end of 1820-style "romantisme hypocondriaque" [hypochondriac romanticism], it sees therein, as Moreau says, "the triumph of true romanticism."[129] Compare Guizot to Fauriel, in 1820, on the "mania of chopping truth in two and only wanting half."[130] Compare Jouffroy saying the Romantics "thought that people were tired of the beautiful. They therefore made the ugly."[131] Staël, Constant, and Fauriel, like Ladvocat's theater collaborators, rework their romantic translations to find this new Berlin synthesis of classic and romantic art.[132] Or compare Berlioz—who for Gautier belongs with Hugo and Delacroix in the "Romantic trinity"—on a scene he stole from Shakespeare for *Les Troyens*: "and I virgilified it."[133] Beethoven,

---

126 Nodier, *Contes*, p. 97.

127 Moreau, *Classicisme*, p. 332; "On ne trouvait plus Chateaubriand assez romantique," brats, Sand, *Œuvres* 2: p. 159.

128 "Explique qui pourra le sens de ces mots, que je comprenais fort bien il y a quelques années, et que je n'entends plus aujourd'hui," Mérimée, *Gazul*, p. 759.

129 Barante, *Études* 2: p. 139. Moreau, *Classicisme*, p. 196.

130 "la manie de couper en deux la vérité et de n'en vouloir prendre que la moitié," Guizot in Glachant, *Fauriel*, p. 22.

131 "ont pensé qu'on était las du beau. Ils ont donc fait du laid," Jouffroy, *Cahier*, p. 48.

132 See Isbell, *Birth*, p. 2 and "Présence;" see also Moreau, *Classicisme*, p. 216.

133 "Hector Berlioz paraît former avec Hugo et Eugène Delacroix la trinité romantique," Gautier in Barzun, *Berlioz*, p. 243; "et je l'ai virgilianisée," in Legouvé, *Souvenirs* 2: p. 189.

who seems to Delacroix "romantic to a supreme degree," comments in later years that he can learn only from Bach, while Delacroix, observing his own growing distaste for Schubert, remarks: "I have been enrolled willy nilly in the romantic coterie."[134] Sand notes that "the romantics, having found in him their highest expression, believed that he belonged exclusively to their school."[135] His resistance to this hijacking emerges when asked if he was happy at the romantics' triumph: "Sir," replied Delacroix, "*I am classic.*"[136]

6. Conclusion

This study asks a question which has been sidelined by history with disturbing ease: how can we explain romanticism's repeated disavowals by the very thinkers who had been its pioneers, and indeed its theoreticians, throughout Europe? While traditional narratives talk of this term being tainted in the decades which follow the 'romantic period,' and attacked from outside by a classical old guard, it seems surprisingly clear on reflection that the term never attained a position of acceptance from which to fall, even among its coiners. The durability of our traditional narratives looks increasingly like a simple tribute to the power of myth. As Marilyn Butler argues, "Going out to look for 'romanticism' means selecting in advance one kind of answer." Ultimately, the price of these preconceptions is the way they "interfere with so much good reading."[137] Was it not limiting to reduce Britain's 'romantic age' to six male poets; to discuss the Germans with Goethe absent; to date French romanticism from 1830, while the Italians meanwhile cite two French authors in 1816?

A new reading can perhaps help resituate the pressures on which our systematic disavowals depend. Hesitations glibly read as proof of 'Preromantic' insipidity here emerge, with some support from context, as the result of many factors: the persistence of a classical taste born

134 Delacroix, *Journal* 1: p. 201. "on m'a enrégimenté, bon gré mal gré, dans la coterie romantique," Véron, *Mémoires* 1: p. 273.

135 "Je commence à prendre furieusement en grippe les Schubert, les rêveurs, les Chateaubriand," Delacroix, *Journal* 1: p. 340. "les romantiques, ayant trouvé en lui leur plus haute expression, ont cru qu'il appartenait exclusivement à leur école," Sand in Moreau, *Classicisme*, p. 248.

136 "Monsieur, répondit Delacroix, je suis classique," Andrieux, *Rabbe*, p. 61.

137 Butler, *Romantics*, pp. 186–187.

of old-regime education and reading, the return to norms thought more solid and durable after a period of experimentation, and the understandable distaste of pioneers who see their terms being hijacked by alleged followers with quite different agendas. Ironically, a whole group of 'Preromantic' writers like Staël and Sismondi were subsequently condemned by their successors, precisely for *not* sharing their successors' own concerns. Here, one can meet the different generational roles of the avant-garde and 'grand public' in shaping historical movements, as well as the difficult relationship between romantic desires for a truly popular national art, on the one hand, and the realities of vulgarization on the other. The later shape of the nineteenth century will reflect these particular problematics. Clearly, one might also expect ample evidence in praxis to support this study's conclusions, but to strike at the core of certain persistent myths, the label itself, as actually used by the artists in question, is splendidly explicit.

What then is our new narrative to be? As we survey post-Revolutionary Europe, certain key themes recur. Friedrich Schlegel's call for a new art to replace the antithesis between Europe's older 'classical' and 'romantic' ages—painfully misread by imitators, media, and public alike as a call for 'romantic' war on the past. Butler refers to the younger British romanticists as neoclassicists, while della Chiesa calls romantic and neoclassical art "two interdependent aspects of a single phenomenon."[138] Indeed, as Jordan remarks, "Artz's idea that neoclassicism and romanticism are parallel movements may strike literary scholars as peculiar, though art and music historians are quite familiar with it."[139] As Sötér notes, "the parallel existence of romanticism and classicism matters so much that [...] certain phenomena of both can only be explained from their parallel nature," adding in answer to our somewhat facile teleology that "the classical period of both Goethe and Schiller was as much 'modern' as the poetry of Novalis."[140] Remak calls romanticism "the desire ... to have synthesis follow antithesis." He later stresses our new attention to the romantic fusion of classic and romantic art, emotion and Enlightenment, realism and fantasy, which later ages

138 "due aspetti interdipendenti di un stesso fenomeno," della Chiesa, "Neoclassico," p. 31.
139 Jordan, *Romantic Poets*, p. 88.
140 Sötér, *European*, pp. 52, 72.

forgot, concluding: "In this sense romanticism had better equilibrium than they did".[141]

Lubich points out the crucial place of parody in this narrative, citing *Die Nachtwachen des Bonaventura*, Peacock's *Nightmare Abbey*, and Pushkin's *Evgenii Onegin*. Like Byron's Don Juan, Kreuzgang and Onegin both ridicule the whole storehouse of romantic cliché: "Pushkin uses Onegin [...] to deal an ironic *coup de grâce* against his former poetic self."[142] Peacock's Scythrop is modeled on Shelley; Byron sent Peacock a rosebud in thanks, and Shelley wrote back: "I am delighted with *Nightmare Abbey*. I think Scythrop a character admirably conceived and executed." As Lubich remarks, Shelley "actually named his own rooftop study 'Scythrop's Tower.'[143]" Eichner observes that in the media debate, adversaries added to the semantic confusion and ridicule, providing romantic artists "with a further reason for not applying the term to themselves." If we ignore these subtleties, he notes, "the writings of the romantics will inevitably be misinterpreted."[144] Immerwahr adds that the term could not be cleaned of all its negative implications, contributing to the emergence of 'romantic irony.'[145] Europe's romantics thus connived with their adversaries to wink at their own enthusiasm, from Walpole's *Castle of Otranto* onward. Butler argues in consequence against "the received view that [...] a Romantic Revolution occurred, which worked a permanent change in literature and in the other arts [...] In reality there would seem to have been no one battle and no complete victory. It is not even clear that there were defeats."[146] From this new and wider field, a long series of critical antinomies may lose their sense of urgency: the classic/romantic/realist series for one, along with the amputations and falsehoods it has entailed.

How was this elegant new synthesis lost? Brown is incisive: "Far from being a repudiation of the Enlightenment, romanticism was its fulfilling summation [...] repudiation and triumph are its most visible gestures, which have led to conventional accounts of the war of romanticism

141 Remak, "Key," p. 44; and in Hoffmeister, *Romanticism*, pp. 340–342.

142 Lubich in Hoffmeister, *Romanticism*, p. 321.

143 Lubich in ibid., p. 316.

144 Eichner, *"Romantic,"* pp. 12–13.

145 Raymond Immerwahr, "The Word *Romantisch* and Its History," in *The Romantic Period in Germany*, ed. Siegbert Prawer (London: Weidenfeld and Nicolson, 1970), p. 59.

146 Butler, *Romantics*, p. 183.

against Enlightenment reason."[147] Perkins also points to the sense that the age was new, brought on by the French Revolution: "the 'spirit of the age' was always described as impatient of authority or limits." Ironically, he adds, this periodization cast Wordsworth, Coleridge, Southey, and Scott as revolutionaries, though all were solidly conservative by the 1810s.[148] Our new narrative's second theme is thus the ensuing tug of war between artists who witness this hijacking of their conciliatory or synthetic agenda, and a public drift they cannot control. As Whalley argues, "the specific symptoms of this emerging category seem always to be most pronounced in the *minor* figures."[149] Our third and final theme is the Faustian bargain this media bandwagon represents for artists deeply concerned with a public and national art. What happens to art when it speaks to, and for, the nation? Must artists compromise their program in order to be heard? The radical Shelley's late works went unpublished, as the legislator in him yielded to the nightingale. Blake's verse prologue to *Milton* became a literal hymn of the establishment, still sung during my childhood in Britain's public schools. Even Byron, so much the master of his myth, lost his very name from the title page of *Don Juan*. We speak, and the public ultimately hears what it chooses: indeed, these radical thinkers spoke and saw their politics disallowed. They stood their terms, their books and careful manifestos on Europe's vast and confusing post-Revolutionary stage, and saw them hijacked by forces beyond their control.

Ironically, this new world of contingency is nowhere more evident than when crossing the new national frontiers these artists helped to create. As Simpson remarks, "there has never been a single entity called 'Romanticism,' and this very knowledge may be read out of the Romantic writings themselves."[150] Heine opens *Die romantische Schule* (1833) by stressing that French and German romantics are different animals; Stendhal and Leopardi show Italy's distinctness; Britain's artists and media see 'romantic' as a foreign term.[151] The label 'romantic' is a political coin in Napoleonic and post-Napoleonic Europe, one

147 Brown writing in Curran, *Companion*, pp. 38–42.
148 Perkins, "Construction," pp. 134–136.
149 Whalley, "Literary," p. 236.
150 Simpson in Curran, *Companion*, p. 20.
151 "diese [Schule] in Deutschland ganz anders war, als was man in Frankreich mit diesem Namen bezeichnet," Heine, *Werke*, p. 1169.

whose local value depends on our knowledge of local politics. What van Tieghem calls critics' "esprit exclusivement national" [exclusively national spirit] can therefore lead to a dangerous blindness.[152] And here lies another reason for the term's almost immediate distortion. As Wellek says of France, "just as in Italy, a broadly typological and historical term, introduced by Mme de Staël, had become the battle cry of a group of writers who found it a convenient label."[153] That danger is for us to judge, not to ignore.

At the root of this old misreading, finally, is another fiction, born by a further irony of the deep, if ambivalent, romantic desire to speak to and for the people in unmediated speech: the fiction that artist and consumer are one being. For romanticism is perhaps, above all, a change of audience, the shared fruit of artistic, industrial, and political revolution. Stereotype printing, romantic art, and a vast consumer market are born in symbiosis. In that romantic triangle of artist, product, and consumer, the new bourgeois publics were disturbing bedfellows. Contemporary readers' letters naively reveal their appropriation of the romantic artist. "I recognized myself in it [...] I said to myself: This is me," writes one; "this is not you [...] it is me," writes another to Hugo.[154] Seeing this shift with his usual flair, Hugo uses it the same year in a preface to his romantic readers: "madman! to think I am not you."[155] Yet text and romantic label, as Sismondi's hapless fate makes clear, remain forever separate events; they are as divorced as thing and word, artist and consumer, despite romantic myth and generations of historians. Lovejoy suggests that the term *Romantic* has "ceased to perform the function of a verbal sign."[156] I would argue that this was true, on a European scale, by 1820. Look, for example, at the case of Britain. No artists can govern the myth they launch, that much is the contract of Promethean creation. Yet this, after all, is a strange fate for the great to suffer, to be colonized by their own epithet while they yet lived and protested. Goethe, Tieck, the Schlegels, Sismondi, Manzoni, Leopardi, Pushkin, Byron, Stendhal, Hugo, Delacroix: when Europe's

---

152 Van Tieghem, *Romantisme*, p. 15.

153 Wellek, "Concept," p. 12.

154 "Je m'y suis reconnu ... je me suis dit: C'est moi," A. Julien in Moreau, *Classicisme* 267; "Ce n'est pas vous ... c'est moi," Ulbach in Simon, "Hugo," p. 293.

155 "Ah! insensé, qui crois que je ne suis pas toi," Hugo, preface to *Les Contemplations*.

156 Lovejoy, "Discrimination," p. 253.

romantics line up to reject the "so-called romantic school," how can we so easily have backgrounded their resistance to the label? Every public will impose a persona on its artists, a fictive *Doppelgänger* they only half control. But which, after all, are we here to judge: that strange romantic myth, or its creators?

3. Romantic Novel and Verse Romance: Is There a Romance Continuum?

You're going to need a bigger boat.
Steven Spielberg, *Jaws* (1975)

0. Prefatory Remarks on Terminology

This chapter is a quest, or if you prefer a hypothesis. It treats two Romantic-era corpuses: the novel and the long poem, arguing for their common debt to the medieval and early modern romance tradition. Two alien objects distort our grasp of Romantic-era production: for prose, two centuries of goal-directed work on the 'realist novel,' and for verse, the much longer epic critical tradition. English usage also severs the novel from the romance, and that prompted this project, bothered as I was to see Friedrich Schlegel's magical ideal, as stated in his 1800 *Brief über den Roman* (Letter on the Romance), translated as *novel* while he cites Shakespeare and Ariosto as models. Retranslate his term as romance, and we can argue that his vision for a new art form was indeed carried out by his contemporaries. This will historicize some lingering positivist historiography and perhaps trace a new continuity between Romanticism and the twentieth century—in particular the history of the modern novel, from Joyce to magical realism.

To begin with, *novel* and *romance*. Spanish and Portuguese, French, Dutch, and German, share the word *novela/nouvelle* and variants, meaning in origin a short fiction presented like a news item. The *Oxford English Dictionary* evokes Boccaccio and cites a source from 1566, a century prior to Littré's first source. Swedish, Danish, Norwegian,

 https://doi.org/10.11647/OBP.0302.03

Russian, Serbo-Croatian, and Czech, however, use *roman* and variants for both novel and romance, as Italian uses *romanzo*; their term *romansa/ romans/romance* is for ballads and music, a distinction shared by all twelve languages. In short, half of Europe's major languages have no separate term *novel* to distinguish verse from prose in extended narratives. The French and German term *nouvelle/Novelle* is for a minor genre, the short story, though German keeps *Romanze* for verse. England's anomalous 'novel' category and history evidently misrepresent European Romantic production, a distortion that our usage of the term *romance* will avoid. This also seems truer to the history of the genre; the *Grande dizionario della lingua italiana* (Large Dictionary of the Italian Language, 1961-, 19 vols) opens with an apt historical review, moving from the Greek *Daphnis kai Chloë* (Daphnis and Chloë) to eleventh-century romance-language narratives, "originally in verse" but shifting to prose in the later Middle Ages, to the sixteenth-century verse of Ariosto, then back to Cervantes and Rabelais presented as a prose "transformation of the epic and heroi-comic poem," to what we might call a refilling of that form with new content in the works of Fielding, Richardson, and Defoe.[1] The verse *Childe Harold. A Romaunt* and *Evgenii Onegin. Roman v stikhakh* (Eugene Onegin. A Romance in Verse) are as much a part of that long romance tradition as are Austen, Dickens, Balzac, or Manzoni—or Scott and Fenimore Cooper, for that matter, who called their works *romances*.

A word on the musical form. Central to Spanish literature is the *romance* or short ballad. The form begins before the *reconquista* as narrative fragments from epic poems, on The Cid for instance; the sixteenth-century *romancero* is one of many collections. As Europe rediscovered ballads in the late eighteenth century, France in particular acquired a taste for writing *romances*, borrowed like the word from Spain, sung aloud in Paris salons or embedded in stories where the hero or heroine sing them. The musical fashion, like the word (*romansa*, etc.), reached Europe from France, and Germany and Italy produced famous settings: Beethoven, Rossini, Verdi. Mendelssohn's *Romances sans paroles* (Romances without words) are a paradox Verlaine later exploits in poetry. This short form may seem tangential to our romance vs. novel

1 "originariamente in versi," "trasformazione del poema epico ed eroicomico." *Grande dizionario della lingua italiana*, ed. Salvatore Battaglia, 19 vols (Turin: Unione tipografico-editrice torinese, 1961-), "Romanzo."

investigation—much as a Tasmanian wolf is not a wolf—but it is linked historically, in the breakdown of medieval Spanish 'epic' or romance, thematically, as a narrative form whose favored content is love and chivalry, and generically, since romance ballads are frequently embedded in romance fictions by Romantic authors, even in fictions in verse. Again, I posit that the Romantic era perceived a 'romance continuum' which has since and regrettably been occluded by critical vocabulary. The very word *romantic*, which derives directly from *romance* (as in Scott's 1824 *Essay on Romance*), might have warned against that occlusion.

What, then, is a non-musical romance? It seems worth listing some elements, to compare with Schlegel's list for his *Roman*. The term derives from the Latin *romanice*; a tale in the vernacular. So, it is a tale, a narrative, not a drama or a "How do I love thee?" lyric poem; narrated, it is not an epistolary novel, though those may have romance elements. Since its naming, it has reviewed love and chivalry, or at least courtly etiquette; this also applies to the works of the seventeenth-century *Précieuses* like Mlle de Scudéry, the influential soil from which Defoe and Mme de Lafayette arise, and to the popular romance tradition that continues through the next century alongside canonical male novelists, leading uninterrupted through the 1790s. The romance genre is thus, bizarrely, simultaneously a courtly, popular, and folk tradition: its heroes are courtly, its popular success visibly continues today, and it speaks for a national against a Classical tradition, a sort of people's voice. Its place in the political spectrum, for a Revolutionary-Imperial Europe, is usefully ambiguous, more complex than that of the 'bourgeois' realist novel we have inherited, as it happens, from Champfleury.

Two other themes are wit and imagination. Wit is more than humor; Mlle de Scudéry's fairly serious romances are full of the embedded narratives and arabesques which represent Friedrich Schlegel's ideal, which he finds splendidly expressed in Ariosto or Cervantes. The arabesque is pure form, independent of any mimesis; the romance tradition frees art from imitating reality, and we can trace this freedom in some 'realist novels' we shall mention. One thinks of Lukács's argument that Balzac's realism is based in unreality, or of Baudelaire's bewilderment that people should ever call Balzac a realist.[2] As with

2 Georg Lukács, *La Théorie du roman*, tr. Jean Clairevoye (Paris: Denoël, 1968), pp. 104–105, on Balzac: "Le démonisme subjectif et psychologique qui caractérise son

modern magical realism, an art where the real and the ideal cohabit has more scope than straight realism for showing how will and circumstance—or energy and matter—divide the human condition, in a truth self-evident to Europe after 1789.

The remainder of this chapter briefly reviews various Romantic literatures, focusing on the verse-prose frontier and the presence of 'romance' in this art. Giving a new entelechy to these creations will sometimes be an act rich in ideological consequences, notably in resituating the artwork's relations to the imagination and to the European tradition, both literary and historical. This is a global hypothesis, making minimal use of biographical sources, for instance, which offer ground for further remarks.

1. German Lands

In 1800, Friedrich Schlegel, like Wordsworth the same year in his new preface to *Lyrical Ballads*, writes in reaction to "frantic novels" and "outrageous stimulation." Schlegel's entire *Brief über den Roman* (Letter on the Romance) addresses a woman who has been reading the wrong novels, and Wordsworth's parallel reminds us that Gothic romances were Europe's best-selling fictional genre in the 1790s, and perhaps beyond. Though Schlegel calls her reading *immoral*, this is not a simple stand against a feminized or Gothic reading tradition (contrast Section 2: The British Isles); he instead targets Fielding and the forgotten Lafontaine. Within this didactic space, Schlegel both describes his ideal for the future and anchors it in a past tradition, by means of examples stretching from antiquity to contemporary writing; the whole lies within the larger frame of his *Gespräch über die Poesie* (Talk About Poetry), reminding us that verse and prose are for Schlegel intimately linked.

The text opens with Amalia's remark that Jean Paul's works are not romances (or novels) but instead "a bright jumble of sickly wit."[3] The

---

œuvre constitue pour lui une réalité ultime." And Baudelaire: "J'ai maintes fois été étonné que la grande gloire de Balzac fût de passer pour un observateur; il m'avait toujours semblé que son principal mérite était d'être visionnaire, et visionnaire passionné." "Théophile Gautier," in Charles Baudelaire, *Œuvres complètes*, 2 vols, ed. Claude Pichois (Paris: Gallimard, 1975), II, p. 120.

3 "ein buntes allerlei von kränklichem Witz." Friedrich Schlegel, *Kritische und theoretische Schriften* (Stuttgart: Reclam, 1978), p. 202.

narrator agrees, calling such *grotesques*—one thinks of Hugo—"the only romantic products of our unromantic age."[4] The term *novel* loses both pun and etymology in this famous remark, as in the subsequent "a romance is a romantic book."[5] He links sickly wit to the arabesque, stressing Sterne and Diderot but adding Swift, Ariosto, Cervantes, and Shakespeare in his argument that, in an unfantastic and ironic age, nature poetry emerges as playful wit and arabesque. The terms echo those of Schiller's 1795 *Über naive und sentimentalische Dichtung* (On Naive and Sentimental Poetry), which calls modernity divided. Goethe's "I call the Romantic the sick" also seems apt. Schlegel goes on to praise both the fantastic in art and the ironic reading of bad books as kitsch, the suspension of disbelief or a divided self that winks at its own enthusiasm. He cites the term *Roman*'s history in an apt definition of the *romance*: "that is Romantic which gives us a sentimental content in a fantastic form."[6] He compares Petrarch and Tasso with what he calls Ariosto's *Romanzo*, stating that the spirit of love must be invisibly omnipresent in Romantic poetry. In the visible world, fantasy and wit must intimate the riddle of eternal love. The next words contain Schlegel's epochal distinction, the first in history, between Classical and Romantic poetry. Romantic or romance poetry pays no attention to "the difference between appearance and reality, between play and seriousness."[7] Where the Classics use mythology, Schlegel argues, Romantic poetry rests on history, and romances from the medieval *Roman d'Alexandre* (Romance of Alexander) to *Le Grand Cyrus* (The Great Cyrus) five centuries later are famous precisely for their magical treatment of historical figures. He concludes thus: "I seek and find the Romantic in the older moderns, in Shakespeare, Cervantes, in Italian poetry, in that age of knights, love and fairy tales, whence the thing and the word itself arise [...] As our poetry with the romance, so that of the Greeks began with the epic."[8] Visibly,

4 "die einzigen romantischen Erzeugnisse unsers unromantischen Zeitalters" F. Schlegel, *Schriften*, p. 203.

5 "Ein Roman ist ein romantisches Buch." F. Schlegel, *Schriften*, p. 209.

6 "ist eben das romantisch, was uns einen sentimentalen Stoff in einer fantastischen Form darstellt." F. Schlegel, *Schriften*, p. 206.

7 "auf den Unterschied von Schein und Wahrheit, von Spiel und Ernst." F. Schlegel, *Schriften*, p. 208.

8 "Da suche und finde ich das romantische, bei den ältern Modernen, bei Shakespeare, Cervantes, in der italiänischen Poesie, in jenem Zeitalter der Ritter, der Liebe und der Märchen, aus welchem die Sache und das Wort selbst herstammt [...] Wie unsre

the standard term *novel* will do odd things to this statement. Schlegel opposes this genre to the drama, not an organic whole, and to the epic, lacking wit and an individual's voice. Songs are different: "I can hardly imagine a romance otherwise than mixed with narration, song and other forms."[9] Any theory of the genre must itself be a romance, he adds, with authors as characters; Novalis will do this with *Heinrich von Ofterdingen* (Henry of Ofterdingen, 1801). Romance, Schlegel suggests, should contain the author's quintessence; he praises memoirs and confessions, and values peculiar detail even in the false school of Richardson and Rousseau, so lacking in lived reality. In 'realist' novels' plots, Schlegel values only the closing arabesque where fates are magically tidied. In all this, one thinks of Bakhtin's dialogic imagination.[10]

German authors carried out almost all this agenda. Schiller wrote a romance, *Der Geisterseher. Aus den Papieren des Grafen O* (The Ghost-seer, 1787–1789). Schlegel contrasts fairy tale and *Novelle;* Goethe writes one of each, with those titles. Like Voss's *Luise. Ein ländliches Gedicht* (Luise, 1795), Goethe's *Hermann und Dorothea* (Hermann and Dorothea, 1782) is an idyll rather than a verse romance; *Die Leiden des jungen Werther* (The Sorrows of Young Werther, 1774) is epistolary, and *Die Wahlverwandschaften* (Elective Affinities, 1809) is closer to Henry James, but *Wilhelm Meisters Lehrjahre* (William Meister's Apprenticeship Years, 1795–1796) is the first *Bildungsroman,* tracing a child's rejection of bourgeois utility in favor of the theater's illusion, a self-reflexive meditation on art, illusion, and the self. Like *Faust,* it contains embedded songs. Schlegel reviews *Meister,* and Novalis wrote *Ofterdingen* as a non-realist reply: during the Crusades, the dreamy Ofterdingen (a historical *Minnesinger*) travels with merchants and family, finding his own story and face in an ancient romance manuscript, learning of the poetry hidden in all things—war, mining—and of the coming magical transformation of the world. Embedded tales and eighteen embedded poems dissolve borders between poetry and prose, dream and waking, and disperse the framing narrative into a harmonic pattern which ends unfinished.

Dichtkunst mit dem Roman, so fing die der Griechen mit dem Epos an." F. Schlegel, *Schriften,* pp. 208–209.

9 "Ja ich kann mir einen Roman kaum anders denken, als gemischt aus Erzählung, Gesang und andern Formen." F. Schlegel, *Schriften,* p. 210.

10 Mikhail Bakhtin, *The Dialogic Imagination. Four Essays by M.M. Bakhtin,* trans. by M. Holquist and C. Emerson (Austin, TX: University of Texas Press, 1981).

Tieck's *Franz Sternbalds Wanderungen. Eine altdeutsche Geschichte* (Franz Sternbald's Wanderings, 1798) is a less fantastic reply to *Meister*: it is the artistic wanderings of Dürer's pupil, echoing the delicate meditation on art Tieck co-signed with Wackenroder, *Herzensergießungen eines kunstliebenden Klosterbruders* (Heart's Outpourings of an Art-Loving Monk, 1796). Tieck is more ludic and self-reflexive in plays like *Der gestiefelte Kater. Ein Kindermärchen in drei Akten* (Puss in Boots) or *Leben und Tod des heiligen Genoveva. Ein Trauerspiel* (Life and Death of Saint Genevieve), mixing lyric and drama. His later historical romances like the Shakespearean *Dichterleben* (Poets' Lives, 1826) or *Vittoria Accorombona. Ein Roman* (1840, a year after Stendhal) draw on Scott. Hölderlin's *Hyperion oder der Eremit in Griechenland* (Hyperion or the Hermit in Greece, 1797–1799) is a poet's epistolary novel, a Werther fighting for Greek independence with his lovely "Song of Fate" near the end. Schlegel wrote his own dullish *Lucinde. Ein Roman* (Lucinde. A Romance, 1799).

Jean Paul's dozen good novels are not full of lyric pieces. *Die unsichtbare Loge. Eine Lebensbeschreibung* (The Invisible Lodge, 1793) and its appendix *Leben des vergnügten Schulmeisterlein Maria Wutz in Auenthal. Eine Art Idylle* (Life of the Contented Schoolmaster Wutz, 1793) were, he said, held together by the binding.[11] Von Knör promises his daughter to the man who can beat her at chess; her child is tutored by a man named Jean Paul. *Hesperus* (1795) is narrated by another Jean Paul, a man who lives on a remote island, basing his news on dispatches from his dog. *Blumen-, Frucht- und Dornenstücke oder Ehestand, Tod und Hochzeit des Armenadvokaten F. St. Siebenkäs* (The Marriage, Death and Wedding [...] of the Lawyer Sevencheese, 1796) has the hero, or perhaps his double, writing Jean Paul's *Devil's Papers* for him; we are midway between Sterne and Flann O'Brien. Jean Paul and Siebenkäs reappear in *Titan* (1800–1803), which ends in a wild parody of Fichte. *Des Feldpredigers Schmelzle Reise nach Flätz* (The Field Preacher Schmelzle's Trip to Flätz, 1809) is full of footnotes, "numbered at random and with no reference to anything in the text."[12] A desolate German imitator of Jean Paul, signing himself Bonaventura, produced the brilliant *Nachtwachen* (Night Watches, 1804). So much for Weimar and the Berlin *Frühromantiker*.

11 Jean Paul, *Reader*, p. 12.
12 Ibid., p. 35.

Dickens certainly knew of Jean Paul, whom Carlyle translated, and his influence on the arabesques of E.T.A. Hoffmann is marked, as is his mix of sentiment, wit, and magic. In Hoffmann's *Lebens-Ansichten des Katers Murr nebst fragmentarischer Biographie* [...] *in zufälligen Makularblättern* (Life Insights of Tomcat Murr alongside a Fragmentary Biography, 1819), for instance, the philistine tomcat uses the verso of the violinist Kreisler's tormented memoirs to write his own dull autobiography, and the two stories are published interleaved, both parody and enthusiasm together. *Bleak House* (1852) does something like this, juxtaposing idyllic and ironic chapters. Among Hoffmann's shorter pieces, *Der Sandmann* (The Sandman) opens Offenbach's opera, linking magic and nightmare grotesque as *Nußknacker und Mausekönig* (Nutcracker and Mouse King) does. In Hoffmann's world, heroines are thrown out of windows or bump their heads—*Rat Krespel, Doge und Dogaressa* (Councillor Krespel, Doge and Dogaressa)—in a call to earth from romance. In sum, Jean Paul and Hoffmann fuse the ideal, the real, and the parodic, as Schlegel desired; Hoffmann is rarely self-referential (though his "Don Juan" is), but his tales are full of artists. Chamisso and La Motte Fouqué, fellow Prussian Romantics, produced two more classics in this vein: *Peter Schlemihls wundersame Geschichte* (Peter Schlemihl's Wondrous Story, 1814), in which Schlemihl sells his shadow to the devil, and *Undine* (1811), in which a water sprite weds a mortal, as in Andersen. Two other Berliners: before his 1811 suicide, Kleist presages in his tales another aspect of Hoffmann, the weird combination of deadpan and grotesque, though he lacks the fantastic element; Eichendorff's short *Aus dem Leben eines Taugenichts* (From the Life of a Good-for-Nothing, 1826) has fourteen embedded poems in its idyll reminiscent of Jean Paul. Heidelberg meanwhile produced Brentano's folk tale *Geschichte vom braven Kasperl und dem schönen Annerl* (Story of the Good Kasperl and the Fair Annerl, 1817) and *Godwi oder das steinerne Bild der Mutter. Ein verwilderter Roman* (Godwi or the Mother's Stone Image, 1801–1802), whose hero narrates his own death (like the frenetic Pétrus Borel's 1833 *Champavert. Contes immoraux*), and Arnim's *Isabella von Ägypten* (Isabella of Egypt, 1812) and *Die Kronenwächter* (The Crown-Watchers, 1817–1854), two romances: Isabella enchants Charles V, two noblemen guard the last emperor. Arnim's 1817 preface, "Poetry and History," stresses the value of historical romance, after Scott's *Waverley* (1814) but before Fenimore Cooper or Dumas.

Such is German prose narrative, 1780–1830; German has little prominent verse romance in this period, though Bürger's ballads and Klopstock's epic *Der Messias* (The Messiah) drew attention. Ironic play and aporia, magic, and historical romance—three elements which are largely anathema in 'the realist novel'—run throughout this corpus, midway between Sterne and the twentieth century; Fontane's later realism seems almost a hiccup or diversion. Moreover, this production is routinely seen as the central corpus of the period; even the theater of Schiller draws on elements from this magical tradition (*Die Jungfrau von Orleans*, The Maid of Orleans), as do Goethe and the Romantic dramatists, the great anthologies and translations, and the critical texts. The corpus elaborates a self-conscious German identity, anchored in folk and medievalism in distinction to French classicizing hegemony. The ironic play between will and circumstance seems at its most extreme in Hoffmann, where the sandman's glasses blind Nathanael, but this only crystallizes a gulf between dream and reality that runs throughout this war-torn society and its productions. It is not the commonsense world of Fielding. It is instead the terrible, post-1793 world of romance. This is no tranquil bourgeois ascendancy, though tranquility may be regretted or desired. Much of this local tradition stayed in Germany, but not all: besides Schlegel's epochal distinction, *Werther*, Jean Paul, and E.T.A. Hoffmann had a broad influence on world Romanticism, notably in France, Britain, and the United States (compare Mérimée, Gautier, Dickens, and Poe).

2. The British Isles

A growing consensus has traced a continuous, largely female British romance tradition from approximately Lyly to the Brontës, presenting the realist school of Defoe, Richardson, and Fielding as a "younger sister," to quote an author of 1787—linked, rival, and semi-independent.[13] Williams's 101 eighteenth-century prefaces, extracts, and reviews realign *post hoc* distinctions, calling Fielding's *The History of Tom Jones, A Foundling* a "prose epick composition," like Fielding's own preface to

13 Compare Williams, *Novel and Romance*, Kiely, *Romantic*, McDermott, *Novel*, Langbauer, *Women*, Ross, *Falsehood*, Richter, *Progress*, Hoeveler. *Gothic*. Williams, *Novel and Romance*, p. 341.

The History of the Adventures of Joseph Andrews, or reviewing Richardson's *romances*.[14] Kiely cites Clara Reeve in 1785: "The Novel is a picture of real life and manners, and of the times in which it was written. The Romance in lofty and elevated language, describes what has never happened nor is likely to," an apt definition of Kiely's twelve 'Romantic novels:' Walpole's *The Castle of Otranto. A Gothic Story* (1764), Beckford's *Vathek. An Arabian Tale* (1786), Radcliffe's *The Mysteries of Udolpho* (1794), Godwin's *Things as They Are; or, The Adventures of Caleb Williams* (1794), Lewis's *The Monk. A Romance* (1796), Austen's *Northanger Abbey* (1803), Scott's *Waverley; or, 'Tis Sixty Years Since* (1814), Shelley's *Frankenstein; or, The Modern Prometheus* (1818), Peacock's *Nightmare Abbey* (1818), Maturin's *Melmoth the Wanderer. A Tale* (1820), Hogg's *The Private Memoirs and Confessions of a Justified Sinner* (1824), and Emily Brontë's *Wuthering Heights* (1847).[15] Reeve continues: "Romances at this time were quite out of fashion, and the press groaned under the weight of Novels," but her *The Old English Baron* is subtitled *A Gothic Story*.[16] Walpole, Beckford, Lewis, Shelley, and Maturin use magic directly—Vathek, Lewis's monk, and Melmoth all deal with demons—but as Schlegel stated, Romanticism depends from its outset (which might be Walpole?) on doubt and ironic suspension. Hogg's murderer of his older brother may also have made a satanic pact, but we like him cannot be certain—any more than Radcliffe's and Austen's 'silly' heroines are certain about reality, or than Scott's Edward Waverley or Emily Brontë's narrator quite understand events they encounter. As in Kant or Berkeley, there is an epistemological gap between the perceiving self and perceived reality. Here lies the horror of Caleb Williams—discovering Falkland's murder of Tyrrel, he has crossed that gap into a world he cannot present within a *Tom Jones* plot, and his epistemological isolation makes him a hunted pariah. It is curious that Godwin calls this work *Things as they are*, while his *Imogen: A Pastoral Romance* and *St. Leon: A Tale of the Sixteenth Century* are called romances. Even the straightest contemporary heroic romances, like Scott's *Ivanhoe* (1819), tend to have Gothic elements like prison, torture, and witch trials to them, reflecting the compromising of romance that Schlegel and the Gothic both address. In these terms, Romantic 'parody'

14 Williams, *Novel and Romance*, pp. 126, 437.

15 Kiely, *Romantic*, p. 3.

16 *The Progress of Romance*, p. 1785, in Langbauer, *Women*, p. 64.

has a fantastic, compromising function, less *An Apology for the Life of Mrs Shamela Andrews* than Schlegel. Kiely reflects that view in his inclusion of *Nightmare Abbey*, and we will meet the idea again throughout Europe, from Byron to Stendhal to Pushkin.

If Gothic irony and wit rely on a divided self, this also appears formally in the systematic new use of chapter epigraphs, starting with Radcliffe and Lewis, then followed by countless Romantics—Scott, Shelley, Maturin, Peacock, and Eliot in England, Cooper and Poe in America, Hugo, Mérimée, Vigny, and Stendhal in France, along with Byron and Hemans in poetry. Epigraphs are broadly unknown in the European novel until then. They have countless functions—fetish authenticity for a narrative, a marker for historical continuity (Vigny), a tuning-fork setting for what follows—but three functions closely echo Schlegel. First, ironic play in the Jean Paul tradition, and an invitation to dialectical arabesque; like Scott's "Old Play" attributions or Hugo's *Han d'Islande* (Han of Iceland), Stendhal routinely concocts epigraphs, even "Truth, bitter truth" to open *Le Rouge et le Noir. Chronique du XIXe siècle* (Scarlet and Black).[17] Second, a fracturing, as in Novalis, of linear narrative and the hegemonic self it implies (who *speaks* these epigraphs?). And third, again like Novalis, a breakdown of the borders between poetry and prose, dream and reality. Lewis's taste for epigraphs from Augustan poets neatly reverses priorities, situating their reason amid his satanic chaos. Despite Genette's excellent work, there is more to be said here; epigraphs are, after all, the primary means by which lyric interlude punctuates Romantic prose narrative.

Since Scott and Byron shaped world Romanticism and other British authors broadly did not, they merit focus. One reason for this chapter was Scott's switch in 1814 from best-selling metrical to prose romances, often attributed to Byron's huge success with *Childe Harold* (1812–1818), and perhaps also reflecting the success of Edgeworth's novels. *The Lay of the Last Minstrel* (1805), influenced by Southey, sold 15,000 copies, followed by six other verse romances up to *Harold the Dauntless* (1817)—indeed, Scott wrote verse even after *Waverley*. All sold very well, and as Scott's biographer Lockhart suggested, he likely switched for esthetic, not financial reasons. Byron, he felt, could reveal "a deeper region of the

17 "La vérité, l'âpre vérité." Stendhal, *Le Rouge et le Noir*, epigraph.

soul than his own poetry could stir," an apt verdict that Scott's pooh-poohing of his own poetry supports.[18] Scott's verse narratives seem listless, distracted by form from storytelling, while his twenty-eight prose narratives explode with invention. America and Europe (Cooper, Dumas, Manzoni) followed Scott in using prose romances—*vox populi*—to tell their nations the story of their existence, and the century's historians had equal debts to his work. *Waverley* opens these windows. Whalley's chapter in Eichner traces the rare and contested instances where Britain's major Romantic poets use the term *romantic*, or what you find in a romance. As Pepys wrote, "The whole story of this lady is a romance and all she does is romantic."[19] Kiely finds three instances of the term describing Waverley's initial impressions, each qualified—"almost, not precisely, bordering on"—and concludes that Scott is ironizing an "adolescent fever fed by exotic reading," as do Peacock or Austen.[20] Lukács and others thus argue—as they of course would—that Scott is an antiromantic ironist, reclaiming him for the realist novel. Kiely notes instead how the irony diminishes, and the hero's way of seeing things "is quite literally swallowed up by his new environment," until Waverley can be led forward by a fair Highland damsel, writes Scott, "like a knight of romance."[21] Verse and the Gothic are stylized forms that constrain their authors; Scott in *Waverley* has found a bridge to Coleridgean suspension of disbelief by passing through irony at the outset, and this will simplify the task of his successors. Richter likewise argues that Scott's footnote erudition licensed male readers to enjoy the 'female' romance genre, much as his embedded Gothic narratives offset the comparative 'realism' of a still-Gothic plot, like the epistolary *Redgauntlet*.[22] In England, Bulwer-Lytton, Disraeli, and Thackeray draw, after 1826, on Scott's innovations.

Byron's solution is different. With *Childe Harold*'s subtitle, *A Romaunt*, Byron works to reclaim the long romance tradition, and highlights the t in *romantic*; as in *Sternbald* and *Ofterdingen*, a divided artist encounters Europe, but like Goethe in *Meister* or Chateaubriand in *René*, Byron makes his story contemporary, thus stressing the self-reflexive link

18 Roberts, *Long Poems*, 179ff.
19 McDermott, *Novel*, p. 120.
20 Kiely, *Romantic*, p. 142.
21 Ibid., pp. 138–144.
22 Richter, *Progress*, pp. 102–105.

between author and hero, and ironizing the gap between our dreams and prosaic, post-Waterloo reality. In sum: 'straight' Romantic-era verse romance lacks tension and bite, and I say this regretfully of Mickiewicz's *Pan Tadeusz, czyli ostatni zajazd na Litwie* (Mister Thaddeus; or The Last Foray into Lithuania), and of Longfellow's best-selling *The Song of Hiawatha*. The form seems to require irony to live. It is fitting that *Don Juan*, like *Beppo: A Venetian Story*, is in the *ottava rima* of Boiardo, Ariosto, and Tasso, Italy's three great Renaissance romancers. Just as Ariosto lovingly mocks what Boiardo plays straight, Byron parodies his own Byronic persona.[23] *The Giaour: A Fragment of a Turkish Tale* and *The Corsair: A Tale* (both 1813), and even *Mazeppa* (1819), are largely "straight" Eastern romances with a unilinear narrative, though *Mazeppa* concludes, "The king had been an hour asleep;" the narrator of *Don Juan* (1819–1824) is omnipresent, as Friedrich Schlegel desired, conflating his ostensible plot with an encyclopedic, parodic review of existence, art, and the self in one superb, monstrous arabesque, stretching from love to anthropophagy.

Britain's great female romance tradition—Behn, Manley, Haywood, Lennox, Burney, Smith, Wollstonecraft, Radcliffe, Edgeworth, Owenson, Austen, Shelley, the Brontës—has at its core, Ross implies, a *sensible* female witness, a continuity misread by men insisting in the Gothic on the male villain's primacy, unlike the sentimental novel, and regretting the heroines' search for logic.[24] Ross's broader terms show Radcliffe's and Burney's closely related plots and, as she writes, confound "traditional categories such as 'novel of manners', 'sentimental novel', 'didactic novel' and 'Gothic novel'."[25] "The life of every Woman is a Romance!" writes Burney, but as Don Quixote explains to Sancho, romance subverts the existing order so that it can re-establish divine distinctions that have been lost.[26] It is odd that men should value in their fictions the aping of reality while condemning romance for its freedom—but as Ross remarks, "official truth was merely verisimilitude for women, something lived second hand."[27] In these terms, all these women's heroines, Gothic

23 McGann, *Byron*, p. 28, reviews his comic debunking in *Manfred: A Dramatic Poem*, as in *Beppo*.
24 Ross, *Falsehood*, 143ff.
25 Ibid., p. 136.
26 Burney ctd. Ibid., p. 39. See also ibid., p. 98.
27 Ibid., p. 4.

or sentimental, share a Romantic, even a fantastic epistemological enterprise; to identify reason in the romance they inhabit. Haywood, Lennox, and Austen parody, in short, not romance convention, but its reading of reality; Wollstonecraft's Maria, in *The Wrongs of Woman: or, Maria. A Fragment*, is told by her brutish husband that her sentiments are *romantic;* Radcliffe punctiliously explains each Gothic event she presents; Edgeworth's narrator in *Castle Rackrent* (1800), who cannot read his own stupidity, narrates deadpan a Jewish wife's years of imprisonment by her husband for money; Mary Shelley's *The Last Man* (1826) is an apocalypse reconstructed from ancient fragments; *Wuthering Heights* (1847) is narrated through a double veil, as Nelly Dean talks to the male narrator, and Rochester in Charlotte Brontë's *Jane Eyre* (1847) goes blind.[28] Reality indeed is darkness visible. Yet this is far from all, as Richter reminds us of Lane's Minerva Press, suggesting that roughly 40% of works of fiction published in 1795–1820 "would be classified as Gothic novels."[29]

Is this Schlegel's ideal? Love and epistemology are omnipresent in this tradition. Ironic suspension is recurrent, as is his play "between appearance and reality"—compensating for the dearth of formal play between verse and prose, since that formal play is subsumed within a deeper play between mystery and reason, this perhaps even evident in Austen's great studies of mores. Hazlitt and De Quincey, in the *Liber Amoris: or, The New Pygmalion* (1823) and in the *Confessions of an English Opium Eater* (1821), answer as Hogg does to Schlegel's stress on the possibilities of the confessional genre; Dickens, finally, speaks directly to the romance tradition. As Langbauer illustrates, his "contemporaries and early critics unhesitatingly labeled his work as 'romance,'" and Dickens says as much himself, in the preface to his weekly journal *Household Words*—"in all familiar things [...] there is Romance enough, if we will find it out"—in the preface to *Bleak House* (1852–1853), which dwells "upon the romantic side of familiar things"—and in *The Posthumous Papers of the Pickwick Club* (1836–1837)—"there's romance enough at home without going half a mile for it."[30] Dickens does not mix genres, and his two historical novels out of sixteen are set in the recent past: the French Revolution and the Gordon Riots of 1780 (*A Tale of Two Cities,*

28 Langbauer, *Women*, p. 100.
29 Richter, *Progress*, pp. 90, 101.
30 Langbauer, *Women*, pp. 133, 148.

Barnaby Rudge). Only his Christmas stories have supernatural events, as in *A Christmas Carol in Prose. Being a Ghost Story of Christmas* (1843). Yet magic runs all through his production, from the "Megalosaurus, forty feet long or so" wandering up Holborn Hill on the first page of *Bleak House*, to the way in *Great Expectations* (1859) that every new stranger is someone's lost wife or father, as if in Ariosto. Dickens completes our survey of British novel writing, 1750–1850, and romance has evidently touched every part of it.

Now for the bridge to verse romance. Roberts's catalog of *Romantic and Victorian Long Poems* reminds us just how neglected this genre has been, despite its evident centrality to the age and its authors, who largely considered their short lyrics as occasional and tangential productions: critics are reclaiming the Big Six here—Blake, Coleridge, Wordsworth, Byron, Shelley, Keats—but still neglect Southey, Moore, Campbell, Landor, Hemans, and Tighe, among many. One may regret that Roberts misses both Rogers and Crabbe, along with Combe's lovely *Tour of Dr. Syntax in Search of the Picturesque* (1812), that Hudibrastic verso to Childe Harold's tormented wanderings. Around 1800, the novel's amorphous critical and empirical heritage makes the border of romance fluid, and a centuries-old tradition suggests revising our criteria. The long poem had much sharper boundaries, and idylls, pastorals, or epics are self-evident poetic vessels which romance will do no more than color. Blake's long visionary poems for instance—*Vala, or the Four Zoas* (finally published in 1893), or *Milton. A Poem in Two Books* (1810), or *Jerusalem, Emanation of the Giant Albion* (1820)—are not romances *per se*, but theogony, echoing Klopstock's and Milton's Christian epics in their lack of human *agon*. As Schlegel said, romance rests on history. Yet Blake's vision of giants, palaces, and divine order betrayed until triumphant, is that of Novalis or of Cervantes's *El ingenioso hidalgo Don Quijote de La Mancha* (Don Quixote, 1605); romance, ultimately, inhabits his epic structure. Keats later faces this question in *Endymion: A Poetic Romance* and in *Hyperion. A Fragment* (1818–1820); *Endymion* echoes the Greek shepherd romances of Spenser or Mlle de Scudéry, while *Hyperion* adapts that romance pastoral setting to the fall of the Titans before Olympus. Wolfson's very good chapter on romance in Keats finds the genre central to his project, reviewing his repeated shift from expected "old Romance" to a meta-romance shaped by irony (285): *Isabella, The Eve of St Agnes,* and *La Belle Dame sans Merci*. Shelley's Greece, as in Byron or Hölderlin, is not always antique:

The Revolt of Islam. A Poem (1818), neglected, though twice as long as *Prometheus Unbound. A Lyrical Drama,* is modern romance, following Laon's and Cythna's adventures and struggle against oppression. Coleridge's narratives—*Christabel, The Ancient Mariner*—are perhaps romances in the Spanish sense, and certainly both magical and fantastic, but too short for our criterion. Wordsworth's short pieces are similar—"The Idiot Boy" and "The Ruined Cottage"—but his longer poems raise interesting questions. *The Prelude or Growth of a Poet's Mind* (published 1850), after considering producing "some old / Romantic tale, by Milton left unsung," instead traces, like *Meister,* the artist's formation from childhood, though it eschews the magic of Tieck or Novalis.[31] *The Excursion* (1814), a story of long chats with neighbors, also more closely resembles prose narrative than most contemporary poetry—for instance, Wordsworth like Byron favors first-person narration, unusual in long poems, encouraging Keats's calling his art "the wordsworthian or egotistical sublime."[32]

The popular poet Rogers did not write romances. Crabbe, who was also quite celebrated, did, and both *The Borough* (1810) and *Tales of the Hall* (1810, 1819) deserve a look from students of Wordsworth's terrible and simple tales. Cooper surely knew Campbell's *Gertrude of Wyoming or the Pennsylvanian Cottage* (1809), where evil Mohawks kill all but the last Oneida. Landor's *Gebir* (1798), set mainly in ancient Egypt and the underworld, has a good romance plot of love, magic, betrayal, and obstacles. Campbell and Landor have seen, like Wordsworth and Crabbe, that they can versify material which is common in contemporary prose. Southey and Moore likewise draw on prose orientalist romances, such as *Vathek* or the *Livre des Mille et une Nuits* (Book of the 1,001 Nights)—we can observe Southey doing so in the Arab and Indian *Thalaba the Destroyer* (1801) and *The Curse of Kehama* (1810), like Moore in his playful Persian *Lalla Rookh: An Oriental Romance* (1814). Wilkie notes that Southey carefully distinguished these two *romances* from his three epics.[33] L.E.L.'s *The Improvisatrice* (1824), a response to Staël's *Corinne ou l'Italie* (Corinne or Italy), features embedded romances improvised by the heroine; Hemans's three long poems *Modern Greece. A Poem, The Abencerrage* (a title stolen by Chateaubriand in 1821), and *The Forest*

31 Wordsworth, *Prelude,* I, p. 169.
32 Wolfson, *Presence,* p. 35.
33 Wilkie, *Epic,* p. 36.

Sanctuary (1816–1824) form a curious trio, showing Greece oppressed by Muslims, medieval Spaniards fighting Muslims, and a Spaniard fleeing the Inquisition for the New World. The last two are what Scott called "metrical romances," while the first is a philosophical poem. Tighe's *Psyche; or, The Legend of Love* (1805), a Greek or Spenserian romance, influenced Shelley and Keats. In sum, verse romances are a lost planet in Romantic-era British fiction, standing oddly alongside the prose romances of the age and casting new light, it may be, on the canon in verse and prose alike. One thinks of the word *romance* in Johnson's *A Dictionary of the English Language* (1755), which does not specify verse or prose: "A military fable of the middle ages; a tale of wild adventures in war and love. [...] A lie; a fiction."

3. France

The French eighteenth century produced relatively little in the vein of Madeleine de Scudéry. Paralleling the *Dictionnaire de l'Académie françoise* (Dictionary of the French Academy) on the word *roman*— "A work ordinarily in prose, containing fictions which represent adventures rare in life, and the complete development of human passions"—Prévost, Marivaux, Rousseau, and the epistolary novel trace human passion, while Voltaire's tales have rare adventures.[34] But despite Voltaire's ironic play, Schlegel carefully avoids him, and he rejects Rousseau's *Julie ou La Nouvelle Héloïse. Lettres de deux amants* [...] *au pied des Alpes* (Julie or The New Héloïse) in favor of his *Les Confessions* (The Confessions). As the century's verse demonstrates, the age lacked poetry; it lacked dream. To Diderot, who is one of Schlegel's models, let us add Sade in the 1790s Gothic tradition, though the mission of his heroines is less to interpret than to suffer pain. Bernardin de Saint Pierre's *Paul et Virginie* (Paul and Virginie, 1787) and *La Chaumière indienne* (The Indian Cottage, 1791) gave Europe the term *pariah;* two fine, and very influential, compromised romances, where today's tropics do not protect man from himself. Barthélemy's popular *Voyage du jeune Anacharsis en Grèce* (Voyage of Young Anarcharsis in Greece, 1788) uses a romance frame to present Greek civilization. French eighteenth-century critics stressed

34 "Ouvrage ordinairement en prose, contenant des fictions qui représentent des aventures rares dans la vie, et le développement entier des passions humaines." *Dictionnaire de l'Académie françoise*, 5th edition, 2 vols (Paris: Nicolle, 1813), "Roman."

believability, a refusal of epistemological crisis (they liked Condillac) which is anathema to our subject, and all these authors but Diderot and Sade present a surface less troubled than Wordsworth. Epistemology, not its crisis, is of course central to authors like Mme de Graffigny in her *Lettres d'une Péruvienne* (Letters of a Peruvian Woman, 1747), written in *quipu*, or Laclos, in his splintered *Les Liaisons dangereuses ou Lettres recueillies dans une société* (Dangerous Liaisons, 1782).

Is the French Romantic novel quite different? Staël, Genevan like Rousseau, published in both centuries. She first tells 'romance' stories set in Africa or the West Indies, with embedded sung romances. Moving to longer narratives, she tries letters (*Delphine*, 1802), then later, an exploded form—written alongside Schlegel's older brother—combining lyric interlude, play performance, text copied or read aloud, and diary fragments (*Corinne ou l'Italie*, 1807). Chateaubriand's short romances *Atala* and *René* (1801–1802), set in French Louisiana, are in the *Paul et Virginie* tradition, while *Les Martyrs ou le Triomphe de la religion chrétienne* (The Martyrs, 1809), set in Diocletian's Empire, combines epic catalogs and nations in movement with romance hermits, love, and adventures in what he called a prose epic—seemingly a new creation. Mme Cottin and the equally popular Mme de Genlis, mistress of the duc d'Orléans, wrote historical romances of love and chivalry. *Mathilde* (1805) is set in the Crusades, and *Mademoiselle de Clermont* (1802) in the court of Louis XIV. Critics continue to sever Romantic-era French poetry and prose, a misguided and misleading act given that France's canonical Romantic poets all published novels: Vigny's *Cinq-Mars* (1826) learnedly reviews a key moment in national history, and follows Scott even in using chapter epigraphs (like Hugo, Mérimée, and Stendhal). Also, before Dumas, Mérimée's *Chronique du règne de Charles IX* (Chronicle of the Reign of Charles IX, 1829), with its ending left for the reader to determine, does likewise, as, among other things, does Hugo's *Notre-Dame de Paris 1482* (Notre-Dame Cathedral, 1831). Vigny also wrote two volumes of tales, *Première Consultation du Docteur-Noir. Stello* and *Servitude et grandeur militaires* (Stello, Military Servitude and Grandeur), both of which focused on the divided modern self, like Lamartine's *Raphaël. Pages de la vingtième année* and *Graziella* (1849–1852) and Musset's bleak *Confession d'un enfant du siècle* (Confession of a Child of the Age, 1836). But Musset, like Byron, also wrote *Lettres de Dupuis et de Cotonet* (Letters of Dupuis and Cotonet, 1836–1838) and *Histoire d'un merle blanc* (Story of a White Blackbird, 1842), burlesquing all Romantic cliché. The *Lettres* quite visibly shaped Flaubert's later *Bouvard et Pécuchet* (Bouvard and Péchuchet, 1881). In sum, French Romantic poets combine poetry and prose most directly by writing both. The term *romance* seems applicable to all their above work, and Schlegel's criteria are largely satisfied by their taste for love, (national) history, the self-reflexive growth of a divided self, and the muted presence of irony and formal experimentation—the arabesque. There is also a more frenetic, sentimental-grotesque tradition, seen in Pétrus Borel's *Champavert* (1833) or in Hugo's *Han d'Islande* and *Bug-Jargal* (1823–1826), set in Norway and Haiti, both featuring psychopathic dwarfs who share Quasimodo's red hair. Here Schlegel's arabesque may be more in evidence.

Nodier, Mérimée, Balzac, and Gautier continue this mood in the French Romantic short story, a fantastic genre still neglected in favor of the 'realist' canon. Nodier has explicit magical events, as in his vampire tale *Smarra* (1821). Mérimée prefers fantastic irresolution, as in *La Vénus d'Ille* (The Ille Venus, 1837), where a statue apparently comes alive to kill someone, or *Lokis manuscrit du professeur Wittembach* (Lokis, 1873), whose hero may be both man and bear. This doubt is a good handle on 'realist' tales like *Carmen* (1845), whose events are less simple than they seem to their naïve narrators. Balzac, for his part, wrote Gothic novels in the 1820s, such as *La Peau de chagrin* (The Shagreen Skin, 1831) which sucks its Parisian owner's life with each wish it grants, and *La Fille aux yeux d'or* (The Girl with Gold Eyes, 1833), which hides Sadean crime in contemporary Paris. Balzac and Mérimée are not the canonical realists they have been labelled. In Balzac's superhuman output of eighty-eight novels for his *Human Comedy*, as in Dickens, a magical thread runs throughout a realist universe—not only in the philosophical studies, which feature *Melmoth réconcilié* (Melmoth Reconciled, 1835), but in modern Paris, as we have seen. Balzac avoids historical novels, but his world is filled with the lost past. *Le Colonel Chabert* (Colonel Chabert, 1832) returns from the Napoleonic wars to find himself written out of history, and the senile Baron Hulot in *La Cousine Bette* (Cousin Bette, 1837) calmly sets up shop with his pubescent mistress Atala—an acid nod to Chateaubriand!—in ghetto Paris as if in Tahiti, while his desperate family searches for him. These are magnificent novels, where reality is transformed by poetry and savage irony, and the price of existence is marked.

Sainte-Beuve's *Vie, poésies et pensées de Joseph Delorme* (Joseph Delorme, 1829), often seen as a lyric anthology, is perhaps France's closest link to the Germans in its fusion of a *Bildungsroman* prose frame and extensive lyric interlude. *Volupté* (Delight, 1834) has another self-reflexive, divided narrator. The poets Gautier and Nerval, two other Romantics of 1830, also wrote novels, as did all the French canon. Gautier's large and diverse oeuvre includes three historical novels, notably *Mademoiselle de Maupin* (1835), whose heroine cross-dresses, with its famous art for art's sake preface attacking the bourgeoisie. Nerval's *Sylvie. Souvenirs du Valois* (Sylvie, 1852) is perhaps the romance Schlegel wanted: a love story full of illusion and occult meaning at the urbane Romantic narrator and hero's expense, constantly undercut by irony, both playful and tragic, and with the present filled by the generations of the past.

Like Nerval, Sand inflects the pastoral, though realist critics have read her uninflected. *La Mare au diable* (The Devil's Pool, 1846) and *La Petite Fadette* (Little Fadette or Little Fairy, 1848) show folk reality always edging on the magical, as in her masterpiece *Les Maîtres Sonneurs* (The Master Pipers, 1852), where Joset may well have sold his soul to the devil. We cannot know, as we found in Mérimée or Hogg. Sexist critics have understandably preferred these 'domesticated' pastorals to Sand's novels of revolt—*Indiana, Lélia, Mauprat* (1831–1837). In those texts, Sand's idealism is more patent. Schor has argued that a realist canon served male critics who chose to exclude magic from the ledger. Sand's more than twenty novels are her data, but even Stendhal is, splendidly, not what he has seemed: in the realist classic *Le Rouge et le Noir* (1830), for instance, Julien Sorel finds a newspaper clipping with his own name in anagram (Louis Jenrel) and the story of his eventual execution. This precisely matches what Ofterdingen encountered. Stendhal's irony, like Mérimée's or Nerval's, reads differently when set alongside Schlegel's divided self. *La Chartreuse de Parme* (The Charterhouse of Parma, 1839) also pulls between irony and romance idyll, between will and circumstance, and with another alienated hero escaping oppression through a devoted lady. Stendhal has simply tilted the scales of compromised romance: his Promethean heroes retreat into isolation, then die, leaving poetry defeated or ridiculed—as Mathilde rides off on the final page with Julien Sorel's severed head in her lap.

Dumas wrote more than Balzac, including eighty historical novels, but three famous novels will serve: Milady ends *Les Trois Mousquetaires* (The Three Musketeers, 1844) beheaded by her first lover, now a public executioner; in *Le Comte de Monte-Cristo* (The Count of Monte-Cristo, 1844–1845), a man betrayed, but made fabulously wealthy by a prison confidence, wreaks his opium-calmed revenge upon society; *La Reine Margot* (Queen Margot, 1845) saves La Mole's severed head, just as La Mole's descendant Mathilde saved Julien's. These texts are anchored in French history, as Schlegel desired, even *Monte-Cristo* depending on Napoleon and Waterloo, and Dumas can indeed be read as serious national history. Dumas's avowed aim was to offer France a living heritage: accused of violating French history, Dumas said, but look at the children I have given her. His history is transformed by romance at every step, far more so than in Scott; *Rob Roy* is not *The Three Musketeers*. This chapter uses Schlegel to explain and justify its search for Romantic era European romance; Dumas is very far from Schlegel, but romance is the core of his enterprise. This also seems the moment to name Eugène Sue, who wrote serialized popular historical novels—*Mathilde* (1841)—and Gothic novels—*Les Mystères de Paris* (The Mysteries of Paris, 1842–1843), *Le Juif errant* (The Wandering Jew, 1844–1845)—to immense and now-neglected success.

Unlike Britain or Germany, France produced almost no extended verse romance in this period. Hugo, Vigny, Musset, Sainte-Beuve, and Nerval wrote none; Lamartine wrote *Dernier chant de pèlerinage d'Harold* (The Last Song of Harold's Pilgrimage, 1825), after Byron, and *Jocelyn. Épisode* and *La Chute d'un ange. Épisode* (An Angel's Fall, 1835–1838), two fragments of a Christian epic with romance elements—love, disguises, obstacles—set at first during the French Revolution, then before the Flood. Gautier wrote *Albertus ou L'Âme et le péché. Légende théologique* (Albertus or the Soul and Sin, 1832), a Faustian parody where the devil sneezes, the poet says bless you, and a witches' sabbath disappears. The poet's mutilated corpse, ending the poem, evokes 'Monk' Lewis. Gautier's *La Comédie de la mort* (The Comedy of Death, 1838) also combines magic and burlesque. In our redrawn Romantic-era corpus, with its new focus on the fantastic, on the night side of reality, and on the arabesque, Gautier's romance work may seem more central than it has, a production considerably larger than his canonical *Émaux et camées*

(Enamels and Cameos, 1852), often billed as anti-Romantic. France's dearth of Romantic-era verse romances, and the 'novels' produced by every canonical French Romantic poet (unlike the English, for instance, who wrote none), suggest that these poets found aspects of French verse constricting, and were more able to complete their extended narratives in prose, benefitting from the same amorphousness that attracted Schlegel. This in turn suggests that their novels, or *romances*, deserve more careful study in future reviews of French Romantic poetry, much as in theater these same authors routinely abandoned the Paris stage in favor of closet drama, a *Spectacle dans un fauteuil*, as Musset put it. In this context, the verse-prose overlap, and other resonances of the term *romance*, again seem more useful than a simplistic division between two warring canons, 'the realist novel and the Romantic lyric.'

4. The Italian Peninsula

Italy's Romantic authors—Monti, Foscolo, Manzoni, Leopardi, Pellico—wrote dramas or (Monti) epics, but no verse romances. In their large prose output, three novels are remembered: Foscolo's *Ultime lettere di Jacopo Ortis* (Last Letters of Jacopo Ortis, 1802), a fragmentary epistolary novel indebted to *Werther*, whose 'saintly' hero runs over a stranger, pays off the family without confessing, and accepts their praise; Pellico's *Le mie prigioni* (My Prisons, 1832),wisdom memoirs about ten years of prison which influenced Primo Levi; and Manzoni's *I promessi sposi, storia milanese del secolo XVII scoperta e rifatta* (The Betrothed, 1827), set in plague-stricken Spanish Lombardy in the 1630s. Foscolo and Pellico reflect the vogue for first-person narration that Schlegel favored. Manzoni's *Betrothed* (a Scott title from 1825) is Italy's most famous novel, using Scott better than Vigny or Mérimée do to make past history a national statement, even to its Milanese dialect. In post-Waterloo Europe, all of Scott's imitators offer veiled political manifestos. Vigny the aristocrat condemns emergent royal despotism, while Scott the Tory values a paternalist establishment; using history allows claims about the nation's true identity. Manzoni's Spaniards stand for the Austrians of 1820, as he appeals for national liberation. This nationalist discourse is absolutely central to the Scottian romance vogue throughout Europe and the Americas. Writing in answer to *Ivanhoe*, Manzoni, like the historian Thierry, focusses on the humble, rejecting historical figures. He went on to write a history of the French Revolution and condemn romance's mix of fact and fiction in *Del romanzo storico* (The Historical Novel, 1850). Foscolo wrote two more novels, *Hypercalypseos liber singularis* (Hypercalypseos a Singular Book, 1815) and *Viaggio sentimentale di Yorick lungo la Francia e l'Italia* (Yorick's Sentimental Journey, 1817), being a satire in the language of Dante's *La vita nuova* (The New Life, 1294) and an imitation of Sterne.

Schlegel also called for a theory of the novel (or romance) in novel form, something more than the eighteenth century's routine use of a thin narrative frame for didacticism. Europe's romances focus repeatedly and self-reflexively on artistic creation, as we have seen. Straight criticism mixed with creative play is rarer but extant, from Byron or Hazlitt to Gautier, and to the Milan 1816 debate—notably Berchet's *Lettera semiseria di Grisostomo al suo figliuolo* (Grisostomo's Semiserious Letter to His Son), which ends with a damaged statue of Italy wheeled out to unite opposing parties. In this Romantic genre, criticism is romanced, much as history is in the age's historical novels. Romantic parodies deserve further study in that light.

5. Northern and Eastern Europe

I started this chapter thinking about Europe's and America's foundational Romantic narratives, struck by their deep resemblances, though in verse or prose depending on the country. What Scott, Dumas, and Cooper build in a series of prose romances, Pushkin and Mickiewicz, Shevchenko and Vörösmarty build in extended verse. Without the word *romance*, we chop this phenomenon in half.

We might call Mickiewicz's twelve-book *Pan Tadeusz* (1834) a folk epic with fantastic elements, a genre rare in Western Europe, though one is reminded of Goethe's *Hermann und Dorothea*. In fact, Mickiewicz began his poem with Goethe in mind, then found Scott to be a better model. Between 1795 and 1918, with a brief Napoleonic interlude, 'Poland' did not exist. Westerners, even Germans and Italians, easily lose sight of what Romantic narratives meant for Slavic countries in particular, with no national map or language. Set in Lithuania under Napoleon, *Pan Tadeusz*, like *The Betrothed*, avoids great names in favor of a feud-inflected love story complete with speeches, village battles, and comic interludes. War here brings order to a disharmonious peace.

Norway apparently produced little Romantic romance, though it has fairy tales. Sweden has Tegnér's highly successful *Frithiofs saga* (1820–1825), adapted from the Old Norse, combining metrical virtuosity, sentiment, and thin characterization. Denmark has, besides Andersen, the poet and dramatist Oehlenschläger—who wrote *Vaulundurs saga* (1812) for instance—Grundtvig's long poems, and Hauch's and Ingemann's imitations of Scott. In what was then Russia, Estonia has Kreutzwald's folk epic *Kalevipoeg* (1857–1861), as Finland has Lönnrot's reconstituted oral epic, the *Kalevala* (1835–1849). Latvia and Lithuania, Romania, Bulgaria, Slovenia, Macedonia, and Albania have national stirrings in the period pre-1850, but no romances that I have come across. Greece's Solomos is mainly a lyric poet. Ukraine has Shevchenko's nationalistic Cossack verse, such as the national folk epic *Haidamaki* (1841). Serbia and Croatia have at least two folk epics, Petrović's *Gorski vijenac* (The Mountain Wreath, 1847) and Mažuranić's *Smrt Smail-Aga Čengića* (The Death of Smail-Aga Čengić, 1846), both about the Montenegrin struggle against the Turks. Czech has Kollár's expanding sonnet cycle *Slávy Dcera* (The Daughter of Sláva, 1824–1852), narrating love and national sentiment, Hanka's folk forgeries, influenced by Macpherson and Chatterton, and the very young Mácha's *Máj* (May, 1836), a Byronic verse romance, both nationalist and nihilist, about a murderer awaiting execution. Hungary has folk epics—Kisfaludy, Vörösmarty's *Zalán futása* (1825)—and Jósika's novel *Abafi* (1836), indebted to Scott. Let us simply note the extensive use of folk epics in Northern and Eastern European nationalism, whereas the West favors prose. These folk epics resemble medieval romance.

Pushkin's bitter, joyous *Evgenii Onegin* (1823–1831) surpasses Byron in its fusion of pathos and burlesque. The urbane narrator gently mocks Lensky, his heart "all but crushed with pain," moments before Lensky's best friend Onegin kills him in a duel for after all no reason.[35] Even in English (see bibliography for all translations from the Russian), the poetry is stunning—Lensky "early found both death and glory / In such a year, at such an age"—as Pushkin shifts in dazzling arabesque between sublime and parodic mode, insisting on a discord in reality,

35 "V nem serdtse, polnoe toskoi." A.S. Pushkin, *Evgenii Onegin. Roman v stikhakh* (Moskva: Izdatel'stvo ATRIUM, 1991), p. 162 (6.xix).

whose pain the choice of simple irony would negate.[36] Pushkin's narrator invokes his Muse in Chapter Seven; he reads Apuleius, while Tatyana (he regrets her vulgar name) reads Byron, Nodier, Stendhal, and Lafontaine. Pushkin, suffused with European authors, and Mickiewicz contrast well; Pushkin's is the hard way to construct the 'free romance' he wanted (Deutsch viii), keeping a universe of antinomies in suspension until the closing line: "As, my Onegin, I drop you."[37] *Ruslan i Liudmila* (Ruslan and Liudmila, 1820) is a mildly parodic, magical folk epic. Pushkin's splendid prose lacks this tension between poetry and bathetic reality, though his *Istoriia sela Goriukhina* (History of the Village of Goriukhino, 1837) contains a wonderful seven-line history of poetry in the narrator's series of attempts to poeticize the village, moving from an epic "abandoned on the third verse" to the portrait he decides on.[38] Like Mérimée, Pushkin also enjoys fantastic tales, somewhere between reality and magic: *Vystrel* (The Shot, 1831), say, or *Pikovaia dama* (The Queen of Spades, 1834).

The Ukrainian Gogol's tales share Pushkin's play between poetry and reality, though his tension is grotesque, less elegant than violent, and closer to Hugo or E.T.A. Hoffmann. *Strashnaya mest* (The Terrible Vengeance, 1832) has a sorcerer, a murdered baby, and a woman saying of her husband: "He was buried alive, you know. Oh, it did make me laugh."[39] *Nos* (The Nose, 1836) has a minor functionary lose his nose and converse humbly with it, now disguised as a State Councilor, in Kazan Cathedral—the nose refuses to return. *Portret* (The Portrait, 1835) has a soul caught on a canvas, presaging *Dorian Grey*, while *Shinel* (The Overcoat, 1842), with another minor functionary, foreshadows Dostoevsky and Kafka. Gogol's novel *Mertvye dushi* (Dead Souls, 1842) continues his grotesque realism but eschews the fantastic, contributing to a reputation which has, somewhat one-sidedly, praised Gogol's realism in neglect of his magic. Lermontov's verse romances like

36 "Pogibshii rano smert'yu smelykh,/ V takoi-to god, takikh-to let." Pushkin, *Evgenii Onegin*, p. 180 (7.vi).

37 "Kak ia s Oneginym moim." Pushkin, *Evgenii Onegin*, p. 286 (8.li).

38 "i ia brosil ee na tret'em stikhe." A.S. Pushkin, *Sochineniia*, 3 vols (Moskva: Izdatel'stvo "Khudozestvennaia literatura," 1964), "Istoriia sela Goriukhno," III, p. 287.

39 "Ved' ego zhivogo pogrebli ... kakoi smekh zabiral menia." N.V. Gogol, *Polnoe sobranie sochinenii* (Moskva: Akademia Nauk S.S.S.R., 1940), "Strashnaia mest'," I, p. 273.

Demon. Vostochnaia poviast (The Demon, 1839) face neglect beside his bleak, superb *Geroi nashego vremeni* (A Hero of Our Time, 1840), five interwoven and embedded tales about or by the bored, fatalist Pechorin, who meets smugglers, kidnaps a Circassian girl, and later kills and is killed at random: "Perhaps some readers will want to know my opinion of Pechorin's character. My answer is the title of this book."[40]

6. Iberia and the Low Countries

Portuguese Romanticism begins with the elegant Almeida Garrett's verse romances *Camões* and *Dona Branca* (1825–1826), about the national poet Camoëns and about a Christian princess in love with a Moor, both published in exile in Paris. His later prose recalls both Sterne and Scott, and his *Romanceiro* (1843) parallels Spanish work collecting the *Romanceros* in 1828–1832. Spain produced mainly drama, but Espronceda's dramatic poems *El estudiante de Salamanca* (The Student of Salamanca, 1839) and *El diablo mundo* (The Devil-World, 1841) use *Romancero* format to mix lyric and dramatic forms, magic, and reality, much as Schlegel wanted. *The Student* retells the Don Juan story. Scott also influenced Rivas's twelve-canto romance *El moro expósito* (The Exposed Moor, 1834), based on a medieval legend. The Flemish van Duyse writes mainly lyrics, while Ledeganck writes national tales in verse. Conscience's hundred-odd novels or romances include *De leeuw van Vlaanderen* (The Lion of Flanders, 1838), a violent thirteenth-century romance again indebted to Scott, populist but without Scott's self-aware narrator, and giving prestige to Flemish eight years after the creation of Belgium. In Dutch, Drost's also Scott-influenced *Hermingard van de Eikenterpen* (1832) and Geertruida Bosboom-Toussaint's national romances from *Het Huis Lauernesse* (The Lauernesse House, 1840) onward are famous. Having read Espronceda, Rivas, Garrett, and Conscience, the link between romance and emergent nationalism remains striking, if unsurprising, since romance speaks to medieval locality—what the Germans call *Kleinstaaterei*—in answer to the imperialist neoclassical universalism Napoleon had encouraged, a contrast Scott, writing from the Scottish

40 "Mozhet byt, nekotorie chitateli zakhotiat uznat' moe mnenie o kharaktere Pechorina? Moi otvet—zaglavie etoi knigi." M.I. Lermontov, *Geroi nashego vremeni*, ed. D.J. Richards (Letchworth: Bradda, 1969), p. 74.

borders, aptly represents. There is also some contemporary work in this romance vein in Breton and Occitan, though perhaps not in Erse or Catalan.

7. The Two Americas

All mainland Latin America achieved independence in the years 1806–1826. Romance, though, is scarce: in Argentina, Echeverría's *Elvira o la novia del Plata* (Elvira, 1832) and Mármol's *Cantos del peregrino* (Songs of the Pilgrim, 1846) are Byronic verse romances. Hernández's later *El gaucho Martín Fierro* (Martin Fierro, 1872) is Argentina's national poem. For his part, Nélod lists no Romantic novels in South America or the Caribbean, where most Romantic texts do in fact seem to postdate 1850. Let us however briefly mention Gertrudis Gómez de Avellaneda's fine Cuban novel *Sab*, written in 1841, about a noble slave in love with his mistress, and the novels produced mid-century in Brazil—Joaquim Manuel de Macedo's romance *A Moreninha* in 1844, Manuel Antônio de Almeida's *Memórias de um Sargento de Milícias*, published in serial form in 1852–1853, José de Alencar's indianizing *O Guarani* from 1857—and in Argentina: Sarmiento's *Civilización y barbarie: Vida de Juan Facundo Quiroga (1845)*, an attack from exile on the Rosas regime. In its turn, Anglophone America had little verse romance; Longfellow's *The Song of Hiawatha* (1855), in the *Kalevala*'s loose trochaic tetrameter, is a rare major example.

Porte's *The Romance in America* (1969) opens, "the rise and growth of fiction in this country is dominated by our authors' conscious adherence to a tradition of non-realistic romance sharply at variance with the broadly novelistic mainstream of English writing."[41] His focus is Cooper, Poe, Hawthorne; let us add Irving. Cooper's moments of national crisis, Porte suggests in a key insight, "could not be dealt with in the realistic novel as he knew it."[42] Nation and individual emerge as symbiotic concepts in the Romantic era, and authors shaping nations from Argentina to Estonia—an activity unknown before 1776—do so in the footsteps of Scott. Fielding's hermetic world allows no bridge

41 Porte, *Romance*, p. ix.

42 Ibid., p. 8.

between feminine private destiny, the *oikos*, and the *polis*, between the clerks and the masses, making it droll that ivory-tower critics later rejected Europe's historical romances as escapist, instead reserving their praise for the Fielding tradition. As Frye writes, "There is a strongly conservative element at the core of realism, an acceptance of society in its present structure."[43] Porte cites Simms in 1835: "the modern Romance is the substitute which the people of the present day offer for the ancient epic."[44] This of course also perfectly fits the criteria of Europe's Romantic-Classical distinction.

Of Cooper's fifty-odd romances, the five *Leatherstocking Tales* (1823–1841) gave him international fame. Like Scott, he shows tribal structures dissolving before a larger nationhood, and uses systematic verse epigraphs to multiple effect. But there is an epic tone here which refuses Scott's irony, plus a new insight into local color, and into the alienness even of those who seem very close: the Christian Hawk-eye in *The Deerslayer: or, The First War-Path* (1841) believes chess pieces must be idols. Cooper rejects magic in his preface to *The Pioneers, or the Sources of the Susquehanna* (1823), and refuses comparison with Homer. But his forest is full of romance, though compromised by 'civilization,' and Hawk-eye is a true hero, unerring in virtue as in battle. *The Last of the Mohicans; A Narrative of 1757* (1826) opens with this same careful distinction between "an imaginary and romantic picture of things which never had an existence" and "the business of a writer of fiction," which is "to approach, as near as his powers will allow, to poetry" (Cooper also curiously links Native Americans and the Orient). Hawk-eye is a fiction, but he is possible. Hawthorne's ironic prefaces, by contrast, stress the radical divide between a novel's probability and a romance's exposure to the "truth of the human heart." As Porte notes, he "entitled or subtitled all of his four major fictions *romances*" (95–96). Hawthorne wants to build, says his preface to *The Blithedale Romance*, in art's neutral territory, "Fairy Land." The elf-child Pearl in *The Scarlet Letter. A Romance* (1850) perhaps cannot cross streams. A wolf greets her, "but here the tale has surely lapsed into the improbable" (Chapter XVIII); we fear an evil spirit, and in walks the Dickensian Roger Chillingworth, just as chilling as his name. As often in the fantastic mode, heuristic problems

43 Frye, *Scripture*, p. 164.

44 Porte, *Romance*, p. 39.

produce a divided narrator or, as in *The Blithedale Romance* and in *The Marble Faun or, The Romance of Monte Beni* (1852–1860), increasing focus on heroes struggling with art and illusion. Like almost all of Europe's fantastic writers, Hawthorne refuses to resolve heuristic irresolution into magical certainty. Irving plays likewise between doubt and burlesque: *Rip van Winkle. A Posthumous Writing of Diedrich Knickerbocker* (1819) and *The Legend of Sleepy Hollow. Found Among the Papers of the Late Diedrich Knickerbocker* (1820), which gave him international fame, are folk legends about a man who sleeps for twenty years and about a headless horseman respectively, encountered by narrators as urbane as those of Byron, Pushkin, or Nerval. It is apt that Irving began his career with a burlesque history of New York, and *The Alhambra* (1831) sets orientalist Moorish legends within a similarly urbane arabesque.

If Cooper, Hawthorne, and Irving delicately explore the limits of belief, leaning increasingly toward magic, then Poe completes this series. His narrators are urbane, but so are vampires; he is *there* first-person for Hop-Frog's appalling revenge, and for the House of Usher's fall into the lake. He is in the pit as the pendulum swings, he himself rips his beloved Berenice's teeth from her entombed body, though still alive, and he personally walls Fortunato up alive in *The Cask of Amontillado*— "Yes [...] for the love of God." Surveying the world's Romantics, what is amazing is not their magic, but their almost total refusal to do what Poe does; to stop flirting with magic—or suspending their disbelief—and step wide-eyed into what Schubert calls the Night Side of reality (*Ansichten von der Nachtseite der Naturwissenschaft*). Poe, Novalis, Hoffmann, and yes, the 'realist' Gogol, are almost alone in doing so. The power of the Enlightenment had waned to this extent.

8. Conclusion

Two primary facts emerge from this study: first, that the Romantic border between poetry and prose is less formal than epistemological, a truth the age repeatedly stresses, and second, that romance allows writers a nation-building enterprise that the realist novel cannot make room for. Its folkish tales echo an *oral* form, fitting the folk agenda of Warton, Percy, Goerres, and the Grimms. The age addressed these two agendas, answering to the political and epistemological crises it faced, in two main types of romance, a global term that may be more apt and useful than 'novel' or 'long poem:' the ironic/magical and the national/historical. It chose verse, prose, or both according to circumstance, showing national and individual variation: Slavic and Scandinavian folk epics, Scott, the French Romantics. We might place British women authors in my first, heuristic category; there is of course massive overlap, and narrators throughout this corpus show a divided self, torn between inside and outside, and between Schopenhauer's contemporary will and representation. Recording this crisis in narrative, which is a fictional entity alien to the self, invites parallel self-reflexive meditations on art's role in forming events and perceived reality. *Romance* is a superb tool with which to examine this problem: it is, as Samuel Johnson writes, "a lie," a claim that parallel to our phenomenal world of objects is the observer/narrator's world of thoughts and memories, with its own pull on the present. Waverley and Keats *expect* romance, and they are not alone; it seems likely that all Europe heard romance in the word romantic, as Pepys or Scott did, with its sense that we have all grown up with stories and they influence what we do, for better or worse, but that without them, reality would be an arid and narrow place. This is why romance caused them problems, and why children love Hugo or Dumas.

4. *Racine et Shakespeare*'s Sleeping Partners: The Return of the Repressed

J'écris comme on fume un cigare, pour passer le temps.
Stendhal[1]

New entrepreneurs need venture capital to supplement their limited credit, and a silent partner can help them, fronting capital and contacts while remaining invisible. *Racine et Shakespeare* (1823–1825) has maintained that borrowed invisibility very well; homage to the treatise has been little troubled by precedents for its precedent-setting, though Stendhal published after a decade of polemic which his contemporaries could not ignore. What pushes us to present Stendhal, and not his foreign bedfellows, among the fathers of French Romantic theory? Ideology, in large part; a paradigm set up over a century ago dates Romanticism from the *bataille d'Hernani*: *ergo*, 1820s texts seem first-generation.[2] But if Stendhal writes after a decade of public debate, not to mention twenty years of personal meditation, then we might consider a new paradigm, placing this manifesto not before but *after* a fierce and long Romantic controversy. We may then find new meaning to its

1 "I write as one smokes a cigar, to pass the time." Stendhal, *Racine et Shakespeare*, ed. Pierre Martino, 2 vols (Paris: Champion, 1925), [henceforth *RS*], I, p. 78. Page numbers alone in the text refer to this volume; other Stendhal texts cite the Henri Martineau edition at Paris: Le Divan, unless otherwise indicated. The second half of this article's title, and some excellent advice here, I owe to my former colleague Gil Chaitin. All translations in this chapter are my own.

2 *Hernani*: for instance, Théophile Gautier in *Les Jeunes France*, ed. René Jasinski (Paris: Flammarion, 1974). Romanticism before *Racine et Shakespeare*: Edmond Eggli and Pierre Martino, *Le Débat romantique en France, 1813–1830*, I, *1813–1816* (Paris: Les Belles Lettres, 1933).

 https://doi.org/10.11647/OBP.0302.04

erotics—the games it plays—and to its place in history: failing which, we have only another imitation cited by a national ideology as original. Stendhal's dance around Romantics like Schlegel, Staël, and the Italians, whose discourse frames his argument, will help make this complexity apparent. Interpreting that dance means looking at his life before 1823; by looking at that past, in a sort of *étude génétique*, the subtle brilliance of his Parisian pamphlets may emerge. This review thus splits into three, situating *Racine et Shakespeare* at the end of twenty years' debate.

1. Private Life and Empire: Henri Beyle, 1803–1814

Here del Litto's review remains precious. In 1802–1803, aged twenty, Beyle discovers Shakespeare, seeing the Ducis *Hamlet*, reading *Othello* and, he notes, "*César, le king Lear, Hamlet; Coriolan; Macbeth; Cymbeline; La Tempête; Roméo et Juliette*, les tragédies historiques."[3] Le Tourneur, whose translation the schoolboy studied in 1796, already stresses Shakespeare's *naturel*, but without Beyle's conclusion, repeated twice in 1805: "C'est pour mon coeur le plus grand poète qui ait existé."[4] Shakespeare offers an antidote to the "fausse délicatesse" of the French stage; this view echoes Staël's *De la littérature*, which Beyle annotates in 1803, neglecting her talk of climate and perfectibility but copying passages on tyranny and affectation, and Staël's explicit contrast of Shakespeare with Racine, who is, she writes, less suited to "une nation devenue libre" after a civil war.[5] Beyle notes on that passage, "Ce n'est plus au Français de Louis XIV que nous voulons plaire, mais à celui de 1803"—*Racine et Shakespeare* in a nutshell, twenty years before the *Muse française*.[6]

---

3 "*Julius Caesar, King Lear, Hamlet; Coriolanus; Macbeth; Cymbeline; The Tempest; Romeo and Juliet*, the historical tragedies." *Hamlet*: 12.iv.1803, in Stendhal, *Pensées*, 2 vols (1931) [henceforth *Pensées*], I, p. 88. *Othello*: 29.v.1803, in Stendhal, *Journal*, 5 vols (1937), I, p. 70. See Victor del Litto, *La Vie intellectuelle de Stendhal. Genèse et évolution de ses idées (1802–1821)* (Paris: P.U.F., 1962) [henceforth *Vie*], pp. 70–71, 221. *César*: 24.ix.1803, in Stendhal, *Molière. Shakespeare. La Comédie et le rire*, 1930 [henceforth *Molière*], p. 196.

4 "He is for my heart the greatest poet who ever existed."

5 "false delicacy;" "a nation become free." *Grand poète*: 11.ii.1805, *antidote*: 26.vii.1805; *Journal*, in Stendhal, *Oeuvres intimes*, 2 vols, ed. Victor del Litto (Paris: Gallimard, 1981) [henceforth *OI*], I, pp. 208, 105. Mme de Staël, *De la littérature*, ed. Gérard Gengembre and Jean Goldzink (Paris: Garnier-Flammarion, 1991), p. 217.

6 "It is no longer the Frenchman of Louis XIV's age that we wish to please, but that of 1803." Louis XIV: *Pensées*, I, p. 150.

France and England—Beyle's attacks on Racine parallel his early taste for Shakespeare. In 1803, he writes of "petits hommes" [little men] who prefer Racine to Corneille, a Napoleonic topos which Geoffroy and others repeat.[7] After 1804, Beyle reads Fénelon on *Phèdre* and Clément's *Lettres à Voltaire*, reinforcing his doubts on Racine.[8] Like *Britannicus*, *Andromaque* seems to him "bavarde. Ce défaut est surtout choquant dans les confidants."[9] He likes *Phèdre* despite the descriptions; *Mithridate*'s plot is dull, the characters vulgar and affected; he despises *Iphigénie*, mediocre like those who admire it.[10] By this period, 1804–1805, Beyle already considers Marmontel an "anti-poète," though *Racine et Shakespeare*'s manuscripts cite Marmontel on mimetic illusion.[11] Beyle may still see merits in Racine, Corneille, and Molière, but his break with French *criticism* is made by 1804, calling La Harpe a *nigaud* [fool] as he sets to work to "délaharpiser son goût."[12]

Whence this opposition? As del Litto argues, "L'éloignement pour Racine tient en grande partie à la théorie de la perfectibilité."[13] Beyle cites Staël's famous theme in May-June 1804, arguing as she does that post-Revolutionary France needs a different tragedy than Racine's. Comparing Fabre with Molière, Beyle concludes that "nous pouvons mettre en scène une mélancolie plus touchante" than Racine can offer.[14] Six days earlier, he says the same of Molière, concluding: "c'est ce qui fait dire avec ridiculité, mais peut-être vérité, à Mme de Staël que la littérature a fait des progrès."[15] If perfectibility forms for Beyle "l'essentiel de son *credo* romantique," it emerges in this early dialogue with Staël, a dialogue which Molière, Racine, and Shakespeare already

7 Corneille: *Pensées*, I, p. 130. Geoffroy: *Journal des Débats*, 12 nivôse XIII/12.i.1805.

8 Fénelon: 24.iv.1804, *OI*, I, p. 67. Clément: *Pensées*, I, pp. 95–6.

9 "talkative. This defect is especially shocking in the confidants." *Britannicus*: 29.iii.1805; *OI*, I, p. 305. *Andromaque*: *Vie*, p. 232.

10 *Phèdre*: 22.iv.1805; *OI*, I, p. 319. *Mithridate*: 17.i.1805; *OI*, I, p. 188. *Iphigénie*: 1.v.1804; *OI*, I, p. 71.

11 *Anti-poète*: Victor del Litto, *En marge des manuscrits de Stendhal. Compléments et fragments inédits (1803–1820). Suivis d'un courrier italien* (Paris: P.U.F., 1955) [henceforth *Compléments*], pp. 113, 136–137. Illusion: *RS*, II, pp. 21–22.

12 "de-La Harpify his taste." *Nigaud*: letter to Pauline Beyle, 20.vi.1804, in Stendhal, *Correspondance*, ed. Henri Martineau and Victor del Litto (Paris: Gallimard, 1981) [henceforth *CSten*], I, p. 109. *Délaharpiser*: 21.xi.1804, *OI*, I, p. 152.

13 "The distaste for Racine stems in great part from the theory of perfectibility."

14 "we can put a more touching melancholy on stage." Fabre: 21.i.1805; *OI*, I, p. 192.

15 "this is what makes Mme de Staël say ridiculously, but perhaps truly, that literature has made progress." *progrès*: 15.i.1805; *OI*, I, p. 183.

frame.[16] Echoes in *Racine et Shakespeare* stretch to the exempla: writing in 1805 of how to paint things without their effect, Beyle argues that Staël's *Delphine* "a absolument besoin de moments de repos."[17] For a counter-example, he already cites the passage in *Macbeth* on the beauty of the castle "où le martinet vient faire son nid."[18] Del Litto's stress on Staël's influence thus seems apt.

While thoughts on tragedy move quickly, we often hear that until Beyle reads A.W. Schlegel in 1814, Molière and comedy remain largely synonymous for him.[19] Yet Staël's *Corinne ou l'Italie* offers Beyle not only a series of Italian topoi he later echoes, but also Carlo Gozzi's fantastic comedy, a radical alternative to Molière he discovers through her by 1808.[20] For Corinne, "le vrai caractère de la gaieté italienne, ce n'est pas la moquerie, c'est l'imagination"—another central distinction in *Racine et Shakespeare*.[21] Beyle's long Paris stay of 1810–1811 thus marks the end of a long maturation. For entertainment, he chooses Mozart and Gozzian *opera buffa* over classical tragedy at the Théâtre-Français, and confesses, "Je suis obligé de me forcer pour lire Corneille et Racine."[22] Again, Beyle is not alone, echoed by Geoffroy, who writes of Classical *froideur* and *ennui*.[23] Even the Institut calls, in 1810, for non-Classical subject matter, "plus conforme à notre manière de voir et de sentir."[24] The year 1809 sees Constant's *Wallstein* appear in print, and performances of the Ducis *Macbeth, Hamlet*, and *Othello* at the Théâtre-Français, alongside Lemercier's Shakespearean *Christophe Colomb* at the Odéon, a concerted Romantic offensive which Napoleon ends by pulping Staël's *De*

16 "the essential part of his Romantic credo." See *Vie*, pp. 233 (*perfectibilité*), 235 and note (credo, Molière).

17 "absolutely needs moments of rest." *Delphine* and *Macbeth*: 5.ii.1805; *OI*, I, p. 201. Compare *RS*, II, p. 218.

18 "where the swift comes to make its nest."

19 Molière and Schlegel: *Vie*, pp. 73, 454.

20 Gozzi: Mme de Staël, *Corinne ou l'Italie* (Paris: Folio, 1985), p. 182; also Stendhal to Pauline Beyle, 26.iii.1808; *CSten*, I, p. 442.

21 "the true character of Italian gaiety is not mockery, it is imagination."

22 "I am obliged to force myself to read Corneille and Racine." *Forcer*: 11.v.1810; *OI*, I, p. 582.

23 Geoffroy: *Journal de l'Empire*, 24.iv.1809.

24 "more in conformity with our manner of seeing and feeling." See *Vie*, pp. 343–345 (Gozzi), 394–396 (Institut, 1809 events).

l'Allemagne in 1810. Reviewing and translating Shakespeare with Louis Crozet in 1811, Beyle is oddly silent on this whole polemic.[25]

So, is Beyle a Romantic yet? His praise of *naturel* and attack on *bienséances* may seem precritical, an anti-Classical reaction uncertain of its alternatives; indeed, he notes in 1812 that "mes maximes sur les arts ne sont pas le fruit d'un système."[26] But the same year, Beyle makes his distinction European, contrasting "the French school" in theater with the Italians, Germans, and English who value expression above noble style.[27] In 1813, as Napoleon falls, Sismondi, Schlegel, and Staël—a *Confédération romantique*—publish from Coppet their great Romantic treatises: *De la littérature du Midi de l'Europe, Cours de littérature dramatique, De l'Allemagne.*[28] Beyle is critical in *Rome, Naples et Florence en 1817*: "Sismondi est tiraillé par deux systèmes opposés: admirera-t-il Racine ou Shakespeare?"[29] Yet a series of Sismondian echoes soon recur, in Beyle's first letter on Metastasio, in his parallel between Alfieri and Schiller, his link between Alfieri's defects and his late education, and his talk of Goldoni's baseness. A.W. Schlegel's immediate impact seems even greater, despite the silence in Beyle's journal and correspondence. Del Litto stresses a chapter of Beyle's *Traité de l'art de la comédie*, "Sur le comique romantique," written on 17 December 1813, seven days after the *Cours* went on sale. Schlegel calls old Greek comedy "un jeu fantastique, une vision aérienne et riante;" Beyle writes of "quelque chose d'aérien, de fantastique dans le comique."[30] Beyle then mentions music, echoing his revelation from 1812—that he likes *opera buffa* because

25 Stendhal and Crozet: *Molière*, pp. 199–216, with Stendhal's superb Romantic misreading: "Toute la grandeur de Shakespeare apparaît à ces mots de César: *Let me have men about me that are flat*" (207). Shakespeare says *fat*, after "Yon Cassius hath a lean and hungry look."

26 "my maxims on the arts are not the fruit of a system." *Système*: *Molière*, p. 220.

27 French school: Stendhal, *Histoire de la peinture en Italie*, ed. Paul Arbelet, 2 vols (Paris: Champion, 1924)], II, p. 379.

28 Coppet: John Isbell, "Le Groupe de Coppet ou la Confédération romantique," in *Le Groupe de Coppet et l'Europe*, ed. Kurt Kloocke (Lausanne et Paris: Touzot, 1994) [henceforth *Confédération*], pp. 309–329.

29 "Sismondi is tugged by two opposing systems: will he admire Racine or Shakespeare?" *Tiraillé*: Stendhal, *Rome, Naples et Florence en 1817 suivi de L'Italie en 1818*, 1956 [henceforth *RNF*], p. 168.

30 "a fantastic game, an airy and laughing vision;" "something airy, fantastic in comedy." Greek comedy, *but écarté*: A.W. Schlegel, *Cours de littérature dramatique* (Geneva: Paschoud, 1814), I, pp. 351, 298. *Aérien*: *Molière*, p. 264.

it gives him "la sensation de la perfection idéale de la comédie."[31] This comic liberation echoes Kantian *art pour l'art;* Schlegel writes that "La gaîté [...] ne peut exister que lorsque tout but est écarté."[32] Beyle finds Schlegel so inspiring that he drafts a newspaper review on 18 December, the day after his new chapter. The review opens with an entertaining portrait, the middle-aged Schlegel as a Wertherian young man of wit and reverie with an "air sauvage et sombre."[33] It then moves on to Schlegel's Classical-Romantic distinction. Facing Greece and France, writes Beyle, are Shakespeare, Calderon, Schiller, and Goethe, "du genre *romantique*. A la bonne heure [...] j'admets la littérature *romantique*."[34]

And yet, as so often with Beyle, public and private discourse differ; his marginalia on Schlegel open with the words: "Collection de faussetés."[35] Beyle's private quibble is with religion, continuing, "dans un siècle, aucun Français sachant lire ne croira au christianisme."[36] He regrets Schlegel's lack of Tracy's empiricism. A note on the translator's disagreeable style is dated March 1814, but a nearby comment on Schlegel, *mystique* and an "être triste" [sad being], is dated August 1816, and other comments are undated, though 1816 suggests itself. Alongside Beyle's objections—"Déraison complète," "téméraire, ridicule, mal écrit"—stand other notes—"Très bon," "This is true," even "Sublimement vrai," next to a passage on the public—and new observations.[37] Schlegel describes social cultures which imitate the ancients, and Beyle notes: "Les courtisans de Louis XIV."[38] In the end, the negatives win out; in 1819, Beyle reopens the book for the first time since 1816, adding, "alors

---

31 "the sensation of comedy's ideal perfection." Buffa: to Pauline Beyle, 2.x.1812; *CSten*, I, pp. 659–60.

32 "Gaiety [...] can only exist when every goal is set aside."

33 "a wild and somber air." Schlegel review: Stendhal, *Mélanges de littérature*, 3 vols, 1933 [henceforth *Mélanges*], III, pp. 137–141. See *Vie*, pp. 462–463 (Sismondi details), 464–466 (Schlegel).

34 "of the *romantic* genre. Well then [...] I admit *romantic* literature."

35 "Collection of falsehoods." Schlegel: Stendhal, *Mélanges intimes et marginalia*, 2 vols, 1936 [henceforth *Marginalia*], I, p. 311–326. As with us all, reading often merely confirms Beyle's beliefs; reading Constant's *De l'esprit de conquête*, 22.iii.1814, he notes another central theme of *Racine et Shakespeare*: "La liberté antique ennemie de la comédie suivant un principe vu depuis longtemps par Dominique [i.e., Beyle];" *OI*, I, p. 904.

36 "in a century, no Frenchman who can read will believe in Christianity."

37 "Complete unreason;" "rash, ridiculous, badly written;" "Very good;" "Sublimely true."

38 "The courtiers of Louis XIV."

pas de livre plus impatientant pour moi."[39] Nor is it clear that Beyle really grasps Schlegel's vision of ideal comedy, despite his new chapter. "Gaîté de jeunes filles et non comique of Hobbes," he notes; "L'Auteur prend toujours le fou pour le *Comique*," concluding: "Toujours la même erreur, délire aimable [...] et non production du *Rire*, du comique."[40] In 1821, he reopens the book once more to note: "Cet auteur m'est antipathique au souverain degré."[41] He adds Voltaire, Staël, and Buffon in listing his antipathies. Beyle's reaction to Schlegel is evidently mixed from the outset, though his public retraction arrives only in 1816.

The *Vies de Haydn, de Mozart et de Métastase*, composed in May-June 1814, allow the new Beyle to transform his sources as he loves to do, rendering Carpani's word *romanzesca*, for Haydn, with "imagination *romantique*" [*romantic* imagination], and putting Carpani's Virgil-Ariosto opposition for Haydn's art in new terms as one between Racine, Ariosto, and Shakespeare.[42] The *Vie de Mozart* even talks of a "lutte du genre classique et du genre romantique" and calls the alexandrine a "cache-sottise."[43] This echoes *Des mœurs* on "la pompe des alexandrins" as an obstacle.[44] Another remark, later crucial to *Racine et Shakespeare*, echoes Staël's *De la littérature*: "la nation française a changé de manière d'être depuis trente ans. Rien de moins ressemblant à ce que nous étions en 1780, qu'un jeune Français de 1814."[45] Yet Beyle's explicit mentions of *De l'Allemagne* in 1814 are less flattering: "Malgré une enflure exécrable, il y a des idées, surtout sur les mœurs des dames allemandes."[46] Volume Three, on German philosophy, seems especially bad to him; Beyle has served Napoleon from Brunswick to Moscow, and despite his views on

39 "then no book was more irritating for me."

40 "Young girls' gaiety and not the comic of Hobbes;" "The author always takes the mad for the *Comic*;" "Always the same mistake, amiable delirium [...] and not the production of *Laughter*, of the comic."

41 "This author is repellent to me to a sovereign degree."

42 *Vies de Haydn, de Mozart et de Métastase*, 1928, pp. 59–60 (*romantique*, Racine and Shakespeare), 317 and note (*lutte*, *cache-sottise*), 213 (1780 and 1814).

43 "struggle between the classic genre and the romantic genre;" "stupidity-hider."

44 "the pomp of alexandrines." *Alexandrins*: Mme de Staël, *De l'Allemagne*, ed. comtesse Jean de Pange and Simone Balayé, 5 vols (Paris: Hachette, 1958–1960) [henceforth *De l'Allemagne*], II, p. 248.

45 "the French nation has changed its mode of being in thirty years. Nothing less resembles what we were in 1780, than a young Frenchman of 1814."

46 "Despite an execrable exaggeration, there are ideas, especially on the customs of German ladies." *Enflure*, German philosophy: to Pauline Beyle, 23.v.1814, *CSten*, I, p. 773.

theater, his new adhesion to Coppet's 'Romantic school' is provisional. In 1814, the Allies enter Paris and Beyle leaves for exile in Austrian Milan.

2. The Birth of Stendhal: Romantic Milan, 1814–1818

Beyle returns to his beloved Milan in August 1814, avoiding destitution by publishing under pseudonyms his first books, two compilations on music and art, in 1815 and 1817: the *Lettres sur Haydn* and the *Histoire de la peinture en Italie*. As we have seen, a Romantic discourse transforms Beyle's sources; the *Histoire de la peinture* argues, like Staël or Schlegel, both that the "beau antique" [antique beauty] is incompatible with modern sentiments, and that we moderns are "formés par les romans de chevalerie et la religion."[47] The *Edinburgh Review* calls this theory "metaphysical obscurity," while the *Journal de Paris* remarks of Beyle, "Son but paraît toujours de louer Shakespeare et Schiller et de toujours blâmer Racine."[48] But the book also contains an attack on Schlegel which marks a watershed in Beyle's thought: Romanticism without the Germans. In September 1816, Beyle writes to Crozet that four or five eminent Englishmen "m'ont illuminé;" they showed him the *Quarterly* and *Edinburgh* reviews.[49] He translates twenty-three pages from the reviews, on Greece, Byron, and *De l'Allemagne*, intended for the *Histoire de la peinture*. Crozet may counsel rejecting Beyle's extracts, but he heeds Beyle's call in the same letter for a stop-press note attacking Schlegel's authority: "La note sur le romantique [...] est bien mauvaise. Ces plats Allemands toujours bêtes et emphatiques se sont emparés du système romantique, lui ont donné un nom et l'ont gâté," Beyle writes: on the other hand, the *different* Romantic system practised by Byron and the

47 "formed by romances of chivalry and religion." *Formés*: Stendhal, *Histoire de la peinture en Italie*, ed. Henri Martineau, 2 vols (Paris: Le Divan, 1929) [henceforth *HPI*], II, pp. 231–232; *beau antique*, Books 4–5.

48 "His goal seems always to praise Shakespeare and Schiller and always to blame Racine." Metaphysical obscurity: *Edinburgh Review* 23/64, October 1819 (p. 334). *Son but*: *Journal de Paris*, 12.xi.1817.

49 "illuminated me." *Illuminé*, repeats: to Crozet, 28.ix.1816, 20.x.1816; *CSten*, I, pp. 819, 835. This letter mentions the *Edinburgh Review* 23/45, April 1814 (pp. 198–229), with Jeffrey on Byron's *Corsair* and *Bride of Abydos*, translated in October. Three weeks earlier, on 7–8.ix.1816, Stendhal translates fifteen pages on Greece from the *Quarterly Review* 10/20, January 1814 (pp. 437–475); on 15.ix.1816, two pages on *De l'Allemagne* (pp. 335–409), published in 1928 as *Sur les unités* (see *Vie*, pp. 511–519, on Crozet and Stendhal's extracts).

Edinburgh Review "est sûr d'entraîner le genre humain."[50] Schlegel, Beyle adds, "reste un pédant ridicule," who wishes French literature had just one head to be chopped (not true): "Il faut bien séparer cette cause de la théorie romantique de celle de ce pauvre et triste pédant Schlegel."[51] Beyle repeats his head story in October, glad not to appear "dans le régiment de ce La Harpe."[52] It is ironic, then, that Schlegel's other alleged insult which Beyle repudiates, "Schiller n'est qu'un élève de Shakespeare," will resurface in Beyle's diary, in *Qu'est-ce que le romanticisme?* and even in *Racine et Shakespeare*: "Schiller a copié Shakespeare et sa rhétorique" (47).[53]

What changed Beyle's mind? The *Edinburgh Review* becomes his bible; del Litto notes four debts in the *Histoire de la peinture* to a single Hazlitt review of Sismondi, hidden behind Beyle's usual playful masks—he translates Hazlitt extracts back into French rather than reopening Sismondi, and attributes what Hazlitt says of Dante to Michelangelo.[54] He signs the same Hazlitt extract "Biography of the A.," but "Mémoires de Holcroft" for the frontispiece to *Rome, Naples et Florence*. Yet does Beyle's new distinction of two Romanticisms, good and bad, English and German, depend on reading the *Edinburgh Review*? In October 1816, Beyle apparently knows only the Byron article, thus rejecting Schlegel before reading Hazlitt's guarded Schlegel review. In Romantic Milan, speech will supplement writing, and the hub of this activity is Ludovico di Breme, who knows both Byron and Schlegel personally and dislikes the latter. Beyle meets Breme in July; in September, he writes to Crozet: "il y a depuis deux mois révolution dans mes idées."[55] Breme pulls Beyle from his isolation, introducing him not only to other

50 "The note on the romantic [...] is very bad. Those insipid Germans always stupid and emphatic took hold of the romantic system, gave it a name and spoiled it;" "is sure to carry away humanity." Schlegel attack: *HPI*, II, p. 54; compare *RS*, II, pp. 3–4, 269–270.

51 "remains a ridiculous pedant;" "One must separate this cause of romantic theory from that of this poor and sad pedant Schlegel."

52 "in the regiment of this La Harpe."

53 "Schiller is only a pupil of Shakespeare's." "Schiller copied Shakespeare and his rhetoric." Schiller insult: 18.xii.1820; *OI*, II, p. 49; also *RS*, II, p. 28.

54 Hazlitt: *Edinburgh Review* 23/49, June 1815 (pp. 31–63), on Sismondi, *De la littérature du Midi de l'Europe*.

55 "in the past two months there has been a revolution in my ideas." See *Vie*, pp. 508–510 (Breme's circle), 528–33 (Hazlitt), 536–539 (Schlegel). *Révolution*: to Crozet, 28.ix.1816; *CSten*, I, p. 821.

Milan Romantics—Monti, Pellico, Borsieri, and Berchet—but also to the Whigs Byron, Hobhouse, Lansdowne, and Brougham, as well as to Dumont and Saint-Aulaire from Geneva and Paris—in short, to a European matrix Breme himself acquires by visiting Staël at Coppet. The *Edinburgh Review* is the organ of this European liberal elite. Beyle's gift list for the *Histoire de la peinture* reflects this matrix in its turn; from Coppet's ambit, it features Staël, her friends Constant and Barante, her son-in-law the duc de Broglie, Saint-Aulaire, even Staël's cousin Mme Necker de Saussure, A.W. Schlegel's French translator.[56]

This is the peak of Beyle's commitment to any Romantic movement. Italian Romantic debate, 1816–1818, is largely a war of pamphlets, opening in January 1816 with Staël's thoughts on translation in the *Biblioteca italiana*. Its center is Breme's box at La Scala, and this is Beyle's world after July. Breme's, Borsieri's, and Berchet's 1816 pamphlets all leave clear traces in Beyle's work, starting in September 1817 with *Rome, Naples et Florence en 1817*, signed for the first time "M. de Stendhal." Martineau traces Stendhal copying Borsieri, in particular, word for word.[57] Several themes of *Racine et Shakespeare* also surface here for the first time: Viganò's ballet, "*romantique* par excellence," whereas Shakespeare himself lacks music; Alfieri, Corneille, and other dramatists treating their tragedies "comme un poème" [like a poem], while Shakespeare focuses on human character and passion to touch his public; the public's "disposition à l'illusion" and Alfieri's long tirades which prevent it.[58] Deep in the Breme circle, Stendhal also echoes Staël's still-manuscript *Considérations sur la Révolution française*, ironically or not, on the Old Regime and "les ilotes de cette monarchie qui avaient fait la terreur," and on the egotist Bonaparte who "leva le masque et marcha au despotisme"—"je pense," writes Stendhal unexpectedly and using Chateaubriand's u, "que Buonaparte n'avait nul talent politique."[59]

56 List: to Didot, 5.iii.1817; *CSten*, I, pp. 856–860. On Coppet and Milan, 1816–1818, see Isbell, "Staël and the Italians." Compare George M. Rosa, "Stendhal raconteur: a partly unpublished record of reminiscences and anecdotes," *Studi francesi* 65–66 (1978), p. 358: "upon reading Stendhal's *Lord Byron en Italie* in 1830, Hobhouse denounced the essay as a tissue of distortions and lies and its author as a scoundrel." Stendhal later copied Hobhouse for about 100 pages of his *Vie de Napoléon*.

57 *RNF*, pp. 386–387, 420 (Borsieri debts).

58 "disposition to illusion." *RNF*, pp. 49–50 (Viganò), 113 (Alfieri).

59 "the helots of this monarchy who had made the Terror;" "lifted the mask and marched to despotism;" "I think that Buonaparte had no political talent." *RNF*,

Ten pages later stands his famous passage on Staël and Coppet, "les états généraux de l'opinion européenne."[60] In December 1816, Stendhal writes to Crozet of "the work of Mme de Staël which I know"—eighteen months before publication, thanks to Breme. Her work spurs Stendhal to return to his *Vie de Napoléon*, his major project in 1817–1818.

Meanwhile, Milan's pamphlet war continues, and Stendhal looks to intervene. In January 1818, Breme publishes two important articles on Rossi's translation of Byron.[61] Stendhal reworks Jeffrey's Byron article to supply a Romantic alternative to Schlegel, stressing the Classical-Romantic opposition, before *Racine et Shakespeare*, as that between pedantry and emotion. From 5–9 March 1818, Stendhal drafts his first pamphlet on theater, *Qu'est-ce que le romanticisme?* He raids Marmontel, A.W. Schlegel, and Samuel Johnson on dramatic illusion, with echoes of Sismondi, and Jeffrey also. "Il faut," he writes in persona as an Italian nationalist, "que chaque peuple ait une littérature particulière [...] nous renverserons Shakespeare et son élève Schiller."[62] Yet this pamphlet remains unprinted and unpublished, like Stendhal's other projects between 1818–1820: *L'Italie en 1818*, his reworking of *Rome, Naples et Florence*; the article *Du romanticisme dans les beaux-arts*, 1819, and his treatise *De l'amour*, 1819–1820, first published in 1822 . On 5 June 1818, Stendhal receives Staël's *Considérations sur la Révolution française*. That day, he notes that "Mme de Staël n'est que puérile" in stressing Napoleon's dependence on "l'argent des conquêtes."[63] He then repeats her charge himself, much as he reuses the insult to Schiller. Twelve days later, he submits a refutation of Staël to Pellico, busy launching the famous *Conciliatore*—but Pellico, who admires Staël's analysis of Napoleon,

---

pp. 172–173 (Buonaparte). François-René de Chateaubriand, *De Buonaparte, des Bourbons, et de la nécessité de se rallier à nos princes légitimes* [...] (1814).

60 "the Estates General of European opinion." *RNF*, p. 186 (Coppet; compare pp. 214–217 for Stendhal's profound ambivalence). *I know*: to Crozet, 26.xii.1816; *CSten*, I, p. 844. See *Vie*, pp. 542–543 and notes (pamphlet details).

61 "*Il Giaurro*... Osservazioni di Lodovico di Breme," *Il Spettatore*, January-February 1818 (pp. 46–58, 113–114).

62 "Each people must have their own literature [...] we will overthrow Shakespeare and his pupil Schiller." *Il faut*: *RS*, II, p. 28.

63 "Mme de Staël is only puerile;" "the money of conquest." *Puérile*: 5.vi.1818; *Compléments*, p. 337. Stendhal cites Staël's credit thesis on a copy of Constant's *Principes de politique*: "Grande erreur de Napoléon, qui en cela avait porté sur le *trône* les préjugés d'un sous-lieutenant;" *Marginalia*, p. 367.

refuses it.[64] Undeterred, in September Stendhal submits a manuscript pamphlet on Monti, *Des périls de la langue italienne.*[65] Pellico rejects that too. Yet Breme's Monti articles in the *Conciliatore* echo Stendhal's themes, even citing "l'immortel Tracy;" a small public trace of Stendhal's contribution to Milan debates.[66] After 1818, Stendhal's Milan ties grow problematic. Along with Pellico's refusals comes distance from Breme, begun once again by Staël's *Considérations*. Breme's *Conciliatore* review of her book calls Napoleon an *immortale facinoroso* (criminal). Noting the word, Stendhal remarks: "Tomber sur cette canaille."[67] Stendhal notes that Breme liked him less after his comment that Staël has only one book, *L'Esprit des lois de la société*—a play on Montesquieu's famous 1748 treatise, *De l'Esprit des lois*, and also a remark he repeats about Sismondi in *Rome, Naples et Florence*. In 1820, Stendhal has a moment of injustice for Breme, saying he died "de rage de n'être rien et d'une fluxion de poitrine."[68] Pellico, Borsieri, and Breme would have every reason to feel slighted by their invisibility in *Racine et Shakespeare*—eclipsed by Manzoni and Visconti, whom Stendhal knew later and less well.

3. Paris 1823–1825: *Racine et Shakespeare*

Racine et Shakespeare begins in October 1822 with Stendhal's article for the *Paris Monthly Review* on an incongruity. In August, Penley's troupe playing Shakespeare in English was booed off the stage by young liberals, calling Shakespeare "un aide de camp de Wellington" (141).[69] Citing the incident, Stendhal calls instead for a liberal-Romantic alliance, as at Coppet or in Milan. That article becomes a first chapter. A January article forms the second, with a third chapter in February. *Racine et Shakespeare* I appears on 8 March 1823, in 300 copies. Over two thirds of the first

64 Refutation: 17.vi.1818; *Mélanges*, III, pp. 179–182, 193. Pellico, Monti: *Vie*, pp. 577–579, 596–599.

65 Stendhal's *Des périls* adds two new digs at Staël: *RS*, II, pp. 59–60.

66 "the immortal Tracy."

67 "Fall on this rabble." *Canaille*, Stendhal on Sismondi: *RNF*, pp. 313, 168; *Mélanges*, III, pp. 260–261.

68 "of rage of being nothing and phthisis." *Fluxion*: to Mareste, 30.viii.1820; *CSten*, I, p. 1036. See *Vie*, pp. 608–610 (March 1818), 612 (Stendhal's persona).

69 "an aide de camp of Wellington." Penley's troupe, publication dates: *RS*, I pp. xcv–xcvi; lxxvi, xcvii-ci.

chapter copies Visconti's *Dialogo delle unità* (1819).[70] I have shown elsewhere how Visconti reuses Schlegel, Staël, and the Milan Romantics; what matters is Stendhal's choice of the mediocre Visconti over his many predecessors and Stendhal's own unpublished pamphlets. His own manuscript *Qu'est-ce que le romanticisme?* would have served better, and with less plagiarism. The new pamphlet mocks the concept of 'illusion parfaite' [perfect illusion] with an 1822 news item, the Baltimore soldier who shot Othello on stage. Sadly, this contradicts Visconti's bizarre claim that moments of 'illusion parfaite' define a drama's quality (16–18). In thus copying Visconti, Stendhal flouts a truth repeated since Johnson, reworked in Coleridge's "suspension of disbelief" idea and used by Stendhal on the facing page.[71] Moreover, on 15 March, Fauriel's Manzoni translation—*Carmagnola* and *Adelchi*—appears in Paris with Manzoni's *Lettre à M. Chauvet* and Visconti's *Dialogo.* Caught on the hop, Stendhal adds an ambiguous stop-press credit, "Dialogue d'Hermès Visconti dans le *Conciliatore*, Milan, 1818;" yet in fact he copies the 1819 dialogue, not the 1818 one (10).[72]

What benefits outweigh these drawbacks? Perhaps Visconti's appeal to Viganò and music, which Stendhal admired—though Viganò vanishes in the French. Stendhal also enjoys playing with sources, in fruitful dialogue: Visconti's four real characters become two abstract symbols, "l'académicien" and "le romantique," and Stendhal resituates the dialogue at the rue Chantereine, whither Penley's hissed-at Shakespeareans had moved in 1822 (22). Like Carpani on Haydn, Visconti seems in fact the weakest thing in this chapter, despite

---

70 Visconti and Manzoni debts: *Il Conciliatore. Foglio scientifico-letterario*, ed. Vittore Branca, 2 vols (Florence: Le Monnier, 1965), II, pp. 95–102, and *RS*, I, pp. lxxiv-lxxvi. On Visconti's two dialogues and their borrowings, see Isbell, "Staël and the Italians."

71 On disbelief, contrast Stendhal's own *Qu'est-ce que le romanticisme?*, which opens with seven pages copied directly from Johnson's *Preface to Shakspeare* (1768): "*Il est faux* qu'aucune représentation soit jamais prise pour la réalité" (*RS*, II, 16). Coleridge: *Biographia litteraria*, ed. James Engell and Walter Jackson Bate, 2 vols (Princeton: Bollingen, 1983), II, p. 6. Stendhal's irony makes judging his position tricky, but Johnson, Schlegel, and Coleridge make a strong case for disbelief.

72 "Dialogue of Hermes Visconti in the *Conciliatore*, Milan, 1818." Pietro Paolo Trompeo, *Nell'Italia romantica sulle orme di Stendhal* (Roma: Leonardo da Vinci, 1924) [henceforth *Trompeo*], p. 110, is struck by Stendhal's Visconti note: "in quel primo capitolo la nota in cui è nominato il Visconti, in perfetta contradizione col testo, fu evidentemente aggiunta da Beyle quando s'accorse, grazie a Fauriel di non poter più appropriarsi un lavoro italiano ch'egli credeva noto a lui solo e a' suoi intimi."

Stendhal's improvements. Before, with bold talk of Scott's novels as Romantic tragedies, and of current French theater as epic or perhaps ode, but not drama, comes Stendhal's stirring appeal: "Je m'adresse sans crainte à cette jeunesse égarée qui a cru faire du patriotisme [...] en sifflant Shakespeare" (9).[73] Amid Visconti, Stendhal adds his own talk of "despotes gâtés par deux siècles de flatterie," and his superb summation that Racine's glory is imperishable, but art moves on: "Tout ce que nous prétendons, c'est que si César revenait au monde, son premier soin serait d'avoir des canons dans son armée" (12, 30).[74] After Visconti, the curtain rises for Stendhal's final barb: to read our own heart above the noise of habit, "il faut n'avoir pas quarante ans;" wry, since the author turned forty in January, but splendid propaganda for him, rewriting a war on 'foreign' art as one between generations (22).[75] "A bas les perruques" [Down with the wigs] was the cry at the 1830 *bataille d'Hernani*. These strong lines—trusting our hearts, artistic and political despotism, and Romantic perfectibility—Stendhal owes ultimately to Staël and her Coppet group.

By the second article in January, Penley's débâcle is old news. Stendhal's goal and public, however, remain unchanged: converting France's young liberals to his own *romanticisme*. An authorial 'je' is center stage, taking notes during Molière, reading the liberal *Miroir*, mocking the royalist *Bonnes Lettres*, and calling Louis XIV "le dieu de cette religion" (31–36).[76] Politics is thus already up front in *Racine et Shakespeare I*. With "Le Rire," Bergson *in ovo*, we pass from tragedy to Classical comedy, called "an epistle" (35). The chapter opens with Staëlian stress on German *sérieux*, here ironized. Stendhal quickly tours Europe, quoting Hobbes, picturing a Parisian dandy in the mud, and describing Didot visiting Parma (25–28). His core is A.W. Schlegel's fantastic comedy, discovered in 1814, "une imagination folle qui me fasse rire comme un enfant," but which Molière's ridicule prevents (32).[77] Stendhal compares this to music—his *opera buffa* theme—and his terms

73 "I speak without fear to those misled youths who felt [...] that whistling Shakespeare was being patriotic."

74 "despots spoiled by two centuries of flattery;" "We simply claim that if Caesar returned to Earth, his first concern would be to have cannon in his army."

75 "one must not be forty."

76 "the god of this religion."

77 "a mad imagination that makes me laugh like a child."

are those of his old Schlegel marginalia. The text admits, "la lecture de Schlegel et de Dennis m'a porté au mépris des critiques français," though as we know Stendhal never read Dennis and he despised La Harpe a decade before reading Schlegel.[78] This is perhaps less propaganda than a private joke (32, 176). Certainly, Stendhal is rarely more Schlegelian—"Molière est inférieur à Aristophane," he writes, while French critics are "impuissants à créer."[79] Voltaire and Molière don't make us laugh, Stendhal tells his readers—"si j'en ai;" watching *Tartuffe*, the public laughed just twice (31, 34).[80] Stendhal closes, after a dig at Byron, with *bonheur*, and the sullen English merchant at Tortoni's that he, like Baudelaire, imagines when Coppet thinkers say the future belongs to Protestant republican virtue (35–36).

Chapter Three deftly opens on maximum pleasure, respectively, for us and for our great-grandparents: Romantic and Classical art. Sophocles, Euripides, and Racine were all Romantic, giving the maximum pleasure to their age, as Bentham demands, and with the courage to dare the new. Imitating them today, however, is Classical (39). Visconti calls this vision *ilichiastic*. Lord Byron "n'est point du tout le chef des romantiques," Stendhal now determines.[81] He rejects Scott, Nodier, Legouvé, and Schiller, who "a *copié* Shakespeare et sa rhétorique" (41–42, 47).[82] More rigorous than Staël on the pleasure criterion, Stendhal defines value here not by the happy few, but by public success alone—thus, Pigault-Lebrun, Béranger, and the vaudeville. He mocks alexandrines, using *hyménée* for the rhyme, unable to say "la poule au pot."[83] How can Delille please someone who saw Moscow burn, as Stendhal in fact did in 1812? No people changed more totally than the French from 1780–1823, and art must change to match it—Staël's great theme (42–45). If we must use Shakespeare, Stendhal writes, just as Staël had, let us transform him. Stendhal's preface closely echoes this chapter: on Louis XIV and "pâles imitateurs;" on the alexandrine as a *cache-sottise;* on David and "la veille

78 "reading Schlegel and Dennis brought me to despise French critics."

79 "Molière is inferior to Aristophanes;" "impotent to create."

80 "if I have any."

81 "is not at all the leader of the romantics."

82 "*copied* Shakespeare and his rhetoric."

83 "chicken in the pot"—what Henri IV wanted for the French. Stendhal, *Souvenirs d'égotisme,* in *OI,* II, p. 497, conceals a self-referential alexandrine on this subject: "l'abominable chant du vers alexandrin."

d'une révolution semblable en poésie."[84] To close, after "le galimatias allemand, que beaucoup de gens appellent romantique aujourd'hui," Stendhal uses two Schlegel themes to reject the unities: conspirators plotting in emperors' cabinets and character development limited to thirty-six hours.[85] His remark on Othello's development, weak if done too quickly, more precisely echoes Manzoni's *Lettre à M. Fauriel*—hence perhaps the earlier footnote praising Pellico's and Manzoni's tragedies (47–48, 42).[86] Stendhal almost certainly saw Manzoni's *Lettre* in manuscript at Fauriel's, where he saw *Adelchi* by July 1822; the *Lettre* appeared a week after his pamphlet, on 15 March. He also uses it that year to answer Lamartine, and three articles, 1822–1823, express his ambivalence about Manzoni's theater. The *Vie de Rossini* also quotes seven stanzas of Manzoni's Napoleon ode, *Il cinque maggio*.[87]

Racine et Shakespeare I's 300 copies did not sell, but *La Muse française*, after July 1823, pushed 'establishment' *romantisme* toward controversy. 1824 is a watershed; despite Romantic praise for Charles X, Church, Academy, and State now align to condemn the movement, calling it "le protestantisme en littérature," and the *romantique=la droite* equation is broken, as Stendhal had desired.[88] In April, Auger at the *Académie* attacks Romanticism; in June, *La Muse française* folds as its editor Soumet joins the *Académie*, then Bishop Frayssinous condemns Romanticism for the Church. In September 1824, *Le Globe* is founded, linking Romantics

---

84 "pale imitators;" "the eve of a similar revolution in poetry."

85 "the German nonsense, that many people call romantic today." Schlegel themes: Isbell, *Confédération*, p. 315.

86 Alessandro Manzoni, *Tutte le opere*, ed. Mario Martelli, 2 vols (Florence: Sansoni, 1973), II, pp. 1681–1682, has a long, fine passage on *Othello* and Voltaire's *Zaïre*. Using Manzoni: *RS*, II, p. 259; *Vie de Rossini*, 2 vols, 1929, II, pp. 226–227.

87 Three articles: Stendhal, *Courrier anglais*, 5 vols, 1935, I, pp. 305–316 (April 1822), 337–349 (July 1822), 362–366 (April 1823). See pp. 315–316, 339–340 which cites the manuscript *Adelgizia* (*Adelchi*), though Manzoni "ne l'a pas encore publiée," and 366, announcing Fauriel's volume, conveniently, in April. *Trompeo*, 108–109, cites Mary Clarke to Fauriel on his friend Beyle: "Vous êtes un homme qu'il aime beaucoup à exploiter [...] je ne puis souffrir qu'il vous voie, car pour sûr il tirera toutes choses de vous." Stendhal in *De l'amour* published uncredited an Arab detail from Fauriel's own research.

88 Protestantism in literature." *Protestantisme: Mémorial catholique, March 1824* (in Jean-Jacques Goblot, *La Jeune France libérale. Le Globe et son groupe littéraire, 1824–1830* (Paris: Plon, 1995), p. 619). René Bray, *Chronologie du romantisme* (*1804–1830*) (Paris: Boivin, 1932), also remains useful.

and liberals.[89] During this period, Stendhal writes and rejects no less than seven draft chapters toward a new pamphlet. *Racine et Shakespeare II* eventually appears in March 1825, with both new goals and market. From the full title onward, Stendhal hangs this pamphlet on Auger—"Ni M. Auger ni moi ne sommes connus"—and on the *Académie* (53–55).[90] In the preface—a heavy satire which misrepresents Auger's call for national tragedy—Stendhal credits Staël and Schlegel, for once, as founders of Romanticism, along with Johnson (!) and Visconti, but in the mouth of their enemy Auger (59–60). Pragmatic propaganda here matches Stendhal's personal antipathies; if we want results, 'foreign enemies' like these will need concealment from a nationalist Parisian audience.

Part Two is over twice as long as the first pamphlet, but far less cosmopolitan—with less use of outside sources, fewer new ideas on literature, and less overall use even of Shakespeare, whom Beyle had loved since 1802. This again is pragmatic propaganda, and a careful double battle: Shakespeare for impact in the now-misleading title, which Stendhal keeps instead of finding a new one as we might expect, and French references in the text for Parisian sensibilities. This time, we are firmly based in Paris throughout. Stendhal has learnt from his initial failure, as his rejected chapters reveal. Several Shakespeare plays are named: *Richard III, Roméo et Juliette, Lear,* and *Othello* with its word *mouchoir* (81, 91, 144, 97). Stendhal's Classic cites *Macbeth*'s barbarity and public failure, though his final letter ends praising Hotspur (74–75, 150). The Romantic suggests "*Macbeth* en prose [...] abrégé d'un tiers"—Staël's theme—and asks, "Que deviendront vos tragédies, le jour où l'on jouera *Macbeth* et *Othello*, traduits par Mme Belloc?" (106, 116).[91] Twenty-eight million people love *Macbeth*, he argues, but critics will answer that the English have no "poésie vraiment admirable" (92).[92] Just one paragraph says the Classical-Romantic battle is "entre Racine et Shakespeare," but it also cites "*La Tempête* [...], toute médiocre qu'elle soit" (96).[93] A

89 *Le Globe* is founded on 14.ix.1824, *Racine et Shakespeare II* appears on 19.iii.1825: *RS*, I, p. cxxii.

90 "Neither Mr. Auger nor I is known."

91 "*Macbeth* in prose [...] shortened by a third;" "What will become of our tragedies, the day they perform *Macbeth* and *Othello*, translated by Mme Belloc?"

92 "truly admirable poetry."

93 "between Racine and Shakespeare;" "*The Tempest* [...] mediocre though it is."

cosmopolitan passage stands out: an ignorant critic thinks Shakespeare's Falstaff is a lord; others judge Shakespeare and Schiller "sans les avoir lus," Staël's theme again; the "jeunes libéraux" boo Shakespeare and the English, old history by now (139–141, 148).[94] But a long note follows, calling *Coriolan* a comedy; reviewing English Puritanism, their *cant*, their "bonne foi naïve et un peu bête;" and concluding, "il faut donc s'écarter beaucoup de la manière de Shakespeare" (144–146).[95] "*The table is full*, s'écrie Macbeth," the note adds in rejecting verse, but since Shakespeare is far indeed from prose, the very predicate of *Racine et Shakespeare* is thrown into question. Shakespeare serves Stendhal well against the unities; he serves for *mélange des genres*, but Stendhal rejects that—"Le mélange de ces deux intérêts me semble fort difficile;" he does not serve Stendhal's call for prose (144).[96] Stendhal has thus chosen another doubtful ally in his battles. To complicate matters, this is not the *Paris Monthly Review*, where Part One appeared, and Stendhal now makes special use of nationalist rhetoric. His new play suggestions include *Charles VII et les Anglais*, and *Jeanne d'Arc et les Anglais*, not once but twice, probably thanks to Barante's *Histoire des ducs de Bourgogne*, and his Napoleon play features a drunken English spy (125, 105–122, 152). Mentioning "la *Transfiguration* de Raphaël au Musée," Stendhal adds "Elle y reviendra," a patent sop to national outrage when Napoleon's pillaged paintings went back to their European owners (87).[97] America parallels England, in Stendhal's old Bonapartist shopkeeper theme. Philadelphia cares only for dollars—in these sad republics, "le *rire* est une plante exotique importée d'Europe" (118).[98]

The preface at the *Académie* mentions foreign Romantics. The Classic's first letter famously praises Staël—"Je ne vois réellement que *Corinne* qui ait acquis une gloire impérissable sans se modeler sur les anciens"—but other credits are less overt (74).[99] Lanfranc, who intrigues "avec toute la maladresse du génie," echoes Staël on Tasso; calling love a sentiment unknown to the age of Sophocles is a central topos at Coppet (82,

94 "without having read them;" "young liberals." Judging unread: *De l'Allemagne* II.i, "Pourquoi les Français ne rendent-ils pas justice à la littérature allemande?"

95 "naïve and somewhat stupid good faith;" "one must then distance oneself considerably from Shakespeare's manner."

96 "The mixture of these two interests seems to me very difficult."

97 "She will return there."

98 "*laughter* is an exotic plant imported from Europe."

99 "Really I see only *Corinne* which has acquired an imperishable glory without modeling itself on the ancients."

126).[100] The stage's 'fourth wall,' removed by the "baguette magique de Melpomène," is Schlegel's idea, as is the claim that the tragedy *Le Retour de l'île d'Elbe* would have "un seul événement" (147, 153).[101] Napoleon returning to despotism—not a common Stendhal theme—echoes Staël's 1818 *Considérations*, like the earlier comparison of France to England after 1660 (152, 107). Stendhal borrows *De l'Allemagne*'s objection to Gloucester's blinding on stage in *Lear*, but hides his source, changing Gloucester to "de petits enfants" (144).[102] Concealment thus causes error. Letters V and VIII have special debts to Coppet: Britannicus as "un peu niais et un peu plat" echoes Schlegel; Classical dramatists "chargés de fers," so agile that we think chains useful, rewrites Staël once more, as does the contrast of Classical talent and Romantic pleasure at the theater (103–104, 95–99).[103] The link here of comedy with despotism is an eighteenth-century topos dear to the Coppet group, with its correlative that liberty does not need art: "si jamais nous avons la liberté complète, qui songera à faire des chefs-d'oeuvre?" (119).[104] As a matter of fact, Stendhal's whole call for national tragedy dates from Coppet's three 1813 manifestos, but influence like that is too global to pinpoint, unlike more idiosyncratic details. Stendhal's rejected chapters reveal his labors, inviting an *étude génétique*: Schlegel's Louis XIV as a wigged Hercules will become an arch in 1825 (100, II 235).[105] The *baguette magique* survives in print; an attack on Racine, Schiller, and Manzoni goes, along with another on Staël, Chateaubriand, and d'Arlincourt; Manzoni's *Andromaque* passage departs, along with a note admitting the debt; gone are the Staëlian chapter titles on conversation, on Molière and society.[106] The Coppet topos, Molière the courtesan writing for a

100 "with all the gaucherie of genius." Tasso: *De l'Allemagne*, III, pp. 55–64. Love: see Edmond Eggli, *L'Érotique comparée de Charles de Villers. 1806* (Paris: Gamber, 1927), the text which launched this topos; especially pp. 119–138, on Coppet authors.

101 "the magic wand of Melpomene;" "a single event." Schlegel, Melpomene and action: Isbell, *Confédération*, pp. 314–315; compare *RS*, II, p. 244.

102 "little children." Gloucester: Staël, *De l'Allemagne*, II, p. 222.

103 "a little foolish and a little insipid;" "loaded with irons." Racine: Schlegel, *Cours de littérature dramatique*, II, p. 199: "comment se figurer le parricide Oreste sous l'image d'un amant soumis et dédaigné?" Pleasure: *De l'Allemagne*, II, p. 134: "La poésie des anciens est plus pure comme art, celle des modernes fait verser plus de larmes."

104 "if ever we have complete liberty, who will think of producing masterpieces?"

105 Wigged Hercules: *De l'Allemagne*, III, p. 348 resumes Schlegel: "Dans les tableaux et les bas-reliefs où Louis XIV est peint, tantôt en Jupiter, tantôt en Hercule, il est représenté nu [...] mais avec sa grande perruque sur sa tête."

106 Attacks, Manzoni: *RS*, II, pp. 246–248, 259. Dorothée Christesco, *La Fortune d'Alexandre Manzoni en France. Origines du théâtre et du roman romantiques* (Paris:

despot aiming to "éteindre le courage civil," is condensed, losing the long passage on exceptional women, while ridiculing despotism and enthusiasm—all the center of Staël's work—with its footnote reference to Staël's *Considérations* as "puéril," and to writing as a lance of Achilles which alone heals the wounds it causes.[107] That is *De l'Allemagne*'s metaphor, as Stendhal's ambivalent game with Staël continues. Closing, Stendhal pointedly dedicates this whole passage to Mme Roland.[108]

As leaving Staël and Schegel to Auger reveals, Stendhal is redrawing the road map of Romantic debate. His treatment of French news is equally manipulative. With his claim that "le romantisme a fait d'immenses progrès depuis un an," dated April 1824, we expect some mention of the *Muse française* or Ladvocat (124).[109] We get neither. As if the *Muse* did not exist, Stendhal talks of 1821's *Société des Bonnes Lettres*, "les moins redoutables des ennemis," citing Chateaubriand and Montmorency, no youngsters, and including Lamartine alone amid his list of liberal replacements for the *Académie* (125–127, 131).[110] Stendhal cites Chateaubriand, on religion as *jolie;* he talks of "tout ce qui est lugubre et niais, comme la séduction d'Eloa par Satan" (109, 99).[111] These Romantic fragments mark a censorship underscored by his brusque reply to the Classic: "personne en France n'a travaillé d'après le système romantique, et les bonhommes Guiraud et compagnie moins que personne" (76).[112] Guiraud edited the *Muse française*, whose authors the Classic of all people had put center stage, listing "Nodier, Lamartine, Guiraud, Hugo, de Vigny et consorts" alongside d'Arlincourt, the "vicomte *inversif*" (73–75).[113] Stendhal thus sidesteps rival *romantiques*, rather than confronting them; the Classic also talks of "des champions qui déshonorent la cause qu'ils prétendent servir"

Editions Balzac, 1943), pp. 49–50, collates Stendhal's Manzoni plagiarisms.

107 "extinguish civil courage." Molière the courtesan: *RS*, II, pp. 165–173, 187–207; 199 (*courage civil*). Achilles: Staël, *De l'Allemagne*, IV, p. 404: "le savoir, comme la lance d'Achille, doit guérir les blessures qu'il a faites."

108 *RS*, II, pp. 200–206, which ends, rather oddly: "Sous le nom de madame Roland, je m'indique à moi-même le nom de femmes d'*un génie supérieur* qui vivent encore." Staël had died in 1817.

109 "romanticism has made immense progress over the past year."

110 "the least fearsome of enemies."

111 "all that is lugubrious and foolish, like the seduction of Eloa by Satan."

112 "nobody in France has worked after the romantic system, and those fellows Guiraud and company less than anyone."

113 "*inversive* viscount."

(73).[114] On the Left, Ladvocat's massive 25-volume *Chefs-d'oeuvre des théâtres étrangers*, which Stendhal had praised in 1822, shows up in one footnote, an odd deletion of a high-profile enterprise whose aim was to provide that very "tragédie nationale en prose" whose absence is Stendhal's alleged reason for writing (81, 138).[115] "Faites, monsieur, faites," writes the Classic (102).[116] This pamphlet makes two opposite judgements of at least three established liberal or Doctrinaire authors—Barante, Lemercier, Jouy—but hiding Ladvocat's liberal contributors in a footnote on the reactionary Villemain's stupidity is even stranger (72–93, 76–136, 127–144). We might observe that Ladvocat, like Didot who is also ridiculed here, had, like Breme in Milan, declined Stendhal's offer to publish with him.[117] *Le Globe*, founded in September 1824 and still more explicit in linking Romantics and liberals as Stendhal desires, appears briefly in a letter dated—curiously—April 1824, disproving Stendhal's old argument that young liberals and the journals they favor will attack any Romantic innovation. The immense majority of this youth, he admits, has been converted to Romanticism by Cousin and the *Globe* (123). Stendhal dismisses his contradiction here, remarking that Cousin's class was banned. True, but the *Globe* was not. He thus fabricates controversy by inventing an opponent.

If Stendhal's allies get short shrift, his enemies may fare better. Indeed, Classical-Romantic dialogue structures the second pamphlet, as it had Chapter One of the first, as Stendhal rejects the monologic pronunciamenti the *Académie* favors. But this 'dialogue' means three letters in ten for the Classics, or five pages out of fifty, and Auger's opinions are libeled. Classicism is presented as part of the State's ideological apparatus; true when Staël said it of Napoleon, rather less true in 1825. "La dispute entre Shakespeare et Racine," says *De l'amour* in 1822, "n'est qu'une des formes de la dispute entre Louis XIV et la

114 "champions who dishonor the cause they claim to serve."

115 "national tragedy in prose." Ladvocat: *Paris Monthly Review*, April 1822, in *Courrier anglais*, 5 vols, 1935, I, pp. 305–316.

116 "Do so, Sir, do so."

117 Publishers: to Didot, 5.iii.1817; to Mareste, 26.iv.1824; *CSten*, I 856–860, II, pp. 27–28.

Charte."[118] Stendhal's approach is both astute and entertaining, two central merits of a political pamphlet. Let us not call it virtue.[119]

Meanwhile, Stendhal's own position is reinforced, part of a larger market strategy for his agenda. After a plug for Part One, still in stock, and for the new *Vie de Rossini*, he displays his liberal credentials to his target public (75, 78).[120] Even the brief *Avertissement* mentions Stendhal's taste for American political theories, amid Lafayette's huge U.S. tour.[121] Liberal shibboleths dot the text: a Jesuit in the *Académie*; Greek independence, twice; the Revolution, its children, and the retreat from Moscow; the *Miroir*'s *bonhomme* joke for the *Bonnes Lettres* members, twice; *Tartufe*; public opinion; Béranger, Courier, Cousin, those liberal lions; Constant and the Doctrinaires' claim that "la vie privée des citoyens doit être murée" (60, 115–145, 79–89, 72–126, 93, 132, 123–131, 153–155).[122] Stendhal adds liberal jokes: the list of new members for the *Académie*, the *Globe*'s favorite part of this pamphlet, and the phrase "Girondins de la réaction royaliste" [Girondins of royalist reaction] for the *Débats* (131, 136).[123] His two play sketches are heavily political, from Lanfranc in prison to Napoleon poisoned by the English (82–83, 153). Stendhal's long passage on censorship is pure politics and deeply ironic, not least his misunderstood remark that politics in literature is "un coup de pistolet au milieu d'un concert" (106–120, 107).[124] France's young generation is overwhelmingly liberal, Stendhal repeats in 1825 in the teeth of some evidence, also repeating that the liberal press shapes their opinions (122, 140–141). Even the metaphors link political and artistic despotism, as they once had for Staël; Stendhal talks of bayonets and the "pouvoir despotique" [despotic power] of habit, and of chains borne by the Classical tragedians (88–89, 103). He even borrows Staël's

118 "The dispute between Shakespeare and Racine is just one form of the dispute between Louis XIV and the Charte." Stendhal, *De l'amour*, Cercle du Bibliophile, I, p. 234; cited in Emile Talbot, "Le romantique et le/la politique: autour de *Racine et Shakespeare*," *Stendhal Club* 98, 15.i.1983, p. 228.

119 Dialogue: Michel Crouzet, "Polémique et politesse ou Stendhal pamphlétaire," *Stendhal Club* 89, 15.x.1980, p. 60.

120 Still in stock: *Racine et Shakespeare*, ed. Henri Martineau (Paris: Le Divan, 1938), p. xx.

121 Lafayette's U.S. tour: July 1824-September 1825.

122 "the private life of citizens must be walled off."

123 The *Globe*: Pierre Trahard, *Le Romantisme défini par 'Le Globe'* (Paris: Presses françaises, 1924), p. 40.

124 "a pistol shot in the middle of a concert."

voguish link of Romantics and Protestants, comparing Romantics and the *Académie* with Luther and the Inquisition, and calling Romanticism "la réforme littéraire" (53–55).[125] His draft review of Werner's *Luther*, a play made famous by *De l'Allemagne*, continues this Protestant theme (148). To appropriate Staël's Genevan attack on Classical despotism, in Restoration Paris in 1825, shows touching faith in her continued appeal.

The main beauty of Stendhal's pamphlet may then be dance and realignment. What new ideas does he bring? He is perhaps at his finest in dialogue with others, but some novelties do surface. His generational theme is striking; even the cover puts *Vieillard* and *Jeune homme* in dialogue to define the century.[126] Art, Stendhal says, should suit the Revolution's children, that old Staëlian argument. Meeting a man who prefers *Iphigénie* to Schiller's *Wilhelm Tell*, Stendhal simply asks how old his son is, a new twist; he reworks Visconti's ilichiastic topos, "tous les grands écrivains ont été romantiques de leur temps" (88, 92).[127] Classicism is sterile imitation of the dead—a Coppet topos—as is the following: Classicism, like feudalism, "a eu son moment où il était utile et naturel" (93).[128] Little interested in philosophies of history, Stendhal values brilliance above consistency; but is each young generation Romantic, or did a Classical period exist? Even the Romans were Romantic, he suggests (100). Like Staël and the Italians, Stendhal wants modern art for a modern world. Unlike most Romantics, Stendhal focuses resolutely on what today's public likes. For unity of time and place, Stendhal substitutes multiplicity of time and place, a world of relativity. Is this relativism absolute? He trades, in fact, one problem for another, marked by his talk of taste; we may end up "inintelligibles les uns pour les autres" (90).[129] "On a toujours raison," notes his *Réponse* to Lamartine, "de sentir comme on sent et de trouver beau ce qui donne

125 "the literary reformation." *Luther*: *RS*, II, pp. 223–228; *De l'Allemagne*, III, pp. 132–141.

126 Cover: *RS*, I, p. 51: "Le Vieillard.—'Continuons.' Le Jeune Homme.—'Examinons.' Voilà tout le dix-neuvième siècle."

127 "all great writers were romantic in their time."

128 "had its moment when it was useful and natural." Imitation: *Corinne ou l'Italie*, p. 177: "l'imitation est une espèce de mort." Feudalism: *De la littérature*, p. 145: "La chevalerie [...] dut être considérée comme un mal funeste, dès qu'elle cessa d'être un remède indispensable."

129 "unintelligible to each other."

du plaisir."[130] Rather than argue, Stendhal asks a doubter of Raphaël's beauty how stocks are doing (87). Habit's despotism can blind us to twenty-eight million admirers of *Macbeth*. It can make us find Lekain ridiculous without a wig, and Talma ridiculous with it (22). If the rules required monosyllables throughout, or acting with a limp, our habits would adjust: "Tout ridicule inaperçu n'existe pas dans les arts," he writes incisively (97–98).[131] The converse is what bores the public: *ennui*. Leaving the *Académie*, where "tout dormait," Stendhal remarks: "j'endors le lecteur. Allons chez Tortoni" (55, 67).[132] His 1823 *Réponse* echoes this relativity, with a remark normally misread as a simple bow to Cuvier: tender souls will find in the Jardin des Plantes amphitheater the refutation of Plato's system "sur l'identité du beau ideal chez tous les hommes."[133] Stendhal is actually referring to Sartje, the *Vénus Hottentot* dissected by Cuvier in 1817, and whose stuffed body, after her death, remained on public display in Paris until the 1970s. "Je n'ose," he writes, "conduire le lecteur à l'amphithéâtre."[134]

Thus, we end with the public, who stars in this pamphlet. "Le public s'obstinera," the short *Avertissement* says twice.[135] The Romantic admits the gulf between himself and the writers "en possession de l'admiration publique" (78).[136] Being Romantic, he claims, means "offrir au public les impressions dont il a besoin" (96).[137] As with boredom, proof is incontrovertible; Paris mocked the *roman historique* for twenty years, until Scott made Ballantyne a millionaire (122). The infallible people's voice is a prerevolutionary theme dear to the Groupe de Coppet, who thereby link art, politics, and economics. Stendhal once echoes this political slant; when Napoleon "trompe cette nation, il tombe" (153).[138] Elsewhere, his argument is market-driven, and justifies his praise for vaudeville (112). Success eludes Stendhal, however, despite this

130 "One is always right to feel as one feels and to find beautiful that which gives pleasure." *Réponse*: *RS*, II, p. 258.

131 "Any unseen ridicule does not exist in the arts."

132 "everything was sleeping;" "I am putting the reader to sleep. Let's go to Tortoni's."

133 "on the identity of ideal beauty among all men." Jardin des Plantes: *RS*, II, pp. 239–240.

134 "I dare not lead the reader to the amphitheater."

135 "The public will insist."

136 "in possession of public admiration."

137 "offer the public the impressions it needs."

138 "deceives this nation, he falls." Coppet's interest in public credit begins with Staël's father Necker and his *Compte rendu au Roi*, 1781—France's first public budget.

praise of it, and the motto to Part One, *Intelligenti pauca*, shows that his views are already ambivalent. French Romantic tragedy did not exist in 1825, and Stendhal could not know that his fight for prose drama was doomed. But it was certainly lonely, on Left and Right alike, and he can sound desperate—pamphlets are the comedies of today; forget "haine impuissante" and moaning "niaisement;" write your plays now, and perhaps in 1834, 1845, 1864 they will be stageable (83, 108, 112–114, 151).[139] The 1854 edition, in fact, adds a long footnote with a bizarre claim: "L'emphase de l'alexandrin convient à des protestants, à des Anglais" (215).[140] On a page which returns from the censor "toute barbouillée de la fatale encre rouge," Stendhal notes: "transformez vos comédies en romans et imprimez à Paris" (117).[141] Which, in the end, is exactly what he did.

4. Conclusion

Tout ce qu'il y a dans cette brochure est traduit de l'allemand ou de l'anglais.
Stendhal[142]

Recalling Stendhal's many debts may seem ungracious. But without them, we miss both the nature of his joke and his place within European Romantic debates; we lie to ourselves as we blindly cite propaganda. This pamphlet completes a dialogue begun twenty years earlier, binding cosmopolitan sources in an indissoluble mix—a mix ideology has preferred to call French, in 1823 and since. Stendhal repeatedly echoes Staël the Genevan on enthusiasm, dramatic interest, pleasure, exteriority, imitation, and Germany. A series of examples echo *De l'Allemagne*, and

139 "impotent hatred;" "foolishly." In 1834, Stendhal wrote this, rather tellingly, in the margin of a copy of *Le Rouge et le noir*: "Depuis que la démocratie a peuplé les théâtres de gens grossiers, incapables de comprendre les choses fines, je regarde le roman comme la comédie du XIXe siècle;" quoted in *Racine et Shakespeare*, ed. Roger Fayolle (Paris: Garnier-Flammarion, 1970), p. 43.

140 "The alexandrine's emphasis suits Protestants, Englishmen."

141 "all covered in fatal red ink;" "transform your comedies into novels and print in Paris."

142 "Everything there is in this brochure is translated from the German or the English." *Qu'est-ce que le romanticisme*, author's note: *RS*, II, p. 31. Jean-Jacques Hamm, "Stendhal et l'autre du plagiat," *Stendhal Club* 91, 15.iv.1981, p. 206 quotes the *Vie de Haydn*: "Au reste, il n'y a peut-être pas une seule phrase dans cette brochure qui ne soit traduite de quelque ouvrage étranger." His fine analysis traces Stendhal the plagiarist's desire to be caught.

the text conceals them; for instance, changing Gloucester's blinding to blinded *infants* in Shakespeare. He cites *Corinne* and the "puéril" *Considérations* instead. A.W. Schlegel is also manipulated, attacked explicitly while providing a framework for Stendhal's whole Romantic esthetics. Stendhal borrows Schlegel's objections to Molière and Racine, but also his complex theories of dramatic unity, of illusion and mimesis, of the mixing of genres and its function—the framework of his thought. This debt is marked in manuscript by repeating Schlegel's very examples from 1813: for instance, Louis XIV as Hercules in a wig. Schlegel reaches Stendhal in French translation; through Hazlitt's review; and through Manzoni's use of him in the brilliant *Lettre à M. Chauvet*; German, English, French, and Italian polyphony, a stew only a bold cook would try to separate. Stendhal also combines Manzoni, Visconti (to whom both refer), and the Berchet-Breme-Borsieri pamphlets preceding all three. In fitting irony, Stendhal's sources Staël, Schlegel, and Manzoni, traditionally backstaged in histories of French Romanticism, were in fact published in French, and in Paris: *language* evidently does not make a citizen, in the new age of nationalism which these four Romantics helped to found.[143]

Any fool can borrow good ideas from others. What matter here are Stendhal's reasons, his methods, and his results. From this chapter emerge, to begin with, Stendhal's pragmatic concessions and personal ambivalence, two friends of inconsistency. Part Two is a very different pamphlet from Part One, despite his move to link them, but they follow one pragmatic line: cosmopolitan references bid for sales in 1823, then yield to a nationalist framework two years later; personal contacts and (fabricated) originality guarantee the author's value, while wit and liberal shibboleths speak to his market; allies and enemies are manipulated as Stendhal redraws the Romantic map, trading real battles for fictional ones. Turning a foreign war into a generational one is particularly fine propaganda, but Part One does not succeed, and Stendhal must regroup. In 1825, Letter VIII's long footnote marks this retreat from Part One's Romantic ambitions, surrendering, in order:

143 Schlegel themes: *Confédération*, pp. 314–318; Chetana Nagavajara, *August Wilhelm Schlegel in Frankreich. Sein Anteil an der französischen Literaturkritik 1807–1835* (Tübingen: Niemeyer, 1966), pp. 229–240 (Manzoni and Fauriel), 263–265 (Stendhal). Staël themes: John Isbell, *The Birth of European Romanticism: Truth and Propaganda in Staël's De l'Allemagne* (Cambridge: Cambridge University Press, 1994).

horror on stage; Classical language, which was André Chénier's topos; *mélange des genres*; a bizarre unity of time, with a one-year limit on action; admission of Shakespeare's English barbarity; verse for everything but historical tragedy (144–148). The footnoted sentence begins: "Je voudrais foudroyer les intolérants classiques ou romantiques."[144]

Ironically, that same note talks of failure "dès l'instant qu'il y a concession apparente au public," and throughout the pamphlet, Stendhal signposts his own private failures (148). Art is useless for those over forty, he writes; this dialogue comes from Visconti; my readers, if I have any; Auger and I are equally unknown. Stendhal's opposite verdicts on the liberals his public admires may be less accidental than the signposts of a private game, like his plagiarism or his love for pseudonyms. How can a pseudonym plagiarize? runs an old defense of Stendhal, and the two concepts are indeed linked. In *Quelques idées italiennes*, Stendhal is equally happy to fill out his co-author's reminiscences in the same first person; he gives as readily as he takes. In the republic of letters, words, like ideas, are evidently common property, though I'm sure Stendhal smiled as he rewrote his borrowings or reminisced in his co-author's stead. This polyphony traces Stendhal's complex game of perspective—his dialogue with his own manuscripts; with the Italians, with Staël, Schlegel, and Geneva; with Paris liberals, Paris Romantics, and the establishment; with the British, his initial paying public; with Shakespeare and Racine.[145] Success and failure, Stendhal's twin poles.

Part Two suggests keeping Classical tragedy four days a week at the Théâtre-Français. That would be a parliamentary majority, and it is a remark rarely quoted (105). The man who writes, in 1818, "je suis un romantique furieux," then in 1824 calls Delacroix's *Scène des massacres de Scio* "médiocre par la déraison," has a personal history and agenda, but his case is also paradigmatic.[146] Romantics throughout Europe and

---

144 "I would like to blast intolerant classics and romantics with a thunderbolt." Language: *RS*, II, p. 250. Chénier's "Sur des pensers nouveaux faisons des vers antiques" was echoed in almost every French statement on Romanticism before 1830.

145 "the moment there is apparent concession to the public." Sandra Teroni's critical edition of *Quelques idées italiennes* should establish this detail.

146 "I am a furious romantic;" "mediocre through unreason." *Furieux*: to Mareste, 14.iv.1818; *CSten*, I, p. 909. *Déraison*: Stendhal, *Salon de 1824*, cited in Francis Claudon, "Stendhal et le néo-classicisme," *Stendhal et le romantisme*, ed. Victor del Litto and Kurt Ringger (Aran: Editions du Grand-Chêne, 1984), p. 197.

America use the Romantic label as a flag of convenience, and not one major figure commits to the label throughout their career. Fittingly, success and novelty stand for Stendhal in inverse proportion; Part Two benefits not only from the favorable *conjoncture*, but from Stendhal's pragmatic concessions. Yet despite these efforts, success remains relative—as Champfleury recalls, "Balzac se vendait médiocrement, Stendhal pas du tout"—and Stendhal abandons Romantic drama to Dumas, Hugo, and the *emphase* he detests.[147] Should we then adopt Stendhal's advice, turning for a moment from his pamphlet to what the people actually read—to Béranger, to Scribe, to Dumas? A bold populist suggestion, today, as when Stendhal first made it in 1823.

147 "Balzac sold poorly, Stendhal not at all." Balzac: J.F.F. Champfleury, *Souvenirs et portraits de jeunesse* (Paris: Dentu, 1872), p. 78.

5. Thoughts on the Romantic Hero, 1776–1848

Il prend envie de marcher à quatre pattes quand on lit votre ouvrage.
Voltaire to Jean-Jacques Rousseau, 30 August 1755[1]

Am I not a Man and a Brother?
Josiah Wedgwood, 1787[2]

1. Prelude: Manon Lescaut and Jean-Jacques Rousseau

Giacomo Puccini, that specialist in star-crossed lovers, premiered his opera *Manon Lescaut* in 1893, and the work is a large-scale and romantic production. It is instructive, however, to turn from Puccini to his source, Abbé Prévost's 1731 *Histoire du chevalier Des Grieux et de Manon Lescaut*—a novel narrated by Des Grieux who, it emerges between the lines, is both a criminal and a liar.[3] The term Jesuitical seems apt in describing a person who blames the weapon for his killing a man. It can be difficult to read Prévost's moral tale without the rose-tinted spectacles handed to us by two centuries of Romantic heroes, but a belief in Des Grieux's virtue—Puccini's position—is increasingly hard to sustain when the actual data of the story are weighed. Romanticism has, rather oddly, colonized the narrative; or perhaps, the original moralist narrative has metastasized

1 François-Marie Arouet [Voltaire] (1694–1778), letter to Jean-Jacques Rousseau (1712–1778), in *The Complete Works of Voltaire: Correspondence and related documents, XVI, March-December 1755*, ed Theodore Besterman (Banbury: The Voltaire Foundation, 1971), p. 259.

2 William Wilberforce (1759–1833) helped inspire Josiah *Wedgwood's* anti-slavery medallion of 1787, in white with a black figure, which reads "Am I not a Man and a Brother?"

3 Abbé Prévost, *Histoire du chevalier Des Grieux et de Manon Lescaut* (Paris: Flammarion, 1995), pp. 125, 211—Des Grieux murders two people and shifts blame away from himself each time.

 https://doi.org/10.11647/OBP.0302.05

in a later Romantic environment. French has a long tradition of flawed first-person narrators, including Chateaubriand's René and Constant's Adolphe—those two Romantic heroes—and it is thus all the odder to reflect on how easily Prévost's lesson in dishonesty became a love story for his successors. But Romanticism has that cultural weight. Indeed, the Romantic challenge to first-person narration reaches beyond French borders to Foscolo's Jacopo Ortis in Italy and Hogg's justified sinner in Scotland—a text that scandalized its first critics and was available only bowdlerized until recently.[4]

This chapter aims to lay out some common traits of Romantic heroes, and perhaps a sort of biography for them, established as we tour the nations of the West. Over the centuries, there had been historical precedents which Romantic painters and authors later celebrated—in Goethe's 1790 *Torquato Tasso*, for instance, or Schiller's 1804 *Wilhelm Tell*—but as the example of Des Grieux usefully reminds us, this Romantic search for precedents may involve a radical misreading of the person or text in question. Tasso's madness seems unlikely to have been a cause for celebration to his Renaissance contemporaries, while Tell's heroism was largely unmatched by other national revolutionaries before George Washington centuries later. Indeed, it is possible to see a pivot in history occurring in August 1755, as Voltaire takes pen to paper to express his thoughts to Jean-Jacques Rousseau: for that dean of the Enlightenment, Rousseau's text is largely gibberish. Wordsworth famously wrote in 1815 that "every author, as far as he is great and at the same time *original*, has had the task of *creating* the taste by which he is to be enjoyed."[5] It seems possible that Rousseau, in a series of epochal and best-selling publications, did just that. It matters then that Rousseau was, it seems fair to say, an unusually weird person—for instance, he wrote *Emile*, a detailed and popular treatise on education, while giving his own four children up for adoption to the foundling hospital.

Romantic heroes routinely seem to operate within a value system distinct from the society around them: they are code breakers. This is

4 Ugo Foscolo, *Ultime lettere di Jacopo Ortis* (1802); James Hogg, *The Private Memoirs and Confessions of a Justified Sinner: Written by Himself* (1824). Scandal: *The Cambridge Companion to British Romanticism*, ed. Stuart Curran, 2nd edition (Cambridge: Cambridge University Press, 2010), p. 207.

5 William Wordsworth, "Essay, Supplementary to the Preface," in *The Poetical Works of Wordsworth*, ed. by Thomas Hutchinson and Ernest de Selincourt (Oxford: Oxford University Press, 1964), p. 750.

the case of the self-created Rousseau, of Goethe's Tasso, and of Schiller's Tell. They are, to an extent, outsiders—Des Grieux and Manon, viewed retrospectively, may thus appear Romantic to us today as they depart from a liminal Parisian existence for the new and rather seedy colony of New Orleans. The heroes sometimes seem elected to a fate larger than themselves: they can be vatic, like Staël's Corinne and Vigny's Moïse, or isolated, like Moïse again, Tasso in his madness, or Ossian—that European success—extemporizing in the Scottish Highlands.[6] They are often in touch with passion, with the night side of human nature, which may be one reason scientists are uncommon as heroes of Romantic texts. Galileo had to wait for Brecht to put him onstage, while Mesmer and Galvani, Lavater and Benjamin Franklin, James Watt and Isambard Kingdom Brunel, also don't appear to have inspired Romantic texts to match their contemporary prestige.[7] Mary Shelley's Frankenstein merits a place in this overview, but it seems reasonable to argue that any urge to favor artists over scientists in the past two centuries has debts to a lingering Romantic value system.

Lastly, the Romantic hero can be perceived as one half of a pole, one which reflects an implicit contract in which the protagonist is engaged. This contract is between the protagonist, exceptional enough to have merited a plot, and the voiceless community they embody, which credits them, and for which they speak. In the Romantic age—one this study brackets by two revolutions, 1776–1848—that community is, by and large, the silent nation. Thus, Goethe's Tasso and Staël's Corinne both speak for the occupied and divided Italians, as indeed Schiller's Tell speaks for the Swiss, the Congress of 1787 spoke for the people of the United States, Petöfi spoke for Hungary, Tegnér for Sweden, and Shevchenko for Ukraine. Actual public success, as Shelley's remark on "*unacknowledged* legislators of the world" makes clear, has little bearing on this contract, though it did perhaps make Stendhal, also no best-seller, dedicate his writing to "the happy few."[8] This sociopolitical realignment—we stand at the birth of nationalism—is significantly threatened by counter-narratives only rarely during the long Romantic period: notably by the French *Declaration of the Rights of Man* in 1789 and

6 "Moïse" in Alfred de Vigny, *Poèmes antiques et modernes* (1826).

7 Bertolt Brecht, *Leben des Galilei* (1943).

8 Percy Bysshe Shelley, *A Defense of Poetry* (1840; Boston: Ginn & Co., 1890), p. 46.

by Marx's *Communist Manifesto* in 1848, two epochal texts that oppose universalism to nationalism's more tribal values. But the contract's staying power can be seen in Hugo's preface to *Les Contemplations* (1856)—"Ah! insensé, qui crois que je ne suis pas toi!" [Madman, to think I am not you!]—as in Thomas Mann's words from Nazi-era exile: "Wo ich bin, ist deutsche Kultur" [Where I am, is German culture].[9] A contract first elaborated around protagonists in texts and paintings here remakes those works' creators as they live and breathe. Any talk of 'the Romantic individual' is just one-half of the age's new esthetic coupling, a coupling grounded in Protestant credit theory and in the social contract succinctly elaborated by Rousseau.

2. German Lands

It is sometimes maintained that German *Frühromantik* separates itself from the preceding *Sturm und Drang* movement in its self-awareness. What *Sturm und Drang* celebrated naively, early Romantics inflected. This echoes Schiller's 1795 distinction in *Über naïve und sentimentalische Dichtung*, where he sees history marked by a shift in art from the former mode to the latter. In these terms, it is curious to open, say, F. M. Klinger's *Sturm und Drang* tragedy *Die Zwillinge* (1776), in which, as one twin returns home, the second runs to the other window to fire off a pistol.[10] All generations are, one would assume, equally self-aware, and their art reflects that truth. Klinger's energetic hero is not unproblematized; he is ironized in Klinger's very stage directions. *Sturm und Drang* does indeed have raw energy—one might think of Bürger's 1774 ballad "Lenore," with its refrain "Die Toten reiten schnell" [The dead ride quickly]; of Goethe's 1774 novel *Die Leiden des jungen Werthers*, with its suicide that enthralled Europe; of Schiller's 1782 *Die Räuber*, where Karl Moor becomes a robber when cheated by his brother Franz of his inheritance. Schiller later panned Bürger to suit his agenda, but just as we still read early Goethe and Schiller—and *Die Räuber* is clearly inferior to Schiller's later plays—so we might continue reading these artists, who opened

9 Victor Hugo, *Les Contemplations*, ed. Léon Cellier (Paris: Garnier, 1969), p. 4.

10 Friedrich Maximilian von Klinger, *Die Zwillinge* [The Twins] (1776; Stuttgart: Reclam, 1977), p. 27.

the door on German Romanticism a little earlier than we are sometimes told.[11]

It seems worthwhile to look at the shift in German literature of which *Sturm und Drang* is a symptom—that is, a move away from French Neoclassicism, the abandonment of the alexandrine, and a new kind of German or *national* hero—and see in this moment a watershed of sorts, with the arrival of the Romantic idea in German lands. It matters that Bürger's "Lenore" is already a ballad, like Brentano, and not alexandrine rhyming couplets; that Karl Moor is, like Nerval's later "El Desdichado," disinherited—indeed, reduced to an outcast life as a robber in the woods; that Karl has a code of ethics we are to admire; that Werther's tragic love story made Goethe's name and launched a European *Wertherfieber*.[12] This may not be *Frühromantik*, but to call it anything other than early Romanticism seems to misrepresent what is happening at the time, both in Germany and in the West. It seems clear that the elements of a German Romantic hero were emerging, if not well established, by the time of *Frühromantik* in 1798–1800, dates of the *Athenäum* journal. Let us describe this hero—who, as yet, seems pretty much male by default—and trace his progenitors.

Here we might recall three figures of the hero presented to the world by German lands during this period: Faust, Don Giovanni, and the (somewhat contested) figure of the philosopher seen in Immanuel Kant. All three predate 1798 and German *Frühromantik*.

The hero of Goethe's *Faust* (the *Urfaust* dates from 1772–1775, and the *Fragment* from 1790) sells his soul to the devil: he is an outsider, with a personal moral code. He is also flawed, indeed criminal, both in his treatment of Gretchen and of her brother Valentin—both die in large part thanks to Faust—but apparently redeemed by love. He is a seeker of the new and strange, and as the subject of a deal between God and the devil, he is elect. His experiences give him insight denied to those around him, which parallels Vigny's Moïse. He is Promethean—perhaps his most fundamental attribute. Ultimately, he is larger than life. It seems implausible for, say, Racine or Voltaire to have written a

11 *Panned:* Roger Paulin, *The Life of August Wilhelm Schlegel. Cosmopolitan of Life and Poetry* (Cambridge: Open Book Publishers, 2016), p. 571. Paulin also notes Heine's (false) claim that A.W. Schlegel attacked Bürger.

12 "El Desdichado" in Gérard de Nerval, *Les Chimères* (1854).

tragedy like this: the play is hard to imagine prior to Europe's Romantic pivot.

Mozart's and Da Ponte's Don Giovanni, in 1787, does not sell his soul, but in the opera's final scene, the stone Commendatore calls him repeatedly to repent, and Don Giovanni refuses. The later German Romantic E.T.A. Hoffmann—who composed an opera himself—argues in 1813 that, at first glance, the libretto offers a vulgar tale of a libertine and *bon vivant*. But he sees in Don Giovanni "all that raises man towards divinity," warped by our fallen world into a Promethean striving for love and passion by means of seduction, and then ending in a Promethean challenge for the stone statue to come dine with him.[13] Certainly, Don Giovanni seems possessed by a force he only partly controls; women find him irresistible; statues walk at his bidding; he defies Heaven in his final moments, as Leporello pleads with him to be less brave. Both Faust and Don Giovanni seem inhabited by life force, an almost electric energy which contributes to the larger-than-life impression they give, and which may well be central to their endurance as myths.

Finally, Immanuel Kant in his three critiques, 1781–1790, established three epochal things.[14] First, that sustained thought could elaborate a unified metaphysics, ethics, and esthetics independent of any established church. Second, that the material of our senses is fundamentally other than, but perhaps parallel to, the universe we inhabit: we may never know the things around us, but we do have their phone numbers, as was later said of subatomic particles. Indeed, a disjunction exists between self and world. And third, that the mind which does this thinking has the potential to achieve a certain celebrity. Prior to the Romantics, by and large, heroes in stories are not given to deep thoughts. It is common thereafter, and Kant's success likely had its part in that. It matters, for instance, that *The Cambridge Companion to British Romanticism* has a chapter on German Romantic thinkers; one thinks of the weight of thought in Wordsworth's long poems or, say, of Coleridge's *Biographia*

---

13 Ernst Theodor Amadeus Hoffmann, *Don Juan. Eine fabelhafte Begebenheit, die sich mit einem reisenden Enthusiasten zugetragen* (1813), in *E.T.A. Hoffmanns sämtliche Werke in fünfzehn Bänden*, ed. Eduard Grisebach (Leipzig: Hesse, [n.d.]), I, p. 70: "den Juan stattete die Natur [...] mit alle dem aus, was den Menschen, in näherer Verwandschaft mit dem Göttlichen [...] erhebt."

14 Immanuel Kant, *Critik der reinen Vernunft* [Critique of Pure Reason] (1781); *Critik der praktischen Vernunft* [Critique of Practical Reason] (1788); *Critik der Urtheilskraft* [Critique of Judgment] (1790).

literaria.[15] Moreover, Kant's German successors in philosophy stretch beyond the nineteenth century: in the Romantic era, Fichte, Schelling, Hegel, and Schopenhauer; after that, Nietzsche, Marx, Wittgenstein, and Heidegger. Just as Bach launched German music, so Kant, one may argue, launched German thought. And since Kant, critics have sought out German system in unlikely places—in the thought of Friedrich Schlegel, for instance, that master of the fragment.

Let us now look at other German Romantic heroes. After *Faust*, satanic pacts recur—in Chamisso's 1814 novel *Peter Schlemihls wundersame Geschichte*, for instance, where Peter foolishly sells his shadow and regrets it; in Weber's 1821 opera *Der Freischütz*, where Max makes a pact for accursed magic bullets—confirming the staying power of Promethean heroes compelled by circumstance to a liminal existence. Schiller, that Weimar Classicist who ceased correspondence with the mad Hölderlin, has several striking heroes in his tragedies: beside Karl Moor and Wilhelm Tell, fighters for justice and even for an oppressed nation, stand Joan of Arc, Wallenstein, and also Don Karlos, again an outsider to the system of values of his father's royal court.[16] Don Karlos is also a man whose ethics, informed as they are by passion, are presented as superior. There is some overlap between this worldview and that of Goethe in *Torquato Tasso*—about an outsider with a passion-based ethical system—or in *Egmont*, about another fighter for an oppressed and voiceless nation, the Dutch.[17] The great poet Hölderlin's epistolary novel *Hyperion* (1797–1799) describes yet another national struggle, the contemporary Greek struggle for liberation from the Turks. All these characters choose the common people over the elite, much as Faust chooses Gretchen. Nor is this world of alternative, passion-based, outsider ethics alien to, say, Heinrich von Kleist, both in his tales—*Die Marquise von O*, about rape followed by marriage, and *Das Erdbeben in Chile*, about adultery—and in his later suicide. In addition, his play *Die Hermannsschlacht*, written months after Prussia's defeat by Napoleon at Jena, stages the famous defeat of Rome by Hermann at the Teutoburger Wald. Meanwhile, E.T.A. Hoffmann's heroes are almost universally

---

15 *The Cambridge Companion to British Romanticism*, pp. 82–102.

16 Schiller: David Constantine, *Hölderlin* (Oxford: Clarendon, 1988), pp. 32–36, 81, 159. Johann Christoph Friedrich von Schiller, *Don Karlos, Infant von Spanien* (1787); *Wallenstein* (1799); *Die Jungfrau von Orleans* (1801).

17 Goethe, *Egmont* (1788).

liminal and weird, from his tales—"Der Sandmann"—to the 1819 novel *Lebensansichten des Katers Murr*, with its tormented violinist narrator, Kreisler. Hoffmann tends to contrast their struggles with contented, not to say fatuous, bourgeois interlocutors, like Tomcat Murr himself in the tomcat's verso-page autobiography.

It seems logical for tragedy to feature a good deal of this sort of conflict. Meanwhile, prose writings of the German Romantic era have other priorities. For instance, this period saw the birth of the *Bildungsroman*: Goethe's *Wilhelm Meister* invented the genre, while Novalis's *Heinrich von Ofterdingen* and Tieck's *Franz Sternbalds Wanderungen* were written in answer.[18] Let us note that all three novels involve the protagonist wandering around the (vanishing) Holy Roman Empire: they are, in that sense, all outsiders, and yet anchored in society because this journeyman experience, still available in German lands around 1800, was an important step in a master craftsman's training. The poet Eichendorff's short novel *Aus dem Leben eines Taugenichts* (1826), whose hero does nothing much to advance a career, is also living a liminal existence, but without the goal-driven plot of a *Bildungsroman*. We might add that Caspar David Friedrich's famous 1819 painting, *Wanderer über dem Nebelmeer*, seems perfectly at home in this tradition of liminality, election, and wanderings across German soil.

Many of these Romantic-era heroes, though outsiders, belong by birth to what, for lack of a better word, we may call the establishment: they are familiar with money and power, with deciding things, with being heard. That is emphatically not the case in the Grimm brothers' 1812–1815 fairy tale collections, where popular and juvenile heroes dominate, nor really in Brentano's and Arnim's 1808 edited collection of old German songs, *Des Knaben Wunderhorn*, whose protagonists are also mostly popular. One might add that these two collections of vernacular speech appeared after the French Revolution of 1789, the invasion of the Rhineland in 1795, and the twin German humiliations at Jena and Austerlitz. They appeared in an occupied Germany. It is worth following more closely how every German text after 1789 interacts with French and European events; for now, let us simply note the highly charged political environment, and how French cultural

---

18 Johann Wolfgang von Goethe, *Wilhelm Meisters Lehrjahre* [Wilhelm Meister's Apprenticeship] *(1795–1796); Wilhelm Meisters Wanderjahre* [Wilhelm Meister's Journeyman Years] (1821–1829).

hegemony prior to 1789—Frederick the Great published in French—was replaced by military and political hegemony soon afterward.[19] It seems no coincidence that Zacharias Werner's 1808 drama *Attila*, featured in Staël's 1810 *De l'Allemagne*, was read by many, including Napoleon's police, as an attack on the French Emperor.[20]

There is room, in German Romantic writing, for whimsy and the fantastic: this is true of the Grimms' fairy tales, of E.T.A. Hoffmann's heroes, and certainly of the protagonists of Jean Paul's many novels, with their debts to Sterne.[21] This is perhaps that *Arabeske* or free play of the imagination proposed for the novel by Friedrich Schlegel in his 1800 *Brief über den Roman*.[22] Yet German heroes of the Romantic era seem more often earnest than playful. The fantastic in this corpus typically echoes the eerie Gothic novel instead, while the Grimms' heroes tend to be resourceful and resilient, but not playful, even as children; Hoffmann and Jean Paul are unusual in this vein. There is also a certain German dialogue between enthusiasm and despair: comparing the 1797 *Herzensergießungen eines kunstliebenden Klosterbruders* and the 1804 *Nachtwachen des Bonaventura*, the contrast is glaring, a move from celebration to nihilism.[23]

So, some recurring traits emerge from this thumbnail sketch. German Romantic-era heroes are often outsiders, with a liminal moral code. They often, though not always, belong by birth to the entitled, though their sympathy is with the voiceless. They are sometimes disinherited.

19 Frederick the Great: *Oeuvres de Frédéric le Grand*, ed. J.D.E. Preuss, 31 vols (Berlin: R. Decker, 1846–1857).

20 Friedrich Ludwig Zacharias Werner, *Attila, König der Hunnen, romantische Tragödie* (1808). Compare Aimé Martin, *Le Portrait d'Attila, suivi d'une Epître à M. de Saint-Victor* (Paris: Aimé Martin, 1814), in John Isbell, "Censors, Police, and *De l'Allemagne*'s Lost 1810 Edition: Napoleon Pulps His Enemies," *Zeitschrift für französische Sprache und Literatur* CV/2 (1995), p. 168.

21 Johann Paul Friedrich Richter [Jean Paul], *Leben des vergnügten Schulmeisterlein Maria Wutz in Auenthal. Eine Art Idylle* (1790); *Die unsichtbare Loge* (1793); *Hesperus* (1795); *Leben des Quintus Fixlein* (1796); *Siebenkäs* (1796); *Titan* (1800–1803); *Des Feldpredigers Schmelzle Reise nach Flätz* (1809).

22 *Arabeske*: *Brief über den Roman*, in *Gespräch über die Poesie*, 284–362, in *Friedrich Schlegel II: Charakteristiken und Kritiken I (1796–1801)*, ed. Hans Eichner (1967), p. 331. Friedrich argues that the *Roman* makes no distinction between "Spiel und Ernst" in Friedrich Schlegel, *Kritische und theoretische Schriften* (Stuttgart: Reclam, 1978), p. 208.

23 Wilhelm Heinrich Wackenroder and Ludwig Tieck, *Herzensergießungen eines kunstliebenden Klosterbruders* (1797); Ernst August Friedrich Klingemann, *Die Nachtwachen des Bonaventura* (1804).

They are often exceptional—in energy, in passion, in intellect, in genius. They often display disregard for accepted social niceties or received moral codes. And from this place of election, they often work, like say Egmont, or Tell, or Hermann, or Hyperion, to raise up an oppressed and voiceless nation. The philosopher Fichte does so, for instance, in his 1808 *Reden an die deutsche Nation*. It is also worth noting that, almost without exception, similar topoi can be found in the French texts of Jean-Jacques Rousseau—who died in 1778.

3. France

In a sense, and with hindsight, everything in France in the years just prior to 1789 is prelude. This is teleology, of course, but it is also true to say that the French eighteenth century, in tandem to an emerging fiscal crisis under Louis XVI, saw increasing pressure to reform the social and political order, pressure for which Rousseau and, curiously, Voltaire are towering emblems. The project of neither makes sense without an awareness that they imagined France, in particular, different than it was, and worked day and night to achieve that goal.

The motto of Voltaire—in no way a Romantic—was "écrasez l'infâme," or *crush the infamous*.[24] His 1759 novel *Candide ou l'optimisme*, sent like a bomb into mid-century Europe, ridicules the inert array of social and religious superstition faced by its hero in his brisk tour of the West. But Voltaire, neither an atheist nor a republican, believed in reason—*les lumières*—to solve all problems, which explains his letter to Rousseau about walking on all fours. Because Rousseau was a very different person. It has been said of Rousseau that he was 'born without a skin,' and indeed his sensitivity to affronts verged on paranoia, as in his dispute with David Hume, who had given him refuge in England when pursued by the law. Rousseau wrote brilliant, seminal political pamphlets (*Du contrat social*, 1762), a best-selling novel of sentiment (*Julie, ou La Nouvelle Héloïse*, 1761), and quintessentially Romantic productions (*Les Rêveries du promeneur solitaire*, 1782), but perhaps his most telling opus is, in the end, his *Confessions* (1782). It is modeled on

24 Voltaire often uses "écrasez l'infâme" to end a letter—thus, to Jean Le Rond d'Alembert, 28 September 1763, in *Voltaire: Correspondence, XXVI, February-September 1763*, ed. Theodore Besterman (Banbury: The Voltaire Foundation, 1973), p. 420. Percy Bysshe Shelley cites "écrasez l'infâme" as epigraph on *Queen Mab*'s title page.

St Augustine, but differs from that saint in featuring a moment when Rousseau steals a ribbon and then allows a maid he likes to be fired for it.[25] Rousseau is prepared for a sort of self-laceration which would be alien to Voltaire, but with which the coming century would feel increasingly at home. It seems possible that the man brought something new and strange into the world, which is an almost impossible task. Furthermore, Rousseau pretty clearly wanted a different society—not necessarily the weird dairy-product idyll he presents in *La Nouvelle Héloïse*, but at the least a world of authenticity and perhaps empowerment, as *Du contrat social* proposes. And the French Old Regime depended on a series of convenient myths. When those began to be dismantled on the pages of the *philosophes*, it faced a sort of reckoning with a literate bourgeoisie who found ready-made arguments and narratives at hand here for reform, and more fundamentally perhaps with a courtly world that was itself more than prepared to treat these arguments as reasonable. It is no coincidence that on the night of 4 August 1789, the assembled French nobility volunteered to abdicate all their feudal rights; nor, perhaps more tellingly, that Marie-Antoinette, that ultimate check on Louis XVI's temptations to swing left, spent her days dressing as a shepherdess in the little cottage she had built on the grounds of Versailles.

This then is the world Beaumarchais stepped into, and he did so by giving the French, and Europe, an emblematic modern hero in *Le Mariage de Figaro* of 1778.[26] Figaro is, to begin with, powerless: he is a servant, and the count has his eye on Figaro's fiancée. But Figaro plans both to marry and to save the day, and what he does have in abundance is native wit. The play's subtitle is *La Folle Journée*, and it ends, like any good comedy, with Figaro happily married, like his parents (it is a double marriage). Here, we are deep in the French 'Preromantic' weeds, decades before 1830's *bataille d'Hernani*; but viewed *sub specie aeternitatis*, it seems hard to view Rousseau as anything other than an early Romantic figure, or Figaro as anything other than a sort of early and happy Rigoletto.

Two dates help to define this early period: 1776 and 1789. Louis XVI, conscious of French defeat in the Seven Years' War, was persuaded to help finance American colonial resistance to the British in the 1770s and

25 The ribbon story closes Section I, Book Two of Rousseau's *Confessions*.

26 Pierre-Augustin Caron de Beaumarchais, *La Folle Journée, ou Le Mariage de Figaro* [The Mad Day, or The Marriage of Figaro] (1778).

1780s. Funding a people's ousting of a king may seem shortsighted, especially with a king who a decade later was beheaded by his own people, but the French lionized Benjamin Franklin in Paris, and saw in the American war a soft power objective to match the hard power one of removing America from their European rival. The young Marquis de La Fayette crossed the ocean to be George Washington's aide-de-camp, while, like Ben Franklin, Washington provided France with a personal model for republican government and virtue. In fact, a vision of republican virtue developed in France from the 1770s on—as modeled in the new American republic, in the Dutch, Swiss, and Genevan republics, and for instance in the Roman republican paintings of David, such as 1784's *Serment des Horaces*. It contributed to the success of the Genevan Necker, French minister of finance, whose exile on 11 July 1789 was followed three days later by the Fall of the Bastille and his reinstatement. From early in the doomed reign of Louis XVI, there was a republican logic to French political discourse, making it entirely fitting that after three years of royal cohabitation, a republic was declared in 1792. But talk like this has its own momentum. The French Revolutionary army first marched beyond French borders with the battle of Fleurus in 1794, after two full years of desperate struggle to save their new republic from Europe's crowned heads. But those European monarchs were right to view the Revolution as a threat, since it was spread not only by guns and bayonets, but also by verbs and nouns, which are as light as air. The Revolution had sympathizers across the breadth of Europe, not least because it promised a voice, a meal, a fair deal to every subject of those benighted regimes. France spent five years after 1789 declining to proselytize, but that changed after Fleurus. And Europe awaited.

It is worth noting that France itself saw two more revolutions in the next half-century: in 1830 and in 1848. Asked in 1972 what he thought of the French Revolution, Zhou Enlai replied: "It's too early to tell."[27] From 1794 to 1815, France moved to occupy Europe. This was an epochal event, one that lies at the core of the West's Romantic era. What place, then, was there for Romantic art in Revolutionary or Imperial France? In 1790s Paris, the painter David staged *fêtes révolutionnaires* with hundreds of thousands in attendance: it is hard to imagine a more literal enacting of

27 Zhou Enlai famously said this to Henry Kissinger in 1972.

the people's voice in art.[28] In literature, alongside novelists of sentiment like Mme de Genlis or Mme Cottin, or indeed dutiful Neoclassicism like Barthélemy's *Voyage du jeune Anarcharsis*, stands Bernardin de Saint-Pierre, whose novel *Paul et Virginie* (1788) uses exoticism to make us admire an outsider love story, just as his *La Chaumière indienne* (1791) gave the world the Romantic word *pariah*.[29] Germaine de Staël had emerged to fame in 1788 with her *Lettres sur Rousseau*, and she was prolific, though often exiled from France, throughout this period, writing novels like *Corinne ou l'Italie*—a key moment for Romantic social contract theory, as her double title suggests—and treatises like *De l'Allemagne*, which praised occupied Germany over the triumphant French Empire.[30] Her final years brought *Dix années d'exil*, where she used Napoleon's exile order to recreate herself as a mythic figure. Chateaubriand, who had a long subsequent career, in 1801–1802 published *Atala*, with a Native American heroine, and then *René*, whose brooding hero presages Byron's Childe Harold.[31] And Staël's lover Constant—who had all Paris at his funeral in revolutionary 1830—published his tribute to their liaison, the 1816 novel *Adolphe*, starring a hero powerless to act.[32]

It is odd to see how little energy appears in the men in these novels: in Staël's Léonce and Oswald, from *Delphine* (1802) and *Corinne* (1807) respectively, but also in Constant's and Chateaubriand's Adolphe and René, or in, say, Senancour's 1804 Obermann. In the days of Austerlitz and the retreat from Moscow, this French passivity may well surprise. Staël's heroine Corinne, by contrast, is elect and Promethean, much as German heroes are, if not more so. Napoleon for his part personally worked to maintain Classicism in France, with some success; it is only after his death that a Romantic Napoleon emerges, in the 1823 *Mémorial de Sainte-Hélène*.[33] There is clearly energy in Revolutionary and Imperial

28 David: Mona Ozouf, *Festivals and the French Revolution*, trans. by Alan Sheridan (Cambridge, MA: Harvard University Press, 1988).

29 Jean-Jacques Barthélemy, *Voyage du jeune Anarcharsis* (1788); Jacques-Henri Bernardin de Saint-Pierre, *Paul et Virginie* (1788) and *La Chaumière indienne* (1790).

30 Germaine de Staël, *Corinne ou l'Italie* (1807), *De l'Allemagne* (1810–1813), *Dix années d'exil* (1821).

31 François-René de Chateaubriand, *Atala, ou Les Amours de deux sauvages dans le désert* (1801), *René* (1802); George Gordon, Lord Byron, *Childe Harold's Pilgrimage* (1812–1818).

32 1830 funeral: *Benjamin Constant 1767–1830* [exhibition catalogue] (Lausanne: Bibliothèque cantonale et universitaire, 1967), pp. 108–110.

33 Emmanuel-Auguste-Dieudonné Las Cases, *Le Mémorial de Sainte-Hélène* (1823).

France, but it tends not to reveal itself in contemporary French Romantic texts. For instance, during the Terror, the Girondin Condorcet wrote the brilliant *Esquisse d'un tableau historique des progrès de l'esprit humain* (1795) while in hiding from the guillotine—broadly an Enlightenment text—while André Chénier wrote fine, rather Neoclassical lyric poetry in an identical situation. Volney's *Les Ruines* is Byronic *avant la lettre*, but, like Mercier's contemporary *Tableau de Paris*, lacks a larger-than-life Byronic hero to front it.[34] Xavier de Maistre's 1794 *Voyage autour de ma chambre*, charming in its philosophical approach to imprisonment, lacks energy almost by definition. Margaret Waller's *The Male Malady* documents this curious French phenomenon, echoing on through Musset's 1836 *Confession d'un enfant du siècle*, which we may oppose to *frénétiques* like Pétrus Borel.[35]

After 1815 and Waterloo, the returning Louis XVIII—younger brother of the guillotined Louis XVI—continued official support for Classical art, while Romantic voices briefly fell silent. Staël died; Constant chose politics; Chateaubriand chose Neoclassicism and politics. Stendhal, who was later to fill his novels—*Le Rouge et le Noir, La Chartreuse de Parme*—with Promethean heroes, was still in Italy.[36] A new generation emerges in the 1820s, the days of *La Muse française*: Lamartine in lyric, then the novel, Hugo and Vigny in lyric, then the theatre and the novel.[37] Dumas too finds stage success in 1829, before his serious work of novel-writing.[38] Alongside these young Romantics are sympathizers—the slippery Nodier, Mérimée, Sainte-Beuve—and some who achieved fame later—Gautier, Nerval. Other successful contemporaries largely eschewed the Romantic debate—Scribe in theatre, Béranger in lyric and song—while

34 Constantin François Chasseboeuf, comte de Volney, *Les Ruines, ou méditations sur les révolutions des empires* (1791); Louis-Sébastien Mercier, *Le Tableau de Paris* (1781–1788).

35 Margaret Waller, *The Male Malady. Fictions of Impotence in the French Romantic Novel* (New Brunswick: Rutgers University Press, 1993); see also Abigail Solomon-Godeau, *Male Trouble. A Crisis in Representation* (London: Thames and Hudson, 1997). Joseph-Pierre Borel d'Hauterive [Pétrus Borel], *Champavert, Contes immoraux* (1833).

36 On Stendhal in Italy, see Chapter Four.

37 *La Muse française* ran 1823–1824. Alphonse de Lamartine, *Les Méditations Poétiques* (1820); Alfred de Vigny, *Poèmes Antiques et Modernes* (1826), then *Cinq-Mars* (1826); Victor Hugo was prolific already before 1830: *Odes et Ballades* (1826), *Hernani* (1830), then *Notre-Dame de Paris* (1831).

38 Alexandre Dumas, *Henri III et sa cour* (1829).

some worked in other fields: painters like Géricault, who died young, and Delacroix and Ary Scheffer, or composers like Berlioz. But looking back at French Romanticism's contribution to the world, it seems hard to avoid the conclusion that it is at its peak in the novel, despite warmed-over talk of Realism, and this mostly begins to emerge after a hiatus starting around 1830.

One short novel from the 1820s seems worth recording: Claire de Duras's 1823 *Ourika*, whose heroine is from Africa. Staël had put African heroines in short stories in the 1780s, but there are few other precedents for this step into otherness, this act of empathy and compassion.[39] Victor Hugo had red-haired dwarves as villains in his two early novels *Han d'Islande* and *Bug-Jargal*, while in *Notre-Dame de Paris* (1831) his hero is a red-haired hunchback: it seems possible that Hugo saw the flaw in his stereotyping there and overcame it.[40] Certainly, Quasimodo is an unusual hero, but then Hugo is an unusual writer. Quasimodo may be Hugo's most mythic creation, more so than Jean Valjean in *Les Misérables*. Dumas gave ten-year-olds the world over no less than three mythic heroes, despite his exclusion from the French canon: in *Les Trois Mousquetaires* (1844), *Le Comte de Monte-Cristo* (1844), and *Le Masque de fer* (1847–1850).[41] Eugène Sue, on the other hand, did not.[42] Nor, one might suspect, are ten-year-olds' dreams peopled by Stendhal's Julien Sorel and Mathilde de la Mole, by Balzac's Eugène de Rastignac or Lucien de Rubempré, or indeed by colonel Chabert, *père* Goriot, or *cousine* Bette, tremendous characters though they may be.[43]

What is true is that the early nineteenth century in France furnished a considerable array of novels—by Dumas, Balzac, Stendhal, Hugo—which have, since the forgotten Champfleury, often been categorized as 'Realist,' not Romantic, but which are filled with Promethean outsiders engaged in titanic struggle with impersonal social forces: "À nous deux

39 Madame de Staël, *Œuvres de jeunesse*, ed. John Isbell with an introduction by Simone Balayé (Paris: Desjonquères, 1997).

40 Victor Hugo, *Han d'Islande* (1823), *Bug-Jargal* (1826).

41 Alexandre Dumas, *Le Vicomte de Bragelonne: Dix ans après* (1847–1850), the final section of which is titled *L'homme au masque de fer*.

42 Eugène Sue wrote serialized novels to great success.

43 Marie-Henri Beyle [Stendhal], *Le Rouge et le Noir: Chronique du XIXe siècle* (1830) contains both Sorel and La Mole; Honoré de Balzac wrote *Le Père Goriot* (1835) with Rastignac, *Illusions perdues* (1837–1843) with Rubempré, *Le Colonel Chabert* (1829), *Le Père Goriot* (1835), and *La Cousine Bette* (1846).

maintenant!" cries Rastignac to the city of Paris to end *Le Père Goriot*. These novels do a tremendous job of peopling the dreams of those older than ten, who have seen perhaps how life can disappoint.[44] Amputating this corpus from the Romantic project makes little sense, denying as it does a central element of the work itself, not to mention the place of the novel in Romantic art as the French Romantics, and the West, conceived it. It also seems worth noting here the French habit of dating nineteenth-century art from 1830 or thereabouts and the *bataille d'Hernani*. Hence, the rather teleological word *préromantique*, which defines an entire corpus purely in relation to an absent Other, of which it could by definition have no knowledge, and the compendious Musée d'Orsay in Paris, whose vision of the nineteenth century it hosts begins at around that late date, effectively excluding a good third of the century in question—including Géricault, Ingres, Ary Scheffer, and the lion's share of Delacroix.

Finally, let us return to the century's two other French revolutions. We have seen how 1830 has been pivotal to the story of Romantic art in France. It also replaced one king with another, a Bourbon *Roi de France* with his Orleanist cousin, a *Roi des Français*. Yet the year 1848 was to prove perhaps even more of a disappointment. It began with the establishment of a Second Republic, forty-four years after the first one perished. That Second Republic lasted all of four years before Bonaparte's nephew 'Napoléon le Petit,' who had never won a battle, proclaimed a Second Empire with himself at its head.[45] History repeats itself "the first time as tragedy, the second time as farce," as Marx said of this moment.[46] The mood of the 1840s is captured in Balzac's *Illusions perdues* (1837–1843), perhaps his greatest novel; but for an acid description of Paris during this, France's third revolution, there are few more gripping scenes than those of Flaubert in his bleak follow-up to *Madame Bovary* (1856), *L'Éducation sentimentale* (1869).[47] Central to the age, in other words, is the image of revolt. It appears in unlikely places—dominating, for instance, Nerval's 1854 lyric sequence *Les Chimères*—but is nowhere more in evidence than in Hugo's 1862 *Les Misérables*.

44 Rastignac's words are on the novel's last page.

45 Victor Hugo, *Napoléon le Petit* [pamphlet] (1852).

46 History repeats itself: Karl Marx, *Der 18te Brumaire des Louis Napoleon* (1852).

47 *Illusions perdues* appeared in 1837–1843 but captures this mood. *L'Education sentimentale* in Gustave Flaubert, *Oeuvres*, 2 vols, ed. A. Thibaudet and R. Dumesnil (Paris: Gallimard, 1952), II, pp. 324–352.

Hugo completed the work, one where Jean Valjean steals a loaf of bread and is pursued for it through war and revolution, in self-imposed exile in Guernsey, before returning to France's Third Republic in 1870 as a *député*, not for the monarchist right where he had begun his career a half-century earlier, but for the socialist left. Victor Hugo, equally at ease in verse, in prose, or on the stage, bestrides nineteenth-century French literature as Voltaire did the eighteenth, like a colossus. Voltaire would have found him incomprehensible.

4. The British Isles

There is clear continuity between the Romantic period and what was once unfortunately called the 'Preromantic' period of the late Enlightenment. In these terms, we might open our survey of the British Romantic era with four texts from the 1760s destined for European impact: Walpole's *The Castle of Otranto* (1764), Macpherson's *The Works of Ossian* (1765), Percy's *The Reliques of Ancient English Poetry* (1765), and Sterne's *The Life and Opinions of Tristram Shandy, Gentleman* (1759–1767). Walpole's *Castle of Otranto,* which may have been written as a joke, thus launches Europe's Gothic novel, with its horror and its fantastical elements.[48] Macpherson's Ossian, a 'third-century' national epic evidently assembled by Macpherson out of oral fragments—just as the German Wolf in 1795 would argue was the case for Homer, or as Lönnrot later pieced together Finland's *Kalevala*—met similar European success as a northern and sentimental alternative to Homer's precedent.[49] Percy's *Reliques* restored the ballad to establishment approval—making, for instance, Wordsworth's and Coleridge's *Lyrical Ballads,* Brentano's and Arnim's *Des Knaben Wunderhorn,* and Almeida Garrett's *Romanceiro* possible, while opening the door to Heine and the brothers Grimm.[50] And Sterne's *Tristram Shandy* brought the free play of the arabesque into the novel—that central *motif* in German and indeed European Romanticism—along with a model for digression in plot that may for instance have shaped Byron's *blasé* and witty *Don Juan* in 1819–1824.

48 Horace Walpole, *The Castle of Otranto* (1764).

49 Friedrich August Wolf, *Prolegomena ad Homerum* (1795).

50 William Wordsworth and Samuel Taylor Coleridge, *Lyrical Ballads, with a Few Other Poems* (1798, 1800).

It is hard to separate the Gothic genre, whose Promethean heroes clearly have their own moral code, from the Romantic corpus, leading as it does to productions like Emily Brontë's 1847 *Wuthering Heights*. Heroes in revolt against conventional morality run like a red thread through Gothic novels, as through Romanticism, often opposed to heroines who appear less Promethean than them and more sentimental, indeed more grounded in reality: in Britain, Lewis's *The Monk* (1796), Ann Radcliffe's *Mysteries of Udolpho* (1794), and Maturin's *Melmoth the Wanderer* (1820) follow this pattern. Mary Shelley's Romantic novel *Frankenstein, or The Modern Prometheus* has such a hero without a prominent heroine. In France, Sade borrows from the Gothic genre in this period for his unpleasant tales, as Lafontaine does in Germany. Byron has learned from the Gothic in productions like *The Giaour* (1813) and *Manfred* (1817), and even in *Childe Harold*. One might also mention his friend Polidori's 1819 *The Vampyre*, the first vampire novel. These heroes, then, are not only outsiders in revolt against things as they are; they are flawed and often criminal, a circumstance which seems less common in the contemporary productions of the Germans, despite their satanic pacts, and of the Revolutionary French. Thus, James Hogg's brilliant *Confessions of a Justified Sinner* (1824) tells the first-person story of a man whose companion and mentor may, or may not, be the devil, and whose belief in Presbyterian election and predestination leads him, among other things, to murder his older brother. But flawed outsiders, even outcasts, run throughout the British Romantic corpus: Wordsworth's Idiot Boy and Coleridge's Ancient Mariner; Blake's Chimney Sweeper and Charlotte Brontë's blind Rochester in *Jane Eyre* (1847); De Quincey's opium eater; even, tellingly, Austen's misjudged Darcy in *Pride and Prejudice* (1813).[51] A touching footnote to this tradition lies in a group of contemporary outsider biographies: Robert Burns, Scotland's folk poet; Thomas Chatterton, the gifted poetic forger who killed himself at seventeen in 1770, earning mention from Wordsworth in 1807's "Resolution and Independence" and a play from Vigny in 1835; John Clare, the farm laborer who wrote "The Badger" and "I Am"—"My friends forsake me like a memory lost"—before his early descent into

51 Wordsworth's "Idiot Boy" and Coleridge's "Ancient Mariner" both feature in their *Lyrical Ballads*. Blake's "The Chimney Sweeper" appears in his *Songs of Innocence and Experience* (1794). Thomas De Quincey, *Confessions of an English Opium-Eater* (1821).

madness.[52] Keats has his place in this story, dying young as leader of the 'Cockney School,' and Shelley and Byron, born into the establishment, also came to live on society's margins and tragically die young, Shelley in a storm at sea and Byron at Missolonghi.

Ossian fits directly into that solitary, melancholy, sentimental outsider narrative, that vision of the expanded Romantic reading public. It matters that he offered Europe's emerging Romantics an alternative canon to the Greeks, becoming for instance Napoleon's favorite author. A great sweep of Europe's Romantic lyric, as we have seen, is meanwhile made possible by Percy's *Reliques*, in which the ballad is fundamental. The tradition reaches across Europe and across the decades from Bürger through Brentano and Arnim, or indeed Hugo's *Odes et ballades*, on to Heine. It seems fair to argue that in, say, the *Lyrical Ballads* of 1798–1800, Wordsworth's and Coleridge's narrators are often fellow travelers to their marginal protagonists. Sterne, meanwhile, in his digressive playfulness, opens the door to Jean Paul, to Friedrich Schlegel's *Gespräch über die Poesie*, to Berchet's *Lettera semiseria*, to Pushkin's *Evgenii Onegin*, to Almeida Garrett's prose fiction, perhaps as said above to Byron's *Don Juan*.

Interest in the Other shapes a good number of British long poems of the period, as discussed in Chapter Three: Moore's *Lalla Rookh*; Campbell's *Gertrude of Wyoming*; Southey's *Thalaba the Destroyer* and *The Curse of Kehama*; Percy Shelley's *The Revolt of Islam*; almost anything by Byron.[53] Clearly, there was an appetite for long exotic poems, often with an orientalist subtext. This may be less prevalent in contemporary women poets such as Charlotte Smith, Letitia Landon, or Felicia Hemans, the best-selling poet of her age; British women poets are mostly known for shorter lyric works.[54] It is perhaps instructive to contrast the exotic locations of Gothic and orientalist narrative, verse, and prose, with the British local color favored both in the first-person Jacobin novel of the 1790s—Godwin's brilliant *Caleb Williams* (1794)—and in the anti-Jacobin

52 Alfred de Vigny, *Chatterton* (1835).

53 Thomas Moore, *Lalla Rookh* (1817); Thomas Campbell, *Gertrude of Wyoming; A Pennsylvanian Tale* (1809); Robert Southey, *Thalaba the Destroyer* (1801), *The Curse of Kehama* (1810); P.B. Shelley, *The Revolt of Islam* (1817); Byron *passim*.

54 Felicia Hemans in *British Women Poets of the Romantic Era. An Anthology*, ed. Paula R. Feldman (Baltimore: Johns Hopkins University Press, 1997). But see the female British long poems reviewed in Chapter Three.

or nation-building novels which followed: Maria Edgeworth in her groundbreaking Irish novel *Castle Rackrent* (1800); Jane Austen in England, from *Mansfield Park* (1814) to *Emma* (1815); Sir Walter Scott in his Scottish novels like *Waverley* (1814) or *Kenilworth* (1821).[55] The fundamentally English Charles Dickens follows in this tradition, though his relation to the Jacobin/anti-Jacobin divide is complex: Pip narrates *Great Expectations*, as David narrates *David Copperfield*, but Dickens is hardly a Jacobin author.[56]

Perhaps the British radical tradition, 1789–1832, merits a closer look, given our focus here on compassion and the outsider as we consider the Romantic hero. The movement, with its roots in authors like Milton or Locke, continues in Thomas Paine, author of *Common Sense* (1776) and *The Rights of Man* (1791)—participant in two revolutions—whose funeral just six people attended. In the 1790s, it touches Godwin and Wollstonecraft, but also Charles James Fox in parliament and the young Wordsworth and Coleridge, who later became less revolutionary in sympathies. It touches Blake and it marks the dramatist and novelist Thomas Holcroft. It marks the Utilitarians, James Mill and Jeremy Bentham, who advocate among other things for prison reform and an end to rotten boroughs, part of a campaign eventually leading to the Reform Act in 1832. These are the years of William Wilberforce's campaign against the Atlantic slave trade, which ended in Britain in 1807. As the French Republic became an empire, the British Jacobin threat to the establishment ebbed, but radical thought did not vanish overnight, from John Thelwall and John Horne Tooke, tried for treason in the 1790s by Pitt's edgy government and then acquitted, to William Cobbett, author of *Rural Rides* (1830). There is a continuity to this tradition, which also marks the thought of Britain's second generation of Romantics—Byron and the Shelleys—as indeed it marks the brilliant William Hazlitt, the essayist Charles Lamb, or Leigh Hunt, founder of *The Examiner*. It determines the career of the satirist and bookseller William Hone, who won his battle against government censorship in

55 Jacobin and anti-Jacobin novels: *The Cambridge Companion to British Romanticism*, pp. 192–199. William Godwin, *Things as They Are; or The Adventures of Caleb Williams* (1794). Nation-building: Sir Walter Scott, *Waverley; or, 'Tis Sixty Years Since* (1814), *Kenilworth. A Romance* (1821).

56 Charles Dickens, *Great Expectations* (1861), *David Copperfield* (1849–1850).

1817 in a blow for freedom of the press. All these thinkers share a vision of practical reform, of a better future for all humanity; all are shaped by the events of 1789.

History frames a good deal of this Romantic-era production. The British eighteenth century saw Hanoverian ascendancy interrupted by two Jacobite incursions and the loss of the Thirteen Colonies. Initial enthusiasm for the French Revolution, challenged early by Burke, then dropped sharply after the declaration of the French Republic, the execution of Louis XVI, and British war with France.[57] This war lasted almost without interruption until 1815, financed in Britain by national credit and made sustainable by Britain's control of the seas, particularly after victory at Trafalgar in 1805, which ended the ongoing threat of French invasion. Against this backdrop, the anti-Jacobin novel plays out. Simultaneously, the industrial revolution and the enclosure movement were reshaping the British countryside: Blake the Londoner was not wrong to see "dark satanic mills" there.[58] The Nottinghamshire Luddite movement of 1811–1816 smashed the new machinery; protesters at St Peter's Fields in Manchester, 1819, were ridden down by mounted troops at "Peterloo." France went into the Revolution as the wealthiest state in Europe, yet the twenty-year war that followed made clear that Britain had access via credit to funds successive French states were denied, while the Industrial Revolution made Britain the most advanced country in Europe, if not the world, in technology and economics. Few are the British Romantics who celebrate these developments.

British Romantic painting, finally, has kept a certain cachet, from Constable and Turner to Fuseli and Blake. There is a gulf between the formal revolution of Blake and that of Turner, but it is worthwhile to compare them both with the work of a cartoonist like Gillray, who is closer to the Augustan tradition that Hogarth exemplifies. As in France with Ingres and Delacroix, as in Germany with Friedrich and Runge, it seems futile to say that either clear line or its absence defines European Romantic painting.

57 Edmund Burke, *Reflections on the Revolution in France* (1790).

58 *Poetry and Prose of William Blake*, ed. Geoffrey Keynes (Bloomsbury: Nonesuch, 1927), p. 464: verse prologue to *Milton*.

5. The Italian Peninsula

Italian Romanticism is in essence a Lombard phenomenon—outside Lombardy, there is Leopardi in the Papal *Marche*, but he began his career by publishing in Milan. It has been argued that Italian Romanticism does not exist—*Il Romanticismo italiano non esiste*, runs Gina Martegiani's arresting 1908 book title.[59] And in fact, the constellation radiating out from the Milanese journal *Il Conciliatore* produced a remarkably small, if impressive, body of significant work: two major novels, a few historical tragedies, a prison memoir, a short, brilliant volume of lyric poems.[60] Also, some elegant and important treatises. One reason for this dearth is Austria. Italy's Milan Romantics agitated for national independence from Metternich's Austrian repression, and in consequence were exiled or imprisoned, almost to a man: Pellico, Borsieri, Berchet, even Gabriele Rossetti, father of Dante Gabriel. By 1820, Foscolo, who was older, had already left for London, and Breme, at whose box at La Scala the Romantics met, died young. Not many Romantic movements have been more comprehensively killed in their cradle.

Let us look at this textual corpus and the circumstances surrounding it. In Foscolo's 1802 novel, *Ultime lettere di Jacopo Ortis*, the narrator and protagonist runs over and kills a man, conceals the crime, and then accepts thanks from the victim's family, fitting the Romantic pattern of flawed first-person narrators that runs like a red thread from Des Grieux through René, Adolphe, and Hogg's justified sinner.[61] Manzoni's later *I promessi sposi* belongs, like the novels of Vigny or Mérimée in France, or Cooper in America, to the quite different tradition of historical novels deriving from Sir Walter Scott's European success: it concerns Lombards under the Spanish yoke in the plague-ridden seventeenth century, with Spain standing in for the Austrians that Garibaldi was soon to eject from the peninsula.[62] These are two splendid novels, though *Ortis* raises interesting questions in ethics. Manzoni also wrote two historical tragedies, *Il Conte di Carmagnola* (1820) and *Adelchi* (1822), both set in

59 Gina Martegiani, *Il Romanticismo italiano non esiste* (Florence: Seeber, 1908).

60 *Il Conciliatore:* Isbell, "Staël and the Italians" reviews this milieu.

61 *Ultime lettere di Jacopo Ortis* in Ugo Foscolo, *Opere*, ed. Mario Puppo (Milan: Mursia, 1966), p. 391.

62 Alfred de Vigny, *Cinq-Mars, ou Une Conjuration sous Louis XIII* (1826); Prosper Mérimée, *Chronique du règne de Charles IX* (1829).

the Italian past and concerning heroic, but flawed, characters, like the proud count of Carmagnola starting work for the Venetian Republic, and various treatises. The prison memoir is Pellico's *Le mie prigioni*, describing his time in different Austrian prisons and quite moving in his faith-based acceptance of unchangeable circumstance. He also wrote four historical tragedies, including *Francesca da Rimini* (1818), based on Dante. And the chiseled lyric poems are Leopardi's, written and revised over two decades and published shortly before his early death. Leopardi also wrote considerable amounts of prose, notably the Pascalian *Zibaldone* (1898).[63] Foscolo and Manzoni put flawed heroes into their art, but in his memoir Pellico is himself very much an outsider—indeed, a prisoner, like Dumas's count of Monte-Cristo or Man in the Iron Mask. It takes a leap of compassion to visit here, and it is a leap largely unseen before the Romantic era. A generation earlier, Casanova's Venetian prison reminiscences, for one, are rather different in tone.

Other Italian figures left less behind for posterity—Giordani, Breme, and Berchet who wrote the lively *Lettera semiseria*—but it seems reasonable to argue that Austrian intervention had its part in this silence. Two foreigners also played roles in this Italian tale: Staël's 1816 article in the *Biblioteca italiana* is routinely cited as the launching point for the Italian Romantic movement, while Stendhal (the young Henri Beyle) came to know several of these Italians and tried in vain to publish with them. We might also mention Manzoni's *Lettre à M. Chauvet* (1820/1823) as we review seminal Italian Romantic texts. The text had its impact in France where it was first published, both in its own right and when plagiarized in Stendhal's *Racine et Shakespeare*.[64]

Finally, the bystanders. The poet Monti, slightly older, less tied to the group, and something of a political trimmer, features on occasion in modern lists of Italian Romantics, a reminder of how Romanticism and Neoclassicism intersect. The two playwrights Gozzi and Alfieri do not feature, and that seems a pity: the charming Venetian *commedia dell'arte* playwright Gozzi, author notably of *Turandot* (1762), was known in Germany and figures in A.W. Schlegel's lectures on drama, an exemplar of the free play of the imagination that Schlegel values in comedy. He became important to Stendhal for a similar reason. The

63 Giacomo Leopardi, *Canti* (1835), *Zibaldone* (1898).

64 On Stendhal, see Chapter Four.

severe Piedmontese tragedian Alfieri, a little older, is Neoclassical much as David is in painting, belatedly and in terms of Roman republican virtue. The sculptor Canova, who enjoyed European fame, is similarly Neoclassical in a way alien to the Rococo, while in music it is hard to describe Rossini as anything but a Romantic composer. The same is true of the great Verdi, of course, but that is later.

6. Eastern and Northern Europe

The map of Eastern Europe, in the long century between the final Partition of Poland in 1795 and the Balkan Wars of 1912–1913, was simple. Broadly, except for Serbia and Greece—independent after 1817 and 1832 respectively—the region was divided between Prussia, Austria, and Russia to the North and the Ottoman Empire to the South. Hungary gained equal status in the Austro-Hungarian Empire after 1867, while other nationalities and language groups of Eastern Europe—the Poles, Czechs, Slovaks, Slovenes, Croats, Romanians, Bulgarians, Ukrainians, the various Baltic peoples, and the Finns—were voiceless. This is the backdrop to Eastern European Romanticism, a *national* art almost by definition. Let us review the silent and unrepresented peoples first, then the speakers for nations which had a voice.

The Slovak Ján Kollár published his groundbreaking *Reciprocity between the Various Tribes and Dialects of the Slavic Nation* in German in 1836, but he also published Czech fairy tales and 615 Czech sonnets, while Karel Hynek Mácha, who died young, wrote lyric poetry. Mácha's well-wrought long poem *Máj*, also 1836, was judged to be too bleak, however—prison, parricide, dismemberment—to suit Czech national tastes. Mickiewicz, born in Lithuania, published his epic *Pan Tadeusz*—the Poles' national epic—in Parisian exile in 1834, alongside his fellow-exile Chopin. He wrote the short epic poem *Konrad Wallenrod* in earlier Russian exile, and the drama *Dziady*, completed after Poland's November insurrection in 1830–1831. In Serbia, the philologist Vuk Karadžić collected and reformed the Serbian vernacular, paving the way for a group of Romantic Serbian-language authors. Ljudevit Gaj did similar work on the Croatian language, followed in 1846 by Mažuranić's Croatian national epic *Smrt Smail-age Čengića*, about the Montenegrin war for independence. Romanticism in Romania arrived after 1848; but in Ukraine, the national poet Taras Shevchenko, who began life as a serf, published his first book of Ukrainian poems in 1840 and his Ukrainian epic *Haidamaky* the following year.

Bulgarian Romanticism between 1762 and 1878—the date of independence from Turkey—conforms to this book's revolutionary and national theses, featuring two saints who published in Bulgarian followed before 1850 by a lexicographer, Nayden Gerov, a folklorist and poet, Petko Slaveykov, and a revolutionary poet, Dobri Chintulov, who survived an assassination attempt and had to burn his manuscripts twice.

Petöfi and Vörösmarty faced different circumstances. Hungary already had a certain autonomy within the Habsburg Austrian Empire, though the Magyar language was contested—it seems that just 42% of the Hungarian kingdom spoke Hungarian in 1804.[65] Yet the two follow a similar path, with Petöfi publishing *János Vitéz* in 1845, a folk epic about plain John's love, exile, and tall tales, while Vörösmarty, in his 1825 epic *Zalán futása*, draws on Hungarian history for his matter.

Turning north to Denmark, beside the Romantic playwright Oehlenschläger—who appears in Staël's *De l'Allemagne*—stands Hans Christian Andersen. Andersen's fairy tales, like the Grimms', commonly feature resourceful children as heroes, who face an amount of suffering that may seem gratuitous—a Victorian plea for genteel compassion—until we recall that Andersen was sent off to a school for the poor by his mother at the age of eleven. In Bernadotte's new Sweden, which took Norway from Denmark in 1814, Tegnér's 1825 *Frithiofs Saga*, based on an Old Norse original, presents a Norwegian hero denied his bride by the king and sent to Orkney while the king burns down his home. Tegnér's metrical virtuosity—the 24 books each have a different meter—is offset by a certain sentimentalism and lack of depth in character, but Frithiof's dilemma is well realized, and he is an outsider hero in the best Romantic vein, a man in revolt—he burns down Baldur's temple—and with his own code of ethics. Goethe admired this much-translated poem.[66] In

65 42%: *European Romanticism. A Reader*, ed. Stephen Prickett, Simon Haines (London: Continuum, 2010), p. 41.

66 See *Goethes sämtliche Werke*, 20 vols (Leipzig: Insel, [n.d.]), XIII, pp. 115–116, "Frithiofs Saga" in *Über Kunst und Altertum*, on Tegnér's "alte, kräftige, gigantisch-barbarische Dichtart [...]."

Norwegian Romantic nationalism, again rather characteristically, after independence from Denmark in 1814, folklorists between 1840 and 1867 collected fairy tales in the Grimms' footsteps (Peter Asbjørnsen and Jørgen Moe), folk songs (Magnus Landstad and Olea Crøger), folk tunes (Ludvig Lindeman), and later, folk artifacts, while the linguist Ivar Aasen codified Nynorsk, a national language largely independent of Danish influence, from the speech patterns of Western Norway. Finnish national poetry opened with Lönnrot's reconstitution of the vernacular oral epic *Kalevala* (1835–1849), while in Estonia, Kreutzwald published his version of the related Estonian epic *Kalevipoeg* in 1853–1862. Common to these national traditions is a Romantic fondness for folk epic with folk heroes—*the people's voice*—and also a focus on the philological work involved in creating, like a Dante or Chaucer, a working national vernacular suitable for high art. This is a quintessentially Romantic enterprise; it is no coincidence that many Eastern European Romantics were polyglot.

Pushkin's splendid *Evgenii Onegin* features earlier in this book, but Gogol and Lermontov also deserve a moment. Gogol is often presented as a 'Realist' author—Soviet scholarship used the term somewhat indiscriminately—but that will not explain his tale where a man meets his nose in Kazan Cathedral and argues with it as it refuses to return to his face.[67] Gogol was not averse to the fantastic, not to say the macabre, and like Balzac, his 'Realist' texts such as the novel *Mertvye dushi* (Dead Souls, 1842) gain weight and clarity when seen to open onto a world of energy, free will, and consequence. Finally, Lermontov's brilliant Pechorin, that Hero for Our Time, leaves the bitter aftertaste that one expects from antiheroes or 'superfluous people,' as the Russian saying went. Like Onegin, he kills his friend in a duel; he is killed; Lermontov wonders if we might ask his opinion of the man, and says, "My answer is the title of this book."[68]

67 Nikolai Vasil'evich Gogol (1809–1852), "The Nose" (1836). "The Terrible Vengeance," in Nikolai V. Gogol, *The Overcoat and Other Tales of Good and Evil*, trans. by David Magarshack (New York: Norton, 1957/1965), p. 50; *Mertvye dushi* [Dead Souls] (1842).

68 Mikhail Iurevich Lermontov, *Geroi nashego vremeni* [A Hero of Our Time] (1840), trans. by Vladimir and Dmitri Nabokov (New York: Knopf, 1992), p. 68.

7. Iberia and the Low Countries

Turning to Spanish Romanticism, this study has argued that Goya's place in Romantic civilization may be more significant than that of, say, Rivas, Larra, Espronceda, or Zorrilla under Spain's Bourbon Restoration. But they deserve a look. Rivas's 1835 *Don Alvaro*, the Spanish *Hernani*, stars the child of a Spanish viceroy and an Inca princess, a hero born in prison, who successively kills all his beloved's male family; it gave Verdi *La Forza del destino*. Larra's 1835 *Articulos de Costumbre*, before his early suicide, reviews customs and aspects of Spanish daily life. It is both full of local color and national in its attention to what is characteristic in the folk. Espronceda's 1840 *El Estudiante de Salamanca*, a retelling of the Don Juan legend combining lyric poetry and dramatic dialogue, is Romantic both in its Promethean revolt and in its eclectic meter, reminiscent of Tegnér or Hugo; and we might add the reactionary Zorrilla's *Don Juan Tenorio* (1844), a drama which again retells the Don Juan legend. Both retellings have their debts to Mozart and Da Ponte. Espronceda had manned the Paris barricades in July 1830; meanwhile, Ferdinand VII's absolutist regime misread A.W. Schlegel in his Vienna lectures as reactionary and Catholic—he was neither—and extended its official *aegis* over this somewhat misconstrued Romantic vision.

Portugal's Almeida Garrett receives a section here on the prose memoir *Viagens na minha terra* (1846). He published earlier Romantic texts, including numerous plays and his *Romanceiro*—a collection of folk poems and ballads, both his own and traditional, in the tradition of Percy's *Reliques*—after his stay in liberal exile in France.[69] From the Low Countries, Conscience receives a section on the Flemish *De Leeuw van Vlaanderen* (1838), one of the hundred-odd novels and novellas he produced. In the young Kingdom of the Netherlands—no longer a republic after 1806—Romantic reference points include the woman author and historical novelist Geertruida Bosboom-Toussaint, the poet Willem Bilderdijk, who had tutored the French Emperor's brother King Louis in Dutch, Hiëronymus van Alphen, who wrote verses for children that are still taught in kindergartens all over the country, and Hendrik

69 João Baptista da Silva Leitão de Almeida Garrett (1799–1854), *Romanceiro e Cancioneiro Geral* (1843).

Tollens, who celebrated the deeds of Dutch history in a series of verse romances.

8. The Americas

In the new United States, Romantics seem to turn up in the northern half of the thirteen original colonies: Boston, Baltimore, upstate New York. Their work ranges from whimsical and folksy—Washington Irving—socially conscious—Nathaniel Hawthorne—nation-building and epic—James Fenimore Cooper—or solitary and freethinking—Henry David Thoreau—to grotesque and macabre—Edgar Allan Poe. Emerson shaped the New England Renaissance primarily as an essayist, though he wrote a good deal of verse, while Longfellow, like Melville, published later. There are debts to be mentioned—in Cooper, to Scott; in Thoreau, perhaps to Rousseau; in Poe, to E.T.A. Hoffmann and the Gothic—but Irving and Hawthorne seem in many ways quintessentially American. The United States was lucky not just in its founding fathers, but also in its first generation of canonical authors. They are a diverse bunch, as dead white males go, but united in establishing an American mode of speaking that would hold good over the next two centuries. It is then worth noting the delay faced by poetry in speaking with the same authority: Emerson's poetry does not, to my mind, match his fine essayistic prose; Longfellow is, in 1855's canonical *Song of Hiawatha*, perhaps more well-intentioned than stimulating for a modern reader; Poe as a poet is memorable but somewhat overripe and not prolific. The country had to wait for Dickinson and Whitman to find the same authoritative American voice in poetry it had found in prose a half-century earlier.

Latin America and the Caribbean parallel this story. The years between 1791 and 1826 saw the independence—under Bolívar, San Martín, Toussaint Louverture—of Haiti and all the region's mainland colonies, and indeed, in the ensuing decades, a variety of authors emerged promoting a national discourse in terms familiar to Europe. However, Latin America's Romantic authors mostly published after 1850, just as with Longfellow's *Hiawatha* or Melville's *Moby-Dick* to their north. Prior to that date, Latin American Romantic texts appear in Cuba, Brazil, and Argentina, but not apparently in any other Caribbean or Latin American country. Cuban anti-slavery tales include Gertrudis Gómez de Avellaneda's bleak novel Sab in 1841 (not published in Cuba until 1914), about a noble slave in love with a mistress who marries a lesser man, and Anselmo Suárez y Romero's *Francisco*, written in manuscript between 1839–1840, though also published much later, while José María Heredia y Heredia was outspoken in exile. In newly independent Brazil, meanwhile, a Romantic movement began in 1836, promoted by the expatriate poet Gonçalves de Magalhães. Other Brazilian poets such as Casimiro de Abreu started experimenting with national and Romantic topoi soon afterward, as, after 1840, did novelists like Joaquim Manuel de Macedo (*A Moreninha*, 1844), Manuel Antônio de Almeida (*Memórias de um Sargento de Milícias*, 1852–1853), and José de Alencar (*O Guarani*, 1857). In Argentina, Esteban Echeverría returned from Paris in the 1830s as a promoter of democracy and Romantic literature, which he helped launch there. He died in exile in Uruguay. The leading figure in mid-nineteenth-century Argentine literature was probably Domingo Faustino Sarmiento, later President of Argentina, notably in 1845's *Civilización y barbarie: Vida de Juan Facundo Quiroga*, a vehement attack from exile on *caudillos* and the Rosas regime.

9. The Drama

Throughout much of Western Europe, though less so outside it, the stage became a battleground on which champions of Classical and Romantic art faced off. This largely reflects the continued prestige of French Classical drama—from Racine, Corneille, and Molière to Voltaire—as a vehicle of French cultural hegemony prior to Revolution, Napoleonic invasion, and the discovery of Shakespeare and (to a lesser extent) the Spanish *siglo de oro* of Lope de Vega and Calderón. This is true early in Germany and in England (where Shakespeare remained a model), later in Italy and Spain—all countries influenced by French Classicism—and in France itself, culminating legendarily in France's 1830 *bataille d'Hernani* between Classics and Romantics.

German objections to French models roll on from Lessing in his theater—from his *bürgerliches Trauerspiel, Minna von Barnhelm* (1767) to *Nathan der Weise* (1779), a parable about tolerance—and also in his influential treatise, the *Hamburgische Dramaturgie* (1767–1769), through *Sturm und Drang* dramas with their array of outsider and even criminal heroes—Klinger's *Die Zwillinge* (1776), Wagner's *Die Kindermörderin*

(1777), Goethe's *Goetz von Berlichingen* (1773) and *Urfaust* (1772–1775), Schiller's *Die Räuber* (1782)—to the Romantics. A.W. Schlegel, in particular, is a brilliant translator of Shakespeare and theorist of the drama, notably in his 1809 *Vorlesungen über dramatische Kunst und Literatur*. But it seems arguable that German Romantic theater did not live up to these expectations, though it had high points, for example Tieck's dreamlike *Leben und Tod des heiligen Genoveva* (1799) and Brentano's sweeping *Die Gründung Prags* (1814). For gripping German drama, 1800–1850, one might look beyond the Romantic canon to Kleist in Berlin (*Die Hermannsschlacht*, 1808), to Werner's dynamic *Martin Luther, oder die Weihe der Kraft* (1807) and *Attila, König der Hunnen* (1808), or his wrenching Fate tragedy *Der vierundzwanzigste Februar* (1815)—later borrowed wholesale by Camus in *Le Malentendu*—to Grillparzer's fine Shakespearean tragedies like *König Ottokars Glück und Ende* (1823), Büchner's later and edgy *Woyzeck* (1836–1837), or of course the corpus of great historical tragedies—*Egmont, Don Karlos*—by Goethe and Schiller in their *Weimarer Klassik* period. Indeed, German-language opera in these years is equally pivotal, from Mozart—*Die Zauberflöte* (1791)—through to Beethoven's 1805 *Fidelio*, about freedom, Weber's 1821 *Der Freischütz*, about a satanic pact, and the works of Wagner after 1840. In sum, German dramatic output, 1750–1850, though memorable, does not seem to be found primarily within the established Romantic canon.

In the British Isles, Shakespeare never really disappeared, though Johnson did help to burnish his reputation with his 1765 edition and preface.[70] The late eighteenth-century theater still performed today—Goldsmith's *She Stoops to Conquer* (1773), Sheridan's *The Rivals* (1775)—tends, however, to be Neoclassical in structure. Other significant Regency dramatists include Elizabeth Inchbald and Joanna Baillie, the critically acclaimed author of the *Plays on the Passions* (1798–1812). Among the male Romantics, meanwhile, Blake produced no drama; Wordsworth wrote *The Borderers* in 1796; Coleridge wrote four plays, 1794–1817, notably *Remorse* (1813); Keats wrote *Otho the Great* (1819), which was a critical failure; but Shelley completed two very stageable and rather different dramas, *The Cenci* (1819) and *Prometheus Unbound* (1820), while Byron wrote several verse dramas, among them *Manfred* (1816–1817), *Cain* (1821), *Marino Faliero* (1821), and *Sardanapalus* (1821). In

70 Samuel Johnson, *The Plays of William Shakspeare* (1765).

short, it seems fair to say that canonical British Romantic drama pivots around Byron and Shelley, with their rebel, criminal, or outsider heroes.

The leading names in Italian eighteenth-century theater are Metastasio and Alfieri. The prolific Metastasio, dramatist and librettist for *opera seria*, did little to challenge Neoclassical orthodoxy, while Alfieri did—his tragedies more closely resemble the republican Neoclassicism of David or Canova. Besides opera and Neoclassical tragedy, the Italian stage also saw popular fare like the French melodrama or vaudeville and the Italian *commedia dell'arte*. The Venetian, Gozzi, was a champion of this last genre and a master of whimsical farce, as in *L'Amore delle tre melarance* (1761), which like his *Turandot* (1762) was later adapted into opera. Mozart's and Rossini's Italian operas—*Don Giovanni* (1787), *Il Barbiere di Siviglia* (1816)—also were enjoying European success just as Italian Romantic playwrights began to challenge Italy's Neoclassical orthodoxy, from Foscolo's three Alfierian tragedies (the anti-French *Aiace* of 1811 got him exiled from Padua) to Pellico's four historical tragedies and Manzoni's two, where the influence of Shakespeare is apparent, as so very often.

In Eastern and Northern Europe, new Romantic-era drama seems thin on the ground, with four major exceptions: Mickiewicz, Pushkin, Gogol, and Oehlenschläger. In Poland, Mickiewicz wrote the splendid *Dziady* (Forefathers' Eve) from 1823 to 1832. In Russia, Pushkin wrote the brilliant but unstageable *Boris Godunov* (1831)—there are horses onstage—and Gogol the evergreen comedy *The Government Inspector* (1836). In Denmark, Oehlenschläger, who is hard to find in English, had a career as a Romantic tragedian, and Hans Christian Andersen also saw success onstage. After 1830, Spain produced two new Romantic versions of the Don Juan legend, by Espronceda and Zorrilla, as we have seen, while Rivas in 1835 staged his epochal Romantic drama, *Don Alvaro*. In Portugal, Almeida Garrett wrote numerous plays; apparently no prominent work appeared in the Low Countries. Meanwhile, reviewing the Americas, it seems, somewhat remarkably, that not one major Romantic drama appeared there in the years 1800–1850. Not in the United States, not in the new Latin American and Caribbean republics. The stage does not appear to have been a locus of debate and activity anywhere throughout the formerly colonial New World, whose Romantic authors evidently had other priorities.

Finally, in France, the Neoclassical (or Classical) epicenter, things played out at their own pace. Though Shakespeare appeared in French in the 1770s, he had little impact, and the only prestigious counter-models to Racine and his successor Voltaire seem to be Diderot, in his brilliant novelistic dialogues like *Jacques le fataliste et son maître* (1785), and Beaumarchais in *Le Mariage de Figaro* (1778). Some early Romantics do experiment—Staël, for instance, moves between the 1790s and the 1810s from quite good Voltairean tragedies to Gozzian comedy, and to prose drama inspired, perhaps, by Tieck. Meanwhile, on the boulevards, vaudeville and melodrama draw audiences, and authors outside the Romantic ambit—like Scribe, both dramatist and librettist—have sustained success. We might note here the tradition of grand opera—Scribe and Meyerbeer's *Les Huguenots* (1836), for instance—which also has its part in shaping the Parisian Romantic-era stage. The 1820s prepare a sort of theatrical coup, with Ladvocat's 25-volume *Chefs-d'oeuvre des théâtres étrangers* (1822–1824) and broadsides like Stendhal's *Racine et Shakespeare* (1823–1825) or Mérimée's unstageable and quirky medley, the *Théâtre de Clara Gazul* (1825). The coup, commemorated in countless historiographies, was planned and executed in 1830, year of France's July Revolution, for the premiere of Hugo's Shakespearean tragedy, *Hernani*. Hugo's own *Cromwell* dates from 1827, and Dumas's *Henri III et sa cour* from 1829, but institutions matter, and the Parisian stage fell at *Hernani*'s opening night. Let us add that Vigny—*La Maréchale d'Ancre* (1830)—is a good dramatist, and the young Musset—*Spectacle dans un fauteuil* (1832), that fresh twist on a Romantic cliché, and *Lorenzaccio* (1834), that unsettling tragicomedy—a remarkably good one. *Hernani* rode on others' shoulders, which is only natural.

10. Romantic Women Writers: The State of the Field

Talk of the Romantic hero should not blind us to the 50% of the Romantic population who lacked a Y chromosome but produced their fair, though occulted, share of its art. While it is true that the role of women Romantics varies across nations during the period, it is also true that much brush-clearing remains to be done, in a variety of languages and traditions; compare the story of British Romantic studies over the past few decades, since the publication of *The Madwoman in the Attic* and *Romanticism & Gender*.[71] In the late 1950s, the Comtesse de Pange, President of the *Société staëlienne*, was informed by the series publisher that Staël would never appear in a *Pléiade* edition. Well, now she has. Other French women authors of the era—Olympe de Gouges, who went to the guillotine, Adélaïde de Souza, Sophie Cottin, Sophie Gay and her daughter Delphine de Girardin, Hortense Allart, Claire de Duras (the duchess who wrote *Ourika*), Marceline Desbordes-Valmore, Félicité de Genlis, the Swiss Isabelle de Charrière, the Franco-Peruvian Flora Tristan, Marie d'Agoult who went by the pen name Daniel Stern, and even the great George Sand—another pen name—continue to await sustained attention, and often even modern editions of their works. At present, there is, for instance, not one monograph in any language devoted to French women Romantics as a group. The German situation is similar, while beyond these three national traditions, the state of play is lamentable. Margaret Fuller is name-checked in America, but other American names before Emily Dickinson are hard to come by; and thus far, my research has turned up not one other canonical woman Romantic across Europe or the Americas, apart from Geertruida Bosboom-Toussaint in the Netherlands, who wrote historical romances, and the incisive and rather neglected Cuban abolitionist novelist Gertrudis Gómez de Avellaneda. Flora Tristan, socialist author of *Pérégrinations d'une paria* (1833–1834), published in French and in France. Researchers will never find, clearly, what they have not gone looking for.

For Britain, as noted, much brush-clearing has happened. Researchers have a better and fuller sense of the role of traditional figures—Jane Austen, Mary Shelley, the three Brontë sisters—with new editions of neglected works; Shelley's for instance. We have rediscovered Felicia Hemans, the best-selling lyric poet of her age, alongside Hannah More, whose *Cheap Repository Tracts* sold in great numbers in 1795–1798, or Ann Radcliffe, that master of the Gothic, or Fanny Burney, precursor of Austen and author of *Evelina* (1778), or Maria Edgeworth and Sydney Owenson, who helped to create in Ireland—with *Castle Rackrent* (1800) and *The Wild Irish Girl* (1806)—the 'nation-building' novel in which Sir Walter Scott later achieved glory, or indeed Charlotte Smith, who

71 Sandra M. Gilbert and Susan Gubar, *The Madwoman in the Attic. The Woman Writer and the Nineteenth-Century Literary Imagination* (New Haven: Yale University Press, 1979); Anne K. Mellor, *Romanticism & Gender* (London: Routledge, 1993).

helped relaunch the English sonnet with her *Elegiac Sonnets* in 1784, just in time for the male Romantics. This labor has radically redrawn the map of British Romantic discourse, reminding readers of what actually sold in the period—women's novels, for instance—and of their themes: a certain sensibility, for one thing, and good sense, something of the world long tied to Austen's Elizabeth Bennet, in opposition perhaps to Darcy, that more 'Romantic' character she comes to love. We have, in short, discovered a missing half of the British Romantic universe.

This labor of discovery and documentation has yet to be done for France, despite the names here proffered. What ties Duras to Sand or to Tristan, Staël to Cottin or to Desbordes-Valmore? The question is fundamental and has yet to be answered. Genlis for instance detested Staël, her younger rival. The group is not without its sentimental romances, but that is hardly definitional of it: Gay is witty, Desbordes-Valmore a gifted poet; Duras is in her own way revolutionary; Staël like Tristan is revolutionary to her core, living in exile and among the small handful of Romantics anywhere to enjoy international fame.[72] Sand moved over the years and over her substantial output from novels of revolt—*Indiana, Lélia*—to subtle, symphonic work anchored, like Thomas Hardy's in Wessex, in the Berry countryside she knew and loved—like *Les Maîtres-sonneurs*, where the hero may, once again, have sold his soul to the devil.[73] The French critical tradition frankly has not been without its sexism; Staël now appears in a *Pléiade* volume, but other important French women Romantics still feature on my shelves—Sophie Cottin, Adélaïde de Souza, Delphine de Girardin—in worn old Second Empire editions.

In German lands, the situation is more complicated. For some time now, scholarship has name-checked women Romantic authors who played second fiddle to men in one way or another: Rahel Varnhagen hosted a salon, like many others; Bettina von Arnim made her name by publishing an edited version of her correspondence with Goethe in whose title she calls herself "ein Kind," *a child*.[74] Other German women Romantics deserve sustained attention: Caroline Schlegel-Schelling, Dorothea von Schlegel, Annette von Droste-Hülshoff, Sophie Mereau,

72 See my monograph *The First European: Staël, Romanticism, and Revolution, 1786–1830*, forthcoming with Cambridge University Press.

73 George Sand, *Les Maîtres Sonneurs* (Paris: Gallimard, 1979), pp. 160–161.

74 Bettina von Arnim, *Goethes Briefwechsel mit einem Kinde* (1835).

Karoline von Günderrode, and the prolific Caroline de La Motte-Fouqué. This substantial group remains understudied, compared, say, with the excellent multivolume critical editions of their male counterparts.

As noted, the only other canonical women Romantics I have identified, across Europe and the Americas, are Margaret Fuller—'the Yankee Corinna'—the Dutch novelist Geertruida Bosboom-Toussaint, and the Cuban abolitionist writer Gertrudis Gómez de Avellaneda. There are surely others, Flora Tristan for instance (who wrote in French). Certainly, there are memoirists deserving attention, like France's Adèle de Boigne or Henriette-Lucy de La Tour du Pin; they are doubtless common throughout the West, since, like correspondence or translation, this genre was for centuries acceptable female discourse. Pushkin's Tatiana thus famously writes Onegin a letter.[75] Similarly, the memoirs of Marie-Antoinette exist, and many others will be awaiting study. Fanny Burney's memoirs describe her reading Staël's *De l'Allemagne*: these are very interesting moments, both in Romantic reader-response theory and in women's studies.[76] It may be trite to say there is much to be done, but after two centuries of largely uninterrupted male conversation, in a variety of languages, it seems *à propos* to hand over the microphone.

Finally, what legacy might women Romantics set alongside that of the men who, as yet, continue to be foregrounded? For one, Anne Mellor might argue for a legacy of common sense tempered by sensibility, as in the evergreen Jane Austen. There is also a sort of Heathcliff-Rochester counter-tradition, rooted in Radcliffe and the Brontës, which leads directly to modern romance novels, or 'bodice-rippers' as they have been called, which sell in their millions. This tradition is radically different, but each has its place in our twenty-first century. It seems clear that while the Romantic era is not short of larger-than-life heroines created by women—one thinks of Staël's Corinne, who is all Italy—still, any view we form about silence and societal pressure, for instance, shaping female Romantic discourse, will, for the time being, be necessarily provisional. The multivolume Belknap *History of Private Life* finds ways

75 Alexander Pushkin, *Eugene Onegin. A Novel in Verse*, trans. by Babette Deutsch (New York: Dover, 1943/1998), pp. 53–55.

76 Fanny Burney: *Diary and Letters of Madame d'Arblay* [Fanny Burney], ed. C. Barrett, rev. A. Dobson, 6 vols (London 1904–1905), VI, p. 98: "Such acuteness of thought, such vivacity of ideas, and such brilliancy of expression, I know not where I have met before. I often lay the book down to enjoy for a considerable time a single sentence."

to make this point, as does modern scholarship on women's contested place in the French Revolution. The story is waiting, across the Western world, in letters, memoirs, and texts intended for and often having seen publication, though later buried by received opinion and prejudice, and now unfortunately neglected or forgotten. That story should be told.[77]

11. Conclusion

As we consider the various 'Romantic heroes' who peopled the West, the first thing to say is perhaps this: in a world where Des Grieux or Rousseau, for instance, can serve as arbiters of a higher moral code, our moral compass is visibly defective. And so, the question is: how did this happen? Or failing that, what is the evolutionary payoff for this sad state of affairs?

The answer, I think, lies in empathy. Empathy requires us to step out of our comfort zone and see others in their difference: Pellico in prison, Quasimodo in his cathedral, Clare in his struggles up from farm work and down again into madness. It is quite in keeping for Goethe to devote a play to the mad Tasso, and Vigny to the suicidal Chatterton. The Enlightenment, we may argue, found comfort in encountering others similar to ourselves; the Romantics, recognizing perhaps the relativity of taste, made allowances for others to be quite different, even outcasts, like the Cuban Sab—and then made heroes and role models of them. It is curious, in that era of somewhat tribal national art, to find this drumbeat of empathy running through the canonical texts, but it seems hard to see a better explanation for the troubled heroes who recur endlessly from Ossian to Jean Valjean. Stretching from Russia to Argentina, these figures somehow stand outside the social order—Karl Moor, Egmont, and Faust; Corinne, Adolphe, Julien Sorel and Rastignac, Monte-Cristo and Quasimodo; Childe Harold, Frankenstein and his creature, Percy Shelley's Prometheus, even Austen's Darcy; Jacopo Ortis, Carmagnola,

77 *A History of Private Life. From the Fires of Revolution to the Great War*, ed. by Michelle Perrot, trans. by Arthur Goldhammer (Cambridge, MA: Belknap, 1990). *Women in Revolutionary Paris 1789–1795*, ed. and trans. by Darlene Gay Levy, Harriet Branson Applewhite, and Mary Durham Johnson (Urbana: University of Illinois Press, 1980); Olwen H. Hufton, *Women and the Limits of Citizenship in the French Revolution* (Toronto: University of Toronto Press, 1990); *Rebel Daughters. Women and the French Revolution*, ed. Sara E. Melzer and Leslie W. Rabine (Oxford: Oxford University Press, 1992).

Pellico himself; Pechorin and Onegin; Frithiof, Almeida Garrett, Natty Bumppo, and Hester Prynne. In that space of exile, they rely on a personal and different moral code to guide their actions. They are, profoundly, individuals and unique. Furthermore, in order to present characters from outside the social pale, it is convenient to present them as somehow criminal—actually criminal, like Jean Valjean and Pellico, or allegedly so, like Caleb Williams and Frankenstein, or indeed born in prison, like Rivas's Don Alvaro. And thereby the social order that condemns these heroes is held up to judgment.

Beyond the myriad of local national traditions, a handful of pan-Western models stand out. After all, only a few Romantics achieved success beyond their national borders. Rousseau with *La Nouvelle Héloïse*; Macpherson with Ossian; Goethe with *Werther*; Staël with *Corinne*; Byron with *Childe Harold*; Scott with *Waverley*—it is a short list. In this short list, certain themes recur: authenticity and melancholy; national identity; a certain compromising of the hero. It is thus common to find heroes who are in some way flawed or failed: René, Obermann, Ortis; Hogg's justified sinner; Onegin, Pechorin, the narrators of Hoffmann or Poe. And this theme, somewhat notoriously, runs through a series of Romantic biographies: Byron, Shelley, Keats; De Quincey and Coleridge; the Brontës; Rousseau and Nerval; Hölderlin, Kleist, Schiller, Hoffmann; Heine; Breme, Leopardi, Pellico; Poe; Pushkin and Lermontov—all these authors faced drugs, madness, scandal, and/or an early death. Multiple Romantics met with scandal or rejection, and others chose exile—Foscolo, Hugo, Heine, Byron—or endured it—Pushkin, Mickiewicz, Staël, Almeida Garrett, Echeverría, Sarmiento. It seems unsurprising that such lives would produce such art, with empathy as a red thread running through it, from Blake or Wordsworth to Hugo or Longfellow. This is the world of Wedgwood's famous abolitionist medallion— "Am I not a Man and a Brother?"—as of Duras's short African novel *Ourika*, duchess that she was. In France, Napoleon and Chateaubriand are conveniently written *post hoc* into this Romantic narrative of suffering and compassion, Napoleon in Las Cases's 1823 *Mémorial de Sainte-Hélène*, and Chateaubriand, by the man himself, in his 1848 *Mémoires d'Outre-Tombe*.

What does it mean to see these figures as Romantic? The term is perhaps irrelevant; but beyond its function as coin of the realm—with precisely the value that any coin has—we may note its etymology in romance and in vernacular or popular speech, two elements fundamental to what this study calls Romantic art. So then, as a genre, romance differs from epic in having more scope for love and sentiment; in having protagonists who are less grandiose; in its closeness to song. Unlike epic, it favors stanzaic meters, as in Petöfi, Byron, or Pushkin. Several Romantic 'folk epics' have romance elements, such as the love story told in Tegnér's modernized Old Norse *Frithiofs Saga*. And use of the vernacular—Croatian, Estonian, Flemish—is fundamental to almost all Romantics: throughout occupied Eastern and Northern Europe, through Russia and the nations of the West, throughout the new republics of the Americas. It seems reasonable to describe that as a definitional Romantic enterprise.

But Romanticism means more and does more, and several other topoi have appeared in these pages. Above all stands the nation-contract described above. Our study is bracketed by two dates, 1776 and 1848: the dates of two major revolutions, but also of two watershed texts, the *Declaration of Independence* and the *Communist Manifesto*. Jefferson's brave new world of national self-determination, built as it is on a vision of the represented people, yields seventy-two years later to a different vision, one anchored in a class war which partitions each nation from within and seeks to tie foreigners together in class solidarity. But if communism looks to supersede Jefferson's holistic national vision, Romanticism instead conveys it to posterity. Text after text shows an exceptional figure—the Romantic hero, let us call him—speaking on behalf of the masses. He or she represents them, as in the preamble to the United States Constitution: "We, the People [...]." Put simply, Romantic art from Russia to Latin America presents itself as the (perhaps rather bourgeois) people's voice. This is evident in the then-unrepresented people of Europe's East and North, that concert of silent nations. It is fundamental to, say, Conscience in Flanders, Cooper in the United States, and Gonçalves de Magalhães in the new Empire of Brazil. It is there in the very title of Staël's *Corinne ou l'Italie*, which sold across the West. It is why Romantics collected vernacular ballads, fairy tales, oral epics—from Percy and Macpherson, through the Grimms to Almeida Garrett and Lönnrot, Kreutzwald and Tegnér, and all through the Slavic lands. Ongoing focus on the Romantic individual, in sum, is one half of the Romantic plot. That 'unique creative genius' we like to call Romantic derives its weight from the hitherto silent nation David assembled *en masse* for his *fêtes révolutionnaires*, from the national bargain or indeed *contrat social* that the Romantics saw at work across this vast area's string of new republics, and which they sought to emulate in song and story. "Poets," we have heard say, "are the unacknowledged legislators of the world." And this new representation depends on credit: without credit to back it up, the coin mentioned above is just a lump of nickel. Credit was a fairly new topic in this period—it won the Napoleonic Wars for Britain and lost them for France—and only a few Romantic authors saw its value. Staël, daughter of the finance minister Necker, anchors her pivotal 1818 *Considérations sur la Révolution française* in credit theory.[78] This bargain, frankly, is why there are statues to Romantic authors from Buenos Aires to Moscow. It elects our representatives and pays our celebrities. It is omnipresent in the modern world.

Romantic art, we have seen, has a way of colonizing figures who were not Romantic to begin with, much as Frankenstein's creature long ago colonized his own creator. Or, put another way, Romanticism tends to metastasize, as we saw with Manon and Des Grieux, as we can observe happening to Napoleon—that man who had sought to end Romanticism, who had pulped Staël's *De l'Allemagne*—in the *Mémorial de Sainte-Hélène*. The movement is happy to roam through the centuries looking for figures to recuperate, from Wilhelm Tell to the tragic Chatterton. Similarly, non-writers can acquire a Romantic tinge—America's Founding Fathers; Simón Bolívar; Toussaint Louverture. Few figures seem more Romantic than Thomas Paine, La Fayette, or Garibaldi, all three of whom fought in multiple revolutions. Offered control of Paris in July 1830—La Fayette's third revolution—the old general, much vilified by later Jacobin historians, remarked, "my conduct at seventy-three will be what it was at thirty-two;" he then climbed to the balcony of the Hôtel de Ville to hand over power to Louis-Philippe.[79]

Lastly, there is the question of empire. The Romantic era saw Spain and Portugal lose their American empires, while Britain, which did the

78 On credit in *Staël's Considérations sur la Révolution française*, see my forthcoming monograph with Cambridge University Press, *The First European: Staël, Romanticism, and Revolution, 1786–1830*.

79 "ma conduite sera à soixante-treize ans ce qu'elle a été à trente-deux." Lafayette, 29 July 1830, in *Mémoires, correspondance et manuscrits du général Lafayette, publiés par sa famille*, 6 vols (Paris: Fournier, 1837–1838), VI, p. 389. See Laurent Zecchini, *Lafayette héraut de la liberté* (Paris: Fayard, 2019), pp. 458–461, on Lafayette during the *Trois glorieuses*.

same, acquired a new one to the East. The French Republic abolished slavery in 1794; Napoleon, whose wife Joséphine was a Martinican planter's daughter, sent troops to Haiti to try to reintroduce it. That is the reason why Wordsworth has a sonnet dedicated to Toussaint Louverture in his cold Pyrenean prison.[80] Staël and Constant fought the slave trade, while Chateaubriand's grand Breton château was bought with proceeds from that evil business.[81] Bristol, where the *Lyrical Ballads* appeared, was a slave port; Austen's *Mansfield Park* has slavery discreetly hidden in its narrative. Britain abolished the trade in 1807, and the practice in 1834; France finally followed suit once more in 1848, under the short-lived Second Republic. Duras's 1823 *Ourika* is part of that struggle. It seems fitting that none of the United States' early Romantics came from the Southern slave states, while Cuba's early Romantics in their turn were abolitionists. Back in Russia, Pushkin's African ancestors did not mean exclusion for him from the canon, while in France, Dumas's similar background evidently did. French scholarship still seems at ease not taking Dumas seriously as an author, despite his lasting and indeed global success. These are of course blind spots, and the Romantic relation to the Other in fact does pose fundamental questions. In 1837, the liberal Echeverría has bloodthirsty Indians kidnap his *Cautiva*; even without such blatancy, much Romantic orientalism deserves weighing as to appropriation or what we might term tourism. But here, let us return to Ourika, to Pellico, to Quasimodo for that matter; empathy goes a long way, and many Romantics evidently found a way to do this more deeply than their predecessors had. Indeed, this seems, to some extent, definitional for the movement, and both its biggest flaw—Heathcliff a hero? Really?—and also perhaps its greatest achievement. Today, and at least since the 1920s, this contract with the silent remains the core appeal of nativist demagogues around the globe. But it is born earlier, in hope and expansion of the heart, in empathy for the poor, the outcast, the downtrodden, the wretched of the Earth. That may be its two-edged legacy to the West.

80 Wordsworth, *Works*, p. 242.

81 On Staël, Constant, Chateaubriand, and slavery, see my "Voices Lost? Staël and Slavery, 1786–1830," in *Slavery in the Francophone Caribbean World. Distant Voices, Forgotten Acts, Forged Identities*, ed. Doris Y. Kadish (Athens, GA: University of Georgia Press, 2000), pp. 39–52.

Romanticism Outside the Western Ambit

To end, at the last: how global is the present overview? A search for, say, Slovenian, Albanian, or Ecuadorean Romanticism quickly turns up representative figures for each national tradition. In other words, Romanticism is remarkably and thoroughly colored inside the lines, and this is just as we might expect, given the movement's metastatic force. Within the Western ambit, national models or writers are necessary, this book argues, and can be identified *post hoc*, as they visibly have been. But that is not the case outside the West, a region which requires different treatment. Outside Europe and the newly independent republics of the two Americas, there is indeed evidence of, for instance, Turkish, Japanese, and South Asian Romanticism—each with its own characteristics, as is to be expected. We might pause a moment over these three different Asian cases, to see what is going on.

Let us begin with Ottoman Turkey—a state for which Romantic nationalism posed an existential threat, much as it did for the Austro-Hungarian Empire after 1867. There is, simply put, no Ottoman Romanticism. What we find instead are Romantic models for the subsequent and much smaller Turkish nation, with comparative silence elsewhere in the sultanate—in Egypt or Morocco, for instance. But are these models home-grown? An interesting question. The Ottoman capital, Constantinople (or Istanbul after 1930), was split between Europe and Asia—it looked to Albania, Bulgaria, or Greece (until 1832), as it did to Syria, Tunisia, or the Persian Gulf. Centuries of cross-border trade and influence cannot be discounted as they can for, say, Japan, when accounting for an emergent Westernized Turkish literature; this influence was then focused on France after the Crimean War of 1854–1856. The first novel published in Turkey is thus dated either to 1851

 https://doi.org/10.11647/OBP.0302.06

(in Armenian: *Akabi Hikâyesi* [Akabi's Story]) or to 1872 (in Turkish: *Taaşuk-u Tal'at ve Fitnat* [Tal'at and Fitnat in Love]).

In Meiji Japan (1868–1912)—a nation with centuries of novel-writing behind it, forcibly opened to the West by Commodore Perry's gunboats after further centuries of isolation—Europe arrived like a gunshot, bringing rapid industrialization and a variety of European models, from free verse to Enlightenment, Classicism, and Realism. In 1889, the novelist Mori Ōgai's anthology of translated poems brought Romanticism to Japan. He was followed in this by Tōson Shimazaki and by new literary magazines. Certain parallels are curious, such as Natsume Sōseki's humorous novel *Wagahai wa neko de aru* [I Am a Cat] in 1905), which employed a cat as the narrator, just as Hoffmann had done with Tomcat Murr. In brief, Romantic art reached Japan by gunboat and was not indigenous to that nation.

Lastly, across the wide linguistic expanse of South Asia—within the British Imperial administration of the Raj—foundational Romantic authors can and have been traced by interested scholars. In the years 1857–1945, they include writers in Kannada, Telugu, and Gujarati, and the great Muhammad Iqbal in Urdu, and Rabindranath Tagore—who won the Nobel Prize—in Bengali and English. Two further foundational groups seem worth noting, in Malayalam and in Hindi with the Chhayavaad movement of neo-Romanticism in poetry, 1922–1938. Outside of Chhayavaad, I hesitate to call these authors Romantic. However, the quintessentially Romantic role of language here—giving voice to the voiceless—is visibly primordial for all.

One may perhaps conclude thus: onto the very disparate soils of the non-Western world, Romanticism arrived like an alien seed. It was brought in by the free exchange of ideas, as Adam Smith might have celebrated, and by simple conquest. And then—as Goya had pointed out in Spain in 1814, as Bolívar or San Martín had pointed out in the Americas—it provided tools across the colonized globe for the wretched of the Earth—those *damnés de la Terre*, as Fanon has it—to find a path out of European empire to national self-determination.

Bibliography

Andrieux, Louis. 1927. *Alphonse Rabbe*. Paris: Lahure.

Anonymous, "Château of Coppet." *Blackwood's Edinburgh Magazine*, (November-December 1818): 198–201, 277–280.

Auerbach, Erich. 1957. *Mimesis: The Representation of Reality in Western Literarure*, trans. Willard Trask. Garden City, NY: Doubleday.

Bakhtin, Mikhail. 1981. *The Dialogic Imagination. Four Essays by M.M. Bakhtin*, trans. M. Holquist and C. Emerson. Austin, TX: University of Texas Press.

Balayé, Simone. 1971. *Les Carnets de voyage de Madame de Staël*. Geneva: Droz.

—1984. "Destins de femmes dans *Delphine*." *Cahiers staëliens*, XXXV: 41–59.

Baldensperger, Fernand. 1937. "'Romantique,' ses analogues et ses équivalents: tableau synoptique de 1650 à 1810 ." *Harvard Studies and Notes in Philology and Literature*, 19: 93–95.

Barante, Prosper de. 1859. *Études littéraires et historiques*. 2 vols. Paris: Didier.

Barrère, J.-B. 1951. "Sur quelques définitions du romantisme." *Revue des sciences humaines*, XVI.62–63: 93–110.

Barzun, Jacques. 1982. *Berlioz and His Century*. Chicago: University of Chicago Press.

Baudelaire, Charles. 1975. *Œuvres complètes*, ed. Claude Pichois. 2 vols. Paris: Gallimard.

Béguin, Albert. 1960. *L'Âme romantique et le rêve*. Paris: Plon.

Behler, Ernest. 1968. "The Origins of the Romantic Literary Theory." *Colloquia Germanica*, 2: 109–126.

Blake, William. 1927. *Poetry and Prose of William Blake*, ed. Geoffrey Keynes. London: Nonesuch.

Bottasso, Enzo. 1984. "La rottura fra Breme e Foscolo: L'imprevista conseguenza d'un giudizio troppo sbrigativo sulla polemica romantica." In *Ludovico di Breme e il programma dei romantici Italiani: atti del convegno di stud. ed. Centro studi piemontesi*. Turin: Centro Studi Piemontesi (pp. 83–104).

Bowman, Frank Paul. 1987. *Le Christ des barricades 1789–1848*. Paris: Editions du Cerf.

Bray, René. 1932. *Chronologie du romantisme (1804–1830)*. Paris: Boivin.

Brentano, Clemens. 1951. *Briefe*, ed. F. Seebaß. 2 vols. Nuremberg: Hans Karl.

Brown, Marshall. 1991. *Preromanticism*. Stanford: Stanford University Press.

Brownlee, Kevin, and Marina S. Brownlee (eds). 1985. *Romance: Generic Transformation from Chrétien de Troyes to Cervantes*. Hanover: University Press of New England.

Burckhardt, C.A.H. 1891. *Das Repertoire des Weimarischen Hoftheaters unter Goethes Leitung 1791–1817*. Hamburg: Voß.

Burney, Fanny. 1904–1905. *Diary and Letters of Madame d'Arblay* [Fanny Burney], ed. C. Barrett, rev. A. Dobson. 6 vols. London: Macmillan.

Butler, Marilyn. 1981. *Romantics, Rebels and Reactionaries*. Oxford: Oxford University Press.

Byron, Lord. 1898–1901. *Letters and Journals*, ed. Lord Prothero. 6 vols. London: Murray.

Carlyle, Thomas. 1884. *Carlyle's Works*. 20 vols. Boston: Estes & Lauriat.

Carroll, Lewis. [n.d.]. *Through the Looking-Glass. The Complete Works of Lewis Carroll*, ed. A Woolcott. London: Nonesuch.

Champfleury. 1872. *Souvenirs et portraits de jeunesse*. Paris: Dentu.

Chateaubriand, François-René. 1859–1861. *Œuvres complètes de Chateaubriand*. 12 vols. Paris: Garnier.

—1946. *Mémoires d'outre-tombe*, ed. M. Levaillant and G. Moulinier. 2 vols. Paris: Gallimard.

—1951. *Lettres à Mme Récamier*, ed. M. Levaillant. Paris: Flammarion.

Chaves, Castelo Branco. *1979. O romance histórico no romantismo português*. Amadora: Instituto de Cultura Portuguesa.

Christesco, Dorothée. 1943. *La Fortune d'Alexandre Manzoni en France. Origines du théâtre et du roman romantiques*. Paris: Editions Balzac.

Claudon, Francis. 1984. "Stendhal et le néo-classicisme." In *Stendhal et le romantisme*, ed. Victor del Litto and Kurt Ringger. Aran: Editions du Grand-Chêne (pp. 191–202).

Coleridge, Samuel Taylor. 1931. *The Poems of Samuel Taylor Coleridge*, ed. Ernest Hartley Coleridge. London: Oxford University Press.

—1983. *Biographia litteraria*, ed. James Engell and Walter Jackson Bate. 2 vols. Princeton: Bollingen.

Constant, Benjamin. 1965. *Wallstein: tragédie en 5 actes et en vers*, ed. Jean-René Derré. Paris: Les Belles Lettres.

—1967. *Benjamin Constant 1767–1830* [exhibition catalogue]. Lausanne: Bibliothèque cantonale et universitaire.

Constantine, David. 1988. *Hölderlin*. Oxford: Clarendon.

Courbet, Gustave. 1930. *Courbet raconté par lui-même*. Geneva: Cailler.

Crouzet, Michel. 1980. "Polémique et politesse ou Stendhal pamphlétaire." *Stendhal Club*, 89: 53–65.

Curran, Stuart (ed.). 1993. *The Cambridge Companion to British Romanticism*. Cambridge: Cambridge University Press.

—2010. *The Cambridge Companion to British Romanticism*. Cambridge: Cambridge University Press.

Dalhaus, Carl. 1991. *Ludwig van Beethoven: Approaches to His Music*. Oxford: Clarendon Press.

Dante Alighieri. 1982–1984. *La Divina Commedia* [The Divine Comedy], ed. Natalino Sapegno. 3 vols. Florence: La Nuova Italia.

Delacroix, Eugène. 1932. *Journal d'Eugène Delacroix*, ed. A. Joubin. 3 vols. Paris: Plon.

del Litto, Victor. 1955. *En marge des manuscrits de Stendhal. Compléments et fragments inédits (1803–1820). Suivis d'un courrier italien*. Paris: Presses universitaires de France.

—1962. *La Vie intellectuelle de Stendhal. Genèse et évolution de ses idées (1802–1821)*. Paris: Presses universitaires de France.

della Chiesa, Angelina Ottino. 1965. "Neoclassico e romantico in Europa." *Il Veltro*, 9: 23–32.

Deschamps, Emile. 1972–1874. *Œuvres d'Emile Deschamps*. 6 vols. Paris: Lemerre.

Dictionnaire de l'Académie française. 1813. 2 vols. Paris: Nicolle.

Duncan, Ian. 1992. *Modern Romance and the Transformations of the Novel: the Gothic, Scott, and Dickens*. Cambridge: Cambridge University Press.

Eggli, Edmond. 1927. *L'Érotique comparée de Charles de Villers. 1806*. Paris: Gamber.

Eggli, Edmond, and Pierre Martino. 1933. *Le Débat romantique en France, 1813–1830, I, 1813–1816*. Paris: Les Belles Lettres.

Eichendorff, Joseph von. 1987–1990. *Werke*, ed. H. Schultz. 6 vols. Frankfurt: Bibliothek deutscher Klassiker.

Eichner, Hans. 1956. "Friedrich Schlegel's Theory of Romantic Poetry." *PMLA*, 71.5: 1018–1041.

—1965. "The Genesis of German Romanticism." *Queen's Quarterly*, 72.2: 213–231.

—1970. "The Novel." In *The Romantic Period in Germany*, ed. Siegbert Prawer. London: Weidenfeld and Nicholson (pp. 64–96).

—(ed.). 1972. *'Romantic' and its Cognates / The European History of a Word*. Toronto: University of Toronto Press.

Eliot, T.S. 1963. *Collected Poems 1909–1962 by T.S. Eliot*. London: Faber & Faber.

Esterhammer, Angela, ed. *Romantic Poetry*. 2002. In *A Comparative History of Literatures in European Languages*. Amsterdam: John Benjamins/Budapest: Akadémiai Kiadó.

Feldman, Paula R. (ed). 1997. *British Women Poets of the Romantic Era. An Anthology*. Baltimore: Johns Hopkins University Press.

Fetzer, John. 1990. "Romantic Irony." In *European Romanticism: Literary Cross-Currents, Modes and Models*, ed. Gerhart Hoffmeister. Detroit: Wayne State University Press (pp. 19–36).

Flaubert, Gustave. 1952. *Oeuvres*, ed. A. Thibaudet and R. Dumesnil. 2 vols. Paris: Gallimard.

Foscolo, Ugo. 1952-. *Edizione nazionale delle opere di Ugo Foscolo*. 22 vols. Florence: Le Monnier.

—1966. *Opere*, ed. Mario Puppo. Milan: Mursia.

Frederick the Great. 1846–1857. *Oeuvres de Frédéric le Grand*, ed. J.D.E. Preuss. 31 vols. Berlin: R. Decker.

Frye, Northrop. 1976. *The Secular Scripture. A Study of the Structure of Romance*. Cambridge, MA: Harvard University Press.

Garber, Frederick, ed. 1988. "Romantic Irony." In *A Comparative History of Literatures in European Languages*. Amsterdam: John Benjamins /Budapest: Akadémiai Kiadó (pp. i, 1–394).

Gautier, Théophile. 1974. *Les Jeunes France: Romans goguenards*, ed. R. Jasinski. Paris: Flammarion.

—1947. *Emaux et camées*. Geneva: Droz.

Genette, Gérard. 1997. *Paratexts: Thresholds of Interpretation*, trans. Jane Lewin. Cambridge: Cambridge University Press.

Gennari, Geneviève. 1947. *Le Premier Voyage de Mme de Staël en Italie*. Paris: Boivin.

Gilbert, Sandra M., and Susan Gubar. 1979. *The Madwoman in the Attic. The Woman Writer and the Nineteenth-Century Literary Imagination*. New Haven: Yale University Press.

Gillespie, Gerald. 1967. "Novella, Nouvelle, Novelle, Short Novel? A Review of Terms." *Neophilologus*, 51: 117–127, 225–230.

—ed. *Romantic Drama*. 2007. In *A Comparative History of Literatures in European Languages*. Amsterdam: John Benjamins/Budapest: Akadémiai Kiadó.

—Engel, Manfred, and Dieterle, Bernard, eds. 2008. "Romantic Prose Fiction." In *A Comparative History of Literatures in European Languages*. Amsterdam: John Benjamins/Budapest: Akadémiai Kiadó (pp. xxi, 1–733).

Gittings, Robert. 1968. *John Keats*. Boston & Toronto: Little, Brown & Co.

Glachant, Paul, and Victor Glachant (eds). 1902. *Lettres à Fauriel conservées à la bibliothèque de l'Institut*. Paris: Nouvelle Revue.

Goblot, Jean-Jacques 1975. "Les mots *protestants* et *protestantisme* sous la Restauration." In *Civilisation chrétienne: Approche historique d'une idéologie*, ed. Jean-René Derré. Paris: Beauchesne (pp. 211–227).

—1995. *La Jeune France libérale. Le Globe et son groupe littéraire, 1824–1830*. Paris: Plon.

Godwin, William. 1988. *Things as They Are; or The Adventures of Caleb Williams*, ed. Maurice Hindle. London: Penguin Books.

Goethe, Johann Wolfgang von. 1948–1960. *Gedenkausgabe der Werke, Briefe und Gespräche*, ed. E. Beutler. 24 vols. Zürich: Artemis.

—1962–1967. *Briefe*, ed. K.R. Mandelkow. 4 vols. Hamburg: Wegner.

—1965–1969. *Briefe an Goethe*, ed. K.R. Mandelkow. 2 vols. Hamburg: Wegner.

—1970–1973. *Goethe. Schriften zur Literatur*, ed. E. Nahler. 7 vols. Berlin: Akademie.

—1827. *Moderne Guelfen und Ghibellinen*. In *Über Kunst und Alterthum*. Stuttgart: Cotta (VI, pp. 164–166).

—[n.d.]. *Goethes sämtliche Werke*. 20 vols. Leipzig: Insel.

Gogol, Nikolai V. 1940. *Polnoe sobranie sochinenii*. Moskva: Akademiia Nauk S.S.S.R.

—1957/1965. *The Overcoat and Other Tales of Good and Evil*, trans. David Magarshack. New York: Norton.

Gombrich, E.H. 1985. *Meditations on a Hobby Horse and Other Essays on the Theory of Art*. Oxford: Phaidon.

Gougelot, Henri. 1943. *La Romance française sous la révolution et l'empire; choix de textes musicaux*. Melun: Argences.

Grande dizionario della lingua italiana, ed. Salvatore Battaglia. 1961-. 19 vols. Turin: Unione tipografico-editrice torinese.

Greene, Donald. 1970. "What Indeed Was Neo-Classicism: A Reply to James William Johnson's 'What Was Neo-Classicism?'" *Journal of British Studies*, 10.1: 69–79.

Guenov, Krâstu. 1968. *Le Romantisme dans la littérature bulgare*. Sofia: Éditions de l'Académie bulgare des sciences.

Hamilton, Paul. 2013. *Realpoetik: European Romanticism and Literary Politics*. Oxford: Oxford University Press.

—ed. 2016. *The Oxford Handbook of European Romanticism*. Oxford: Oxford University Press.

Hamm, Jean-Jacques. 1981. "Stendhal et l'autre du plagiat," *Stendhal Club*, 91: 203–214.

Harvey, Sir Paul, and J.E. Heseltine. 1959. *The Oxford Companion to French Literature*. Oxford: Oxford University Press.

Heine, Heinrich. 1954. *Heinrich Heines Werke. Die Bergland-Buch-Klassiker*. Salzburg: Bergland.

Hoeveler, Diane Long. 1998. *Gothic Feminism: The Professionalization of Gender from Charlotte Smith to the Brontës*. University Park: Pennsylvania State University Press.

Hoffmann, Ernst Theodor Amadeus. [n.d.]. *E.T.A. Hoffmanns sämtliche Werke in fünfzehn Bänden*, ed. Eduard Grisebach. Leipzig: Hesse.

Hoffmeister, Gerhart (ed.). 1990. *European Romanticism: Literary Cross-Currents, Modes and Models*. Detroit: Wayne State University Press.

Hölderlin, Friedrich. 2004. *Poems and Fragments*, trans. Michael Hamburger. London: Anvil.

Holy Bible. 1611. Authorized King James Version.

Horace. 2011. *Satires and Epistles*. Oxford: Oxford University Press.

Hufton, Olwen H. 1992. *Women and the Limits of Citizenship in the French Revolution*. Toronto: University of Toronto Press.

Hugo, Victor Marie de. 1820. *Conservateur littéraire*, 25 March 1820.

—1897. *Préface de Cromwell*, ed. M. Souriau. Paris: Lecène.

—1904–1937. *Œuvres complètes de Victor Hugo*, ed. G. Simon. 35 vols. Paris: Librarie Ollendorf.

—1963. *Romans*. 3 vols. Paris: Seuil.

—1976. *Littérature et Philosophie mêlées*, ed. A.R.W. James. 2 vols. Paris: Klincksieck.

Il Conciliatore. Foglio scientifico-letterario, ed. Vittore Branca. 1965. 2 vols. Florence: Le Monnier.

Ilgner, Richard M. 1979. *The Romantic Chivalrous Epic as a Phenomenon of the German Rococo*. Bern: Peter Lang.

Immerwahr, Raymond. 1970. "The Word *Romantisch* and Its History." In *The Romantic Period in Germany*, ed. Siegbert Prawer. London: Weidenfeld and Nicholson (pp. 34–63).

Isbell, John Claiborne. 1994. *The Birth of European Romanticism: Truth and Propaganda in Staël's De l'Allemagne*. Cambridge: Cambridge University Press.

—1994. "Le Groupe de Coppet et la *Confédération romantique*: August Wilhelm Schlegel, Madame de Staël et Sismondi en 1814." In *Le Groupe de Coppet et l'Europe, 1789–1830*, ed. Kurt Kloocke. Lausanne: Touzot (pp. 309–329).

—1995. "Censors, Police, and *De l'Allemagne*'s Lost 1810 Edition: Napoleon Pulps His Enemies." *Zeitschrift für französische Sprache und Literatur*, CV/2: 156–170.

—1996. *The People's Voice: A Romantic Civilization, 1776–1848*. Bloomington, IN: Lilly Library.

—1997. "The Italian Romantics and Madame de Staël: Art, Society and Nationhood." *Rivista di letterature moderne e comparate*, L.4: 355–369

—1998. "Présence de Coppet et romantisme libéral en France, 1822–1827." *Le Groupe de Coppet et le monde moderne*, ed. Françoise Tilkin. Geneva: Droz.

—1999. (ed.) *The People's Voice: A Romantic Civilization, 1776–1848: Essays on European Romanticism*. Monash Romance Studies 4, ed. Andrea Ciccarelli and Brian Nelson. Melbourne: School of European Languages and Cultures, Monash University.

—2000. "Voices Lost? Staël and Slavery, 1786–1830." In *Slavery in the Francophone Caribbean World. Distant Voices, Forgotten Acts, Forged Identities*, ed. Doris Y. Kadish. Athens, GA: University of Georgia Press (pp. 39–52).

—Forthcoming. *The First European: Staël, Romanticism, and Revolution, 1786–1830*. Cambridge: Cambridge University Press.

Johnson, Paul. 1991. *The Birth of the Modern. World Society 1815–1830*. New York: HarperCollins.

Johnson, Samuel. 2006. *A Dictionary of the English Language*. London: Folio Society.

Jordan, Frank, Jr. (ed.). 1972. *The English Romantic Poets: A Review of Research and Criticism*. New York: MLA.

Jouffroy, Théodore. 1924. *Cahier vert*, ed. P. Poux. Paris: Presses françaises.

Keats, John. 1944. *The Poetical Works of John Keats*, ed. H. Buxton Forman. Oxford: Oxford University Press.

Kelly, Gary. 2010. "Romantic Fiction." In *The Cambridge Companion to British Romanticism*, ed. Stuart Curran. Cambridge: Cambridge University Press (pp. 187–208).

Kiely, Robert. 1972. *The Romantic Novel in England*. Cambridge, MA.: Harvard University Press.

Klinger, Friedrich Maximilian von. 1977. *Die Zwillinge* [The Twins]. 1776; Stuttgart: Reclam.

Köpke, R. (ed.). 1855. *Ludwig Tiecks Nachgelassene Schriften*. 2 vols. Leipzig: Brockhaus.

La Fayette, Marie-Joseph Paul Yves Roch Gilbert du Motier de. 1837–1838. *Mémoires, correspondance et manuscrits du général Lafayette, publiés par sa famille*. 6 vols. Paris: Fournier.

Lamartine, Alphonse de. 1881–1882. *Correspondance de Lamartine*, ed. V. de Lamartine. 4 vols. Paris: Hachette.

Langbauer, Laurie. 1990. *Women and Romance: The Consolations of Gender in the English Novel*. Ithaca: Cornell University Press.

Legouvé, Ernest. 1888. *Soixante ans de souvenirs*. 4 vols. Paris: Hetzel.

Leopardi, Giacomo. 1969. *Tutte le opere*, ed. W. Binni. 2 vols. Florence: Sansoni.

—2010. *Canti: Poems*, trans. Jonathan Galassi. New York: Farrar, Straus, and Giroux.

Lermontov, Mikhail Iurevich. 1969. *Geroi nashego vremeni*, ed. D.J. Richards. Letchworth: Bradda.

—1992. *Geroi nashego vremeni* [A Hero of Our Time] (1840), trans. Vladimir and Dmitri Nabokov. New York: Knopf.

Levi, Primo. 1979. *If This Is a Man and The Truce*. London: Penguin/Sphere.

Levy, Darlene Gay, Harriet Branson Applewhite, and Mary Durham Johnson (eds and trans). 1980. *Women in Revolutionary Paris 1789–1795*. Urbana: University of Illinois Press.

Lovejoy, Arthur O. 1924. "On the Discrimination of Romanticisms." *PMLA*, 39: 229–253.

—1941. "The Meaning of Romanticism for the Historian of Ideas." *Journal of the History of Ideas*, 2.3: 257–278.

Lucas, F.L. 1936. *The Decline and Fall of the Romantic Ideal*. Cambridge: Cambridge University Press.

Lüdeke, H. (ed.). 1930. *Ludwig Tieck und die Brüder Schlegel: Briefe*. Frankfurt: Baer.

Lukács, György. 1955. *Der historische Roman*. Berlin: Aufbau.

—1968. *La Théorie du roman*, trans. Jean Clairevoye. Paris: Denoël.

MacFarland, Thomas. 1987. *Romantic Cruxes*. Oxford: Clarendon.

Manzoni, Alessandro. 1973. *Tutte le opere*, ed. Mario Martelli. 2 vols. Florence: Sansoni.

Martegiani, Gina. 1908. *Il Romanticismo italiano non existe*. Florence: Seeber.

Martin, Aimé. 1814. *Le Portrait d'Attila, suivi d'une Epître à M. de Saint-Victor*. Paris: Aimé Martin.

Martini, Fritz. 1951. *Deutsche Literaturgeschichte von den Anfängen bis zur Gegenwart*. Stuttgart: Kröner.

Massey, Irving. 1965. "The Romantic Movement: Phrase or Fact." *The Dalhousie Review*, 44: 396–412.

Matenko, P. (ed.). 1933. *Tieck and Solger: The Complete Correspondence*. New York: Westermann.

Mauskopf, Seymour H. 1995. "Lavoisier and the improvement of gunpowder production." *Revue d'histoire des sciences*, 48.1–2: 96–122

McDermott, Hubert. 1989. *Novel and Romance: The Odyssey to Tom Jones*. Totowa: Barnes & Noble.

McGann, Jerome. 1983. *The Romantic Ideology*. Chicago: University of Chicago Press.

—1999. *Byron and Wordsworth*. Nottingham: University of Nottingham School of English Studies.

McKenzie, Kenneth. 1940. "Romanticism in Italy." *PMLA*, 55.1: 27–35.

Mellor, Anne K. 1990. "Why Women Didn't Like Romanticism." In *The Romantics and Us*, ed. G.W. Ruoff. New Brunswick: Rutgers University Press (pp. 274–287).

—1993. *Romanticism and Gender*. London: Routledge.

Melzer, Sara E., and Leslie W. Rabine (eds). 1992. *Rebel Daughters. Women and the French Revolution*. Oxford: Oxford University Press.

Menhennet, Alan. 1981. *The Romantic Movement*. London: Croom Helm.

Mérimée, Prosper. 1978. *Théâtre de Clara Gazul: Romans et nouvelles*, ed. J. Mallion and P. Salomon. Paris: Gallimard.

Mersereau, John, Jr. 1963. "Pushkin's Concept of Romanticism." *Studies in Romanticism*, 3: 38–40.

Metternich, Klemens von. 1883–1886. *Mémoires [...] laissés par le Prince de Metternich*, ed. Richard de Metternich. 8 vols. Paris: Plon.

Mickiewicz, Adam. 1992. *Pan Tadeusz*, trans. Kenneth R. MacKenzie. New York: Hippocrene Books.

Mitchell, P.M. 1972. "Scandinavia/Romantisk—Romantik—Romantiker." In *'Romantic' and its Cognates/ The European History of a Word*, ed. Hans Eichner. Toronto: University of Toronto Press (pp. 372–417).

Moget, Gilbert. 1967. "En marge du bi-centenaire de Mme de Staël 'Classiques' et 'Romantiques' à Milan 1816." *La pensée*, 131: 1–27.

Moreau, Pierre. 1932. *Le Classicisme des romantiques*. Paris: Plon.

Musset, Alfred de. 1963. *Œuvres complètes*, ed. P. van Tieghem. Paris: Seuil/ Intégrale.

Nagavajara, Chetana. 1966. *August Wilhelm Schlegel in Frankreich. Sein Anteil an der französischen Literaturkritik 1807–1835*. Tübingen: Niemeyer.

Nélod, Gilles. 1969. *Panorama du roman historique*. Paris: SODI.

Nerval, Gérard de. 1966. *Œuvres*, ed. H. Lemaitre. Paris: Garnier.

Nodier, Charles. 1956. "Preface." In Maturin, Charles. *Bertram, ou Le Château de Saint-Aldobrand*, ed. M. Ruff. Paris: Corti (pp. 69–72).

—1961. *Contes*, ed. P.-G. Castex. Paris: Garnier.

Novalis. 1842. *Henry of Ofterdingen*, trans. John Owen. Cambridge, MA: Cambridge Press.

—1960–1988. *Novalis. Schriften. Die Werke Friedrich von Hardenbergs*, ed. Paul Kluckhohn and Richard Samuel. 5 vols. Stuttgart: Kohlhammer.

Ozouf, Mona. 1988. *Festivals and the French Revolution*, trans. Alan Sheridan. Cambridge, MA: Harvard University Press.

Pange, Comtesse de. 1967. "Quelques remarques sur l'article de Mme de Staël intitulé: De l'esprit des traductions." *La Rivista di letterature moderne e comparate* [*RLMC*], 20: 215–225.

Paul, Jean. 1992. *Jean Paul. A Reader*, ed. Timothy J. Casey, trans. Erika Casey. Baltimore: The Johns Hopkins University Press.

Paulin, Roger. 1970. "The Drama." In *The Romantic Period in Germany*, ed. Siegbert Prawer. London: Weidenfeld and Nicholson (pp. 173–203).

—1985. *Ludwig Tieck: A Literary Biography*. Oxford: Clarendon.

—2016. *The Life of August Wilhelm Schlegel. Cosmopolitan of Art and Poetry*. Cambridge: Open Book Publishers, https://doi.org/10.11647/OBP.0069.

Pearsall Smith, Logan. 1925. "Four Romantic Words." In *Words and Idioms: Studies in the English Language*. London: Constable & Co. (pp. 66–134).

Peckham, Morse. 1951. "Toward a Theory of Romanticism." *PMLA*, 66: 5–23.

Pellegrini, Carlo. 1926. *Il Sismondi e la storia delle letterature dell'Europa meridionale*. Geneva: Olschki.

Perkins, David. 1990. "'The Construction of the Romantic Movement' as a Literary Classification." *Nineteenth-Century Literature*, 45. 2: 129–143

Perrot, Michelle. 1990. *A History of Private Life. From the Fires of Revolution to the Great War*, ed. And trans. Arthur Goldhammer. Cambridge, MA: Belknap.

Petöfi, Sandór. 2004. *John the Valiant*. London: Hesperus.

Peyre, Henri. 1969. "The Originality of French Romanticism." *Symposium*, 23.3–4: 333–345.

Pierce, Frederick A. 1918. *Currents and Eddies in the English Romantic Generation*. New Haven: Yale University Press.

Pope, Alexander. 1966. *Pope. Poetical Works*. Oxford: Oxford University Press.

Porte, Joel. 1969. *The Romance in America: Studies in Cooper, Poe, Hawthorne, Melville, and James*. Middletown: Wesleyan University Press.

Prawer, Siegbert (ed.). 1970. *The Romantic Period in Germany*. London: Weidenfeld and Nicholson.

Prévost, Abbé. 1995. *Histoire du chevalier Des Grieux et de Manon Lescaut*. Paris: Flammarion.

Prickett, Stephen, and Simon Haines (eds). 2010. *European Romanticism. A Reader*. London: Continuum.

Proffer, Karl R. 1966–1967. "Gogol's Definition of Romanticism." *Studies in Romanticism*, 6: 120–127.

Puppo, Mario. 1985. *Romanticismo italiano e romanticismo europeo*. Milan: Istituto Propaganda Libraria.

Pushkin, Alexander. 1943. *Eugene Onegin. A Novel in Verse*, trans. Babette Deutsch. New York: Ltd. Editions Club.

—1964. *Sochineniia*. 3 vols. Moscow: Izdatel'stvo "Khudozhestvennaia literatura."

—1986. *Pushkin on Literature*, trans. and ed. T. Wolff. London: Athlone.

—1991. *Evgenii Onegin. Roman v stikhakh*. Moscow: Izdatel'stvo ATRIUM.

—1999. *The Collected Stories*, trans. By Paul Debreczeny. New York: Everyman's.

Racine, Jean. 1962. "*Phèdre*." In *Œuvres complètes*. Paris: Seuil (pp. 246–264).

Ragusa, Olga. 1972. "Italy/Romantico—Romanticismo." In *'Romantic' and its Cognates/ The European History of a Word*, ed. Hans Eichner. Toronto: University of Toronto Press (pp. 293–340).

Raimondi, Ezio. 1997. *Romanticismo italiano e romanticismo europeo*. Milan: Mondadori.

Remak, Henry H.H. 1968. "A Key to West European Romanticism?" *Colloquia Germanica*, 2: 37–46.

—1990. "New Harmony: The Quest for Synthesis in West European Romanticism." In *European Romanticism: Literary Cross-Currents, Modes and Models*, ed. Gerhart Hoffmeister. Detroit: Wayne State University Press (pp. 333–351).

Richter, David H. 1996. *The Progress of Romance: Literary Historiography and the Gothic Novel*. Columbus: Ohio State University Press.

Roberts, Adam. 1999. *Romantic and Victorian Long Poems: A Guide*. Aldershot: Ashgate.

Rodger, Gillian. 1970. "The Lyric." In *The Romantic Period in Germany*, ed. Siegbert Prawer. London: Weidenfeld and Nicholson (pp. 147–172).

Rosa, George M. 1978. "Stendhal raconteur: a partly unpublished record of reminiscences and anecdotes." *Studi francesi*, 65–66: 358–364.

Ross, Deborah. 1991. *The Excellence of Falsehood: Romance, Realism, and Women's Contribution to the Novel*. Lexington: University Press of Kentucky.

Sand, George. 1970. *Œuvres autobiographiques*, ed. G. Lubin. 2 vols. Paris: Gallimard.

—1979. *Les Maîtres Sonneurs*. Paris: Gallimard.

Schlegel, August Wilhelm von. 1814. *Cours de littérature dramatique*. Geneva: Paschoud.

—1846–1848. *Sämmtliche Werke*, ed. E. Böcking. 16 vols. Leipzig: Weidmann.

—1966. *Vorlesungen über dramatische Kunst und Literatur* I, ed. Edgar Lohner. In *Kritische Schriften und Briefe* V-VI. Stuttgart, Berlin, Cologne, Mainz: W. Kohlhammer (pp. 1–263, 1–303).

Schlegel, Friedrich. 1929. *Die Botschaft der deutschen Romantik an Europa*, ed. Josef Körner. Augsburg: Filser.

—1936, 1969. *Krisenjahre der Frühromantik*, ed. J. Körner. 3 vols. Brno: Rohrer.

—1957. *Fragmente zur Literatur und Poesie I: Literary Notebooks, 1797–1801*, ed. Hans Eichner. London: Athlone.

—1963. *Kritische Friedrich-Schlegel Ausgabe* 18: *Philosophische Lehrjahre 1796–1806*, I, ed. Ernst Behler. Munich, Paderborn, Vienna: Ferdinand Schöningh, pp. 1–422.

—1967. "Brief über den Roman, in Gespräch über die Poesie." In *Friedrich Schlegel II: Charakteristiken und Kritiken I* (*1796–1801*), ed. Hans Eichner. Munich: Schöningh (pp. 284–362).

—1967–1979. *Kritische Friedrich Schlegel-Ausgabe*, ed. E. Behler. 14 vols. Munich: Schöningh.

—1978. *Kritische und theoretische Schriften*. Stuttgart: Reclam.

Schor, Naomi. 1993. *George Sand & Idealism*. New York: Columbia University Press.

Shakespeare, William. 1974. *The Riverside Shakespeare*. Boston: Houghton Mifflin.

Shaw, Harry E. 1983. *The Forms of Historical Fiction: Sir Walter Scott and His Successors*. Ithaca: Cornell University Press.

Shelley, Mary. 1983. *Frankenstein, or, The Modern Prometheus*. New York: New American Library.

Shelley, Percy Bysshe. 1890. *A Defense of Poetry*, ed. Albert S. Cook. Boston: Ginn & Co.

—1926–1930. *Complete Works*, ed. R. Ingpen and W.E. Peck. 10 vols. London: Benn.

—1952. *The Complete Poetical Works of Percy Bysshe Shelley*, ed. Thomas Hutchinson. Oxford: Oxford University Press.

Shevchenko, Taras. 1977. *Selected Poetry*. Kiev: Dnipro.

Siebers, Tobin. 1984. *The Romantic Fantastic*. Ithaca: Cornell University Press.

Simon, G. 1922. "Victor Hugo et les critiques." *Revue de Paris*, 13 (1 July): 268–307.

Sismondi, J-C.-L. 1813. *De la littérature du midi de l'Europe*. 4 vols. Paris: Treuttel et Würtz.

—1933–1975. *Epistolario*, ed. Carlo Pellegrini. 5 vols. Florence: Nuova Italia.

Smith, C. Colin (ed.). 1964. *Spanish Ballads*. Oxford: Pergamon Press.

Solomon-Godeau, Abigail. 1997. *Male Trouble. A Crisis in Representation*. London: Thames and Hudson.

Solovieff, Georges. 1990. *L'Allemagne et Madame de Staël*. Paris: Klincksieck.

Sondrup, Steven P. and Nemoianu, Virgil, eds. 2004. *Nonfictional Romantic Prose: Expanding Borders*. In *A Comparative History of Literatures in European Languages*. Amsterdam: John Benjamins/Budapest: Akadémiai Kiadó (pp. i–vi, 1–477).

Sötér, I. and I. Neupokoyeva (eds). 1977. *European Romanticism*. Budapest: Akadémiae Kiadó.

Staël, Germaine de. 1834. *Œuvres complètes*. 3 vols. Paris: Treuttel et Würtz.

—1958–1960. *De l'Allemagne* [On Germany], ed. Comtesse de Pange and Simone Balayé. 5 vols. Paris: Hachette.

—1985. *Corinne ou l'Italie*. Paris: Folio.

—1991. *De la littérature*, ed. Gérard Gengembre and Jean Goldzink. Paris: Garnier- Flammarion.

—1997. *Œuvres de jeunesse*, ed. John Isbell with an introduction by Simone Balayé. Paris: Desjonquères.

—2008. *Réflexions sur le suicide* in *De l'influence des passions et autres essais moraux*, ed. Florence Lotterie. Paris: Champion (pp. 341–395).

Starobinski, Jean, 1957. *Jean-Jacques Rousseau, La Transparence et l'obstacle*. Paris: Plon.

Stendhal. 1924. *Histoire de la peinture en Italie*, ed. Paul Arbelet. 2 vols. Paris: Champion.

—1925. *Racine et Shakespeare*, ed. Pierre Martino. 2 vols. Paris: Champion.

—1928. *Vies de Haydn, de Mozart et de Métastase* , ed. Henri Martineau. Paris: Le Divan.

—1929. *Histoire de la peinture en Italie*, ed. Henri Martineau. 2 vols. Paris: Le Divan.

—1930. *Molière. Shakespeare. La Comédie et le rire*, ed. Henri Martineau. Paris: Le Divan.

—1931. *Pensées: filosofia nova*, ed. Henri Martineau. 2 vols. Paris: Le Divan.

—1933. *Mélanges de littérature*, ed. Henri Martineau. 3 vols. Paris: Le Divan.

—1936. *Mélanges intimes et marginalia*, ed. Henri Martineau. 2 vols. Paris: Le Divan.

—1937. *Journal*, ed. Henri Martineau. 5 vols. Paris: Le Divan.

—1938. *Racine et Shakespeare*, ed. Henri Martineau. Paris: Le Divan.

—1956. *Rome, Naples et Florence en 1817, suivi de L'Italie en 1818*, ed. Henri Martineau. Paris: Le Divan.

—1962. *Correspondance*, ed. H. Martineau and V. del Litto. 3 vols. Paris: Gallimard.

—1970. *Racine et Shakespeare*, ed. Roger Fayolle. Paris: Garnier-Flammarion.

—1981. *Oeuvres intimes*, ed. Victor del Litto. 2 vols. Paris: Gallimard.

—1981. *Correspondance*, ed. Henri Martineau and Victor del Litto. Paris: Gallimard.

—1967. *De l'amour*, ed. Daniel Muller and Pierre Jourda. 2 vols. Paris: Cercle du Bibliophile.

Steinberg, S.H., and J. Buchanan-Brown. 1973. *Cassell's Encyclopedia of World Literature*. 3 vols. London: Cassel & Co.

Talbot, Emile. 1983. "Le romantique et le/la politique: autour de *Racine et Shakespeare*." *Stendhal Club*, 98: 227–234.

The Oxford English Dictionary. 1989. Oxford: Oxford University Press.

Tieghem, Paul van. 1969. *Le Romantisme dans la littérature européenne*. Paris: Albin Michel.

Trahard, Pierre. 1924. *Le Romantisme défini par 'Le Globe.'* Paris: Presses françaises.

Trainer, James. 1970. "The *Märchen*." In *The Romantic Period in Germany*, ed. Siegbert Prawer. London: Weidenfeld and Nicholson (pp. 97–120).

Trompeo, Pietro Paolo. 1924. *Nell'Italia romantica sulle orme di Stendhal*. Roma: Leonardo da Vinci.

Véron, Louis. 1853–1855. *Mémoires d'un bourgeois de Paris*. 6 vols. Paris: Gonet.

Voltaire [François-Marie Arouet]. 1971. *The Complete Works of Voltaire: Correspondence and related documents, XVI, March-December 1755*, ed. Theodore Besterman. Banbury: The Voltaire Foundation.

—1973. *Voltaire: Correspondence, XXVI, February-September 1763*, ed. Theodore Besterman. Banbury: The Voltaire Foundation.

Waller, Margaret. 1993. *The Male Malady. Fictions of Impotence in the French Romantic Novel*. New Brunswick: Rutgers University Press.

Weisinger, Herbert. 1946. "English Treatment of the Classical-Romantic Problem." *Modern Language Quarterly*, 7.4: 477–488.

Wellek, René. 1949. "The Concept of Romanticism in Literary History." *Comparative Literature*, 1: 1–23, 147–172.

—1955–1992. *A History of Modern Criticism: 1750–1950*. 6 vols. New Haven: Yale University Press.

—1970. *Discriminations*. New Haven: Yale University Press.

Whalley, George. 1965. "Literary Romanticism." *Queen's Quarterly*, 72.2: 232–252.

—1972. "England/Romantic—Romanticism." In *'Romantic' and its Cognates/ The European History of a Word*, ed. Hans Eichner. Toronto: University of Toronto Press (pp. 157–262).

Wilkie, Brian. 1965. *Romantic Poets and Epic Tradition*. Madison: The University of Wisconsin Press.

Wilkins, Ernest. 1954. *A History of Italian Literature*. Cambridge: Harvard University Press.

Williams, Ioan (ed.). 1970. *Novel and Romance 1700–1800. A Documentary Record*. London: Routledge & Kegan Paul.

Wolfson, Susan J. 1986. *The Questioning Presence: Wordsworth, Keats, and the Interrogative Mode in Romantic Poetry*. Ithaca: Cornell University Press.

Wordsworth, William. 1964. *The Poetical Works of Wordsworth*, ed. Thomas Hutchinson and Ernest de Selincourt. Oxford: Oxford University Press.

Yalom, Marilyn. 1993. *Blood Sisters. The French Revolution in Women's Memory*. New York: HarperCollins.

Zecchini, Laurent. 2019. *Lafayette héraut de la liberté*. Paris: Fayard.

Index

About the Team

Alessandra Tosi was the managing editor for this book.

Cameron Baillie and Melissa Purkiss proof-read the manuscript. Rosalyn Sword indexed the work.

Katy Saunders designed the cover. The cover was produced in InDesign using the Fontin font.

Luca Baffa typeset the book in InDesign and produced the paperback and hardback editions. The text font is Tex Gyre Pagella; the heading font is Californian FB. Luca produced the EPUB, AZW3, PDF, HTML, and XML editions — the conversion is performed with open source software such as pandoc (https://pandoc.org/) created by John MacFarlane and other tools freely available on our GitHub page (https://github.com/OpenBookPublishers).

This book need not end here...

Share

All our books — including the one you have just read — are free to access online so that students, researchers and members of the public who can't afford a printed edition will have access to the same ideas. This title will be accessed online by hundreds of readers each month across the globe: why not share the link so that someone you know is one of them?

This book and additional content is available at:

https://doi.org/10.11647/OBP.0302

Customise

Personalise your copy of this book or design new books using OBP and third-party material. Take chapters or whole books from our published list and make a special edition, a new anthology or an illuminating coursepack. Each customised edition will be produced as a paperback and a downloadable PDF.

Find out more at:

https://www.openbookpublishers.com/section/59/1

You may also be interested in:

Romanticism and Time
Literary Temporalities
Sophie Laniel-Musitelli and Céline Sabiron (eds)

https://doi.org/10.11647/OBP.0232

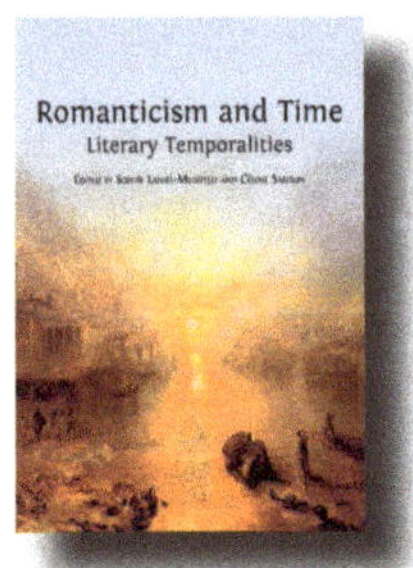

From Goethe to Gundolf
Essays on German Literature and Culture
Roger Paulin

https://doi.org/10.11647/OBP.0258

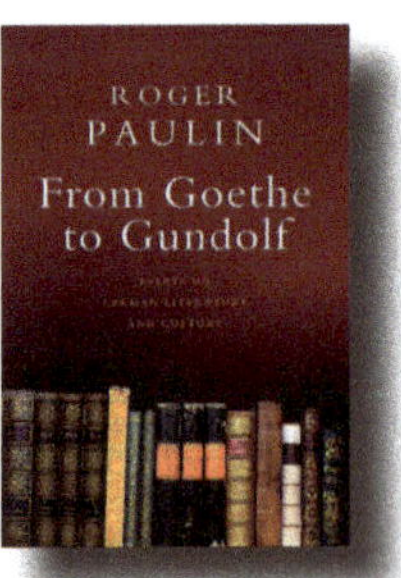

Tennyson's Poems
New Textual Parallels
R. H. Winnick

https://doi.org/10.11647/OBP.0161

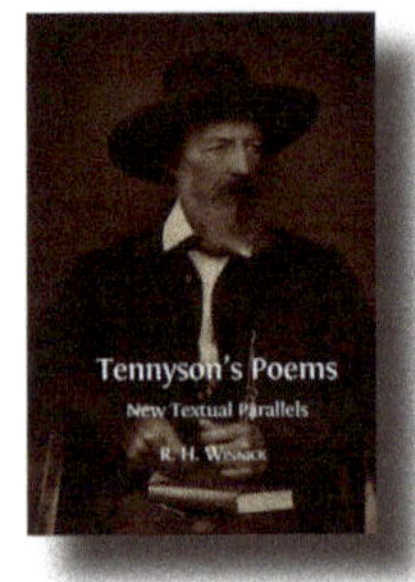

www.ingramcontent.com/pod-product-compliance
Lightning Source LLC
LaVergne TN
LVHW052351100826
845147LV00013B/812
* 9 7 8 1 8 0 0 6 4 7 4 2 8 *